Deeds, Not Words!

Deeds, Not Words!

The Experiences of Two Suffragettes in the
Struggle for the Vote for British Women

Prisons and Prisoners

Constance Lytton and Jane Warton

Pages from the Diary of a Militant Suffragette

Katherine Roberts

LEONAUR

Deeds, Not Words!
The Experiences of Two Suffragettes in the Struggle for the Vote for British Women
Prisons and Prisoners
by Constance Lytton and Jane Warton
Pages from the Diary of a Militant Suffragette
by Katherine Roberts

FIRST EDITION

First published under the titles
Prisons and Prisoners
and
Pages from the Diary of a Militant Suffragette

Leonaur is an imprint
of Oakpast Ltd

ISBN: 978-1-78282-507-4 (hardcover)
ISBN: 978-1-78282-508-1 (softcover)

http://www.leonaur.com

Contents

Prisons and Prisoners

Constance Lytton

Contents

"JANE WARTON" RELEASED.

Home Office Acts on Learning She is Lady Constance Lytton.

Special Cable to THE NEW YORK TIMES.

LONDON, Jan. 23.—Lady Constance Lytton, sister of Lord Lytton and a militant suffragette, was released from jail in Liverpool to-day on orders from the Home Office, following the disclosure of the fact that she had been imprisoned there under an assumed name.

Lady Constance was sent to prison at Newcastle as a suffragette last October, but was released after two days' incarceration by order of Home Secretary Gladstone. She resented this as a concession to her rank, and Mrs. Pethick Lawrence denounced it as political snobbery. Mr. Gladstone, in the House of Commons, declared that Lady Constance was released solely because it was medically reported that she was suffering from serious heart trouble and that forcible feeding might have grave consequences.

At Liverpool Saturday a week ago a suffragette in workingwoman's garb, who said she was Jane Warton, was charged withm breaking windows in the local jail and was fined 10 shillings, with the alternative of fourteen days' imprisonment. She chose the alternative and refused to take food in the prison. She was forcibly fed for four or five days, and not until yesterday was the fact disclosed that Jane Warton was Lady Constance Lytton. When released she was in a very feeble condition.

The case is likely to attract great attention because at the Liverpool trial the police swore to two previous convictions of the socalled Jane Warton, and also because when Lady Constance was released from Newcastle the prison doctor certified that she had a weak heart, whereas the Liverpool prison doctor reported Jane Warton's heart to be all right.

Prisons and Prisoners

DEDICATION TO PRISONERS

When, for a short while, I shared your lot, I asked myself through all my waking hours if there were any friendly thought which could act beneficently for all prisoners, no matter how various the training of their previous lives, no matter whether distress of circumstance, drunkenness, selfish action, cruelty, or madness had been the cause which brought them into prison.

And there seemed this one thing. It is a single idea, but needs many words to give it shape.

Lay hold of your inward self and keep tight hold. Reverence yourself. Be just, kind and forgiving to yourself. For the inner you of yourself is surely the only means of communication for you with any good influence you may once have enjoyed or hope some day to find, the only window through which you can look upon a happier and more lovable life, the only door through which some day you will be able to escape, unbarring it to your own release from all that is helpless, selfish, and unkind in your present self.

Public opinion, which sent you to prison, and your gaolers, who have to keep you there, are mostly concerned with your failings. Every hour of prison existence will remind you of these afresh. Unless you are able to keep alight within yourself the remembrance of acts and thoughts which were good, a belief in your own power to exist freely when you are once more out of prison, how can any other human being help you? If not the inward power, how can any external power avail?

But if you have this comforter within you, hourly keeping up communication with all that you have known and loved of good in your life, with all the possibilities for good that you know of—in your hands, your mind, your heart—then when you are released from pris-

11

on, however lonely you may be, or poor, or despised by your neighbours, you will have a friend who can really help you.

There will be people who visit you in prison, and who watch over you at first when you come out. They will try to help you, but unless they truly understand your lot, understanding your goodness as well as your badness, and sympathising with your badness as well as with your goodness, they will seem far off from you. Who knows, though, but what you may help them? In my ignorance and impudence I went into prison hoping to help prisoners. So far as I know, I was unable to do anything for them. But the prisoners helped me. They seemed at times the direct channels between me and God Himself, imbued with the most friendly and powerful goodness that I have ever met.

Prisoners, I wish I could give to you, for your joy, something of the help you gave to me, and that in many ways I could follow your example.

CHAPTER 1: INTRODUCTION

Some of the experiences which I have to record are of so unusual a character that I think it will help to a better understanding on the part of my readers if I briefly outline the drift of my existence before I became aware of the women's movement, and in touch with that section of it known as the "Militant Suffragettes."

My father had been dead fifteen years and I was thirty-nine years old in 1906, when my narrative begins. I lived with my mother in the country. Two sisters and two brothers had left the home when they were young—the sisters to marry, the brothers to train for and enter their professions. I assumed, as did all my friends and relations, that, being past the age when marriage was likely, I should always remain at home. In my early girlhood I had a yearning to take up music professionally; again, after father's death, when unexpected financial misfortunes caused my mother great anxiety, I had longed to try my hand at journalism; and once more, a few years later, I had the same ambition. But these wishes, finding no favour, had in each case eventually to be repressed, and in 1906 I had neither equipment, training nor inclination for an independent life.

I had been more or less of a chronic invalid through the greater part of my youth. An overmastering laziness and a fatalistic submission to events as they befell were guiding factors in my existence. I was passionately fond of animals and of children, music was a great delight to me; otherwise I was not given to intellectual pursuits. So far as I know, I was an average ordinary human being, except perhaps for an exaggerated dislike of society and of publicity in any form. I had many intimate friends, both men and women, and also children. Such mental training as I have known was chiefly due to intercourse with them. I owed to them, as well as to my mother and many members of my family, a happy life, in spite of considerable physical suffering.

In 1896 and successive years I had given secretarial help to my aunt, Mrs. C. W. Earle, in the writing of her wonderfully delightful books, beginning with *Pot Pourri from a Surrey Garden*. She insisted that, in return for my small and mostly mechanical services, we should share the profits of the sale. The book ran into many editions, and she held to her bargain, but I never felt as if I had a right to the money. Her widely sympathetic and stimulating companionship had a great influence on my mind. Thanks to her investigations in theories of diet, I became a strict vegetarian. My health gained in all directions and I gradually freed myself from the so called "constitutional" rheumatism from which I had suffered since my infancy. I realised, too, that all these years I had caused untold suffering that I might be fed, and determined that in future the unnatural death of an animal should not be necessary to make up my bill of fare. My vitality increased, but the notion of a vocation apart from my family and home remained as foreign to my ideas as it was then to the average British spinster of my class.

In the year 1906 my godmother, Lady Bloomfield, died. She had shown me much kindness and I had never found an opportunity to serve her in any way, the generosity had been all on her side; yet, at her death, she left me some money, without any conditions as to how I should spend it. It gave me a strange new feeling of power and exhilaration. I look back upon this event as being spiritually the starting point in my new life, of which this book will tell, although, from the practical point of view, it seems only by a series of coincidences that my after experiences were evolved from it.

I looked about me with a view to spending the money. I had a fancy to put it to some public use. The commonly accepted channels of philanthropy did not appeal to me. I shifted my inquiries in other directions. I remember that at this time I was chiefly occupied with the idea that reformers were for the most part town dwellers, their philosophy and schemes attuned to those surroundings. There seemed to me need for a counteracting influence to attempt reform and regeneration on behalf of country dwellers. The noiseless revolution which had been worked in a few decades by the system of compulsory education seemed to me tainted throughout by the ideals of townsfolk. The influence of teachers and clergy, of public authorities in general, sets before the nation's children and their parents ideals which mould them into townsfolk.

Country craft and country lore grow less, and are less honoured in every decade. There is no room for them in the national curriculum. This tendency, nevertheless, seems unnatural, imposed by a species of force on a reluctant though inarticulate people. Some temperaments cannot acclimatise themselves to town dwelling. The life of cities will always appear to them artificial, repellent from the physical conditions it imposes and the mental outlook resulting from these. Rain, earth and air are better scavengers than any municipal corporation. The ceaseless cleansing, yet never making clean, of town existence has from my childhood fretted my imagination and produced a sense of incarceration. In towns, the earth is laid over with tombstones, metalled roads or floors of wood. Avenues of bricks and mortar shut out a great part of the sky, limiting into a mere ceiling the heavens which should be our surrounding. A town had always seemed to me a "deterrent" workhouse at best, and often a punitive prison besides.

The monster of industrialism, which followed in the wake of the discovery of steam and the dethroning of handicraft by artificially-propelled machinery, may one day be bridled and controlled so as to be a servant of humanity, a fellow worker in the day-today glory of creation; but for the present it is still a wild beast, a dragon at large, dealing pestilence and death with its fiery breath, combated in panic, its evils evaded rather than faced, its power a nightmare breeding fear and subjection. Instead of harnessing this new force to every branch of our existence, ordering it to serve us at our command, we have cringed before it, left our normal lives and drained our energies to congregate in its grimy temples and worship at its shrine. Poor, blind force that it is, we are determined to make it an idol, and for sake of the return in money which its mechanical rotations produce, we have been willing to sacrifice the interests both of the human beings which should control it and of the soil, the land, which alone can produce the raw material for its task.

How to transform this Moloch from a tyrannous master to a helpful, submissive friend, that was the problem which seemed to cry out for solution above all others. I looked around to see how the needs of country folk were able to express themselves, and everywhere there was presented to my inquiries a complicated machinery of administration both national and local—voting rights for election of parliamentary, municipal, county, district and parish councils. But this machinery was apparently born and bred of urban conditions, superimposed upon the rural districts, in no way native to them, not of spontaneous growth. This succession of councils, instituted with the apparent purpose of watching one another, and, if necessary, bringing pressure to bear upon one another, were for the most part lifeless formalities, having no organic life, no breath of reality to set them in motion.

The only function which gives them any tangible vitality is their power of imposing taxation and levying rates. You find in the country districts that members of these different bodies are the same individuals. The parish councillor who is expected to bring pressure to bear on the district councillor, who again must appeal, if need be, to the county councillor, is one and the same person who, as likely as not, is also the representative of the district on the board of guardians, and he is sure to be selected again to work the administrative machinery of every new device that comes along for the amelioration of social evils. In other words, the elective principle is a farce in rural districts. The electorate are dead both to their powers and their duties.

They live, in fact, under a system which is anything but representative. They live rather, under the devitalised husk of the feudal system, the poorer members of the community dependent, in the worst sense, upon those who are their social superiors, but no longer receiving from them any security of well-being, and neither class extending to the other, with rare exceptions, either the loyalty or devotion which seem to have been bound up with the feudal traditions of our forefathers. Was it possible to wake up this inert mass, so that they should co-operate with one another, and thus be strong enough to grasp the present machinery of national government, and either utilise it or alter it to one better suited to their needs?

Each of my inquiries in turn led me back to the individuals concerned, to the human beings themselves. What were their homes, their ambitions, thoughts, beliefs? What guidance do they give to those who wish to serve them? I groped my way blindly and acquired knowledge only in a negative sense by a series of failures. I gleaned two general precepts from my investigations. They were these: It is useless to try and help the lives of a community without consulting the individuals whom you hope to benefit, and that to benefit the life conditions of men does not necessarily benefit the life conditions of women, although their interests may be apparently identical as to social grade, locality, religious and other beliefs.

After a series of barren experiments, I stumbled by chance on a piece of social radium, a regenerative agency that bore good fruit and that contained an element of spontaneous joy most refreshing compared to the oppressive straightjackets of national or private philanthropists. I heard of the revival of folk songs and dances. I went to see and hear them. The first performance opened the door for me into a new paradise. The Esperance Club of working girls had been the means of bringing to life researches of antiquarian musical students. This club had evidently been for many years an unusually successful social enterprise, but the discovery of a lost treasure in the shape of traditional songs and dances gave it a new inspiration. Both words and tunes of the songs have come, generation after generation, from the heart of the English folk.

Each generation, each individual who has sung them, has added or omitted some little touch, so that in these songs, which have been mostly collected from old men and women over eighty years of age, is expressed the very soul of English national sentiment. The same with the dances. They were traditional in families or localities, they had been handed down from father to son, and were as truly folk dances as the songs were folk songs. Songs and dances alike are full of life on the land and love of the land, of flowers, animals and crops, of the daily lives of men, women and children. Dramatic, tragic and comic incidents find spontaneous expression, and every one of them tells of a vigorous and mainly joyous existence.

The girls of this club learnt the Morris dance first from two Oxfordshire countrymen. Both the dances and songs were acquired easily "by a sort of spiritual sixth sense," as if the rhythm and meaning of them were latent in their being and were easily reawakened. The girls not only learnt quickly, but were inspired to teach others, young girls of seventeen and eighteen showing an amazing facility and power of organisation in this matter. One of these came, at my eager request, to teach in our village, and, after one week, men, women and children were alive with these friendly, joy-giving, native arts. The following year a girl teacher came to us again with renewed success.

In the autumn, 1908, I was invited by the secretary of the club, Miss Mary Neal, herself a wonderful organiser, to share a seaside holiday with her girls. In those days I never left home save for family reasons, or for some very exceptional matter. I, therefore, refused the invitation. I happened to mention the proposal the next day to my mother. She said: "Why don't you go?" I immediately went, little realising that this visit would lead to a most unexpected series of experiences.

CHAPTER 2: MY CONVERSION

It was in August—September, 1908, at "The Green Lady Hostel," Littlehampton, the holiday house of the Esperance Girls' Club, that I met Mrs. Pethick Lawrence and Miss Annie Kenney. I was two or three days in the house with them without discovering that they were Suffragettes or that there was anything unusual about their lives. But I realised at once that I was face to face with women of strong personality, and I felt, though at first vaguely, that they represented something more than themselves, a force greater than their own seemed behind them. Their remarkable individual powers seemed illumined and enhanced by a light that was apart from them as are the colours and patterns of a stained-glass window by the sun shining through it. I had never before come across this kind of spirituality.

I have since found it a characteristic of all the leaders in the militant section of the woman's movement, and of many of the rank and file. I was much attracted by Mrs. Lawrence, and became intimate with her at once on the strength of our mutual friendship for Olive Schreiner. We had, besides, many other interests and sympathies in common. The first Sunday that we were together, the girls of the club were asked to come in early that evening, so that Jessie Kenney, Annie Kenney's sister, who had only recently been released from Holloway, might tell them of her prison experiences. I then realised that I was amongst Suffragettes. I immediately confessed to them that although I shared their wish for the enfranchisement of women, I did not at all sympathise with the measures they adopted for bringing about that reform.

I had, however, always been interested in prisons and recognised from the first that, incidentally, the fact of many educated women being sent to gaol for a question of conscience must do a great deal for prison reform, and I was delighted at this opportunity of hearing first-hand something about the inner life of a prison. I listened eagerly and was horrified at some of the facts recorded. Amongst these I remember specially that the tins in which the drinking water stood were cleaned with soap and brick dust and not washed out, the tins being filled only once or at most twice in twenty-four hours; the want of air in the cells; the conduct of prison officials towards the prisoners.

Having betrayed my disapproval of the Suffragette "tactics," which seemed to me unjustified, unreasonable, without a sense of political responsibility, and as setting a bad example in connection with a reform movement of such prominence, there was naturally something of coolness and reserve in my further intercourse with Mrs. Pethick Lawrence and the Kenneys. But before their brief stay at the club came to an end, I achieved a talk with each of the leaders.

One evening, after incessant rain, Annie Kenney and I marched arm-in-arm round the garden, under dripping trees. I explained that though I had always been for the extension of the suffrage to women, it did not seem to me a question of prime urgency, that many other matters of social reform seemed more important, and I thought class prejudice and barriers more injurious to national welfare than sex barriers. I was deeply impressed with her reply. She said, in a tone of utmost conviction:

Well, I can only tell you that I, who am a working-class woman, have never known class distinction and class prejudice stand in the way of my advancement, whereas the sex barrier meets me at every turn.

Of course, she is a woman of great character, courage and ability, which gives her exceptional facilities for overcoming these drawbacks, but her contention that such powers availed her nothing in the face of sex prejudices and disabilities, and the examples she gave me to bear out her argument, began to lift the scales of ignorance from my eyes. She was careful to point out that the members of her own family had been remarkably free from sex prejudice, and her illustrations had no taint of personal resentment. She explained how the lot of women being, not understood of men, and they being the only legislators, the woman's part had always got laid on one side, made of less importance, sometimes forgotten altogether.

She told how amongst these offices of women was the glorious act of motherhood and the tending of little children. Was there anything in a man's career that could be so honourable as this? Yet how often is the woman who bears humanity neglected at such times, so that life goes from her, or she is given no money to support her child. I felt that through Annie Kenney's whole being throbbed the passion of her soul for other women, to lift from them the heavy burden, to give them life, strength, freedom, joy, and the dignity of human beings, that in all things they might be treated fairly with men. I was struck by her expression and argument, it was straightforward in its simplicity, yet there was inspiration about her. All that she said was obvious, but in it there was a call from far off, something inevitable as the voice of fate. She never sounded a note of sex-antipathy; it was an unalloyed claim for justice and equity of development, for women as for men.

Then Mrs. Pethick Lawrence and I, during a day's motoring expedition, achieved a rare talk out. She met all my arguments, all my prejudices and false deductions with counter-arguments, and above all with facts of which I had till then no conception. I trusted her because of what I had learnt of her personality, her character, mind, wide education and experience, and was to a certain extent at once impressed; still I only half believed many of the things she reported, the real purport of her statements did not yet sink into my soul as they were soon to do, fact upon fact, result upon result, as I found out their truth for myself.

During my stay at Littlehampton I witnessed a scene which produced a great impression upon my conscience. One morning, while wandering through the little town, I came on a crowd. All kinds of people were forming a ring round a sheep which had escaped as it was being taken to the slaughterhouse. It looked old and misshapen. A vision suddenly rose in my mind of what it should have been on its native mountain-side with all its forces rightly developed, vigorous and independent. There was a hideous contrast between that vision and the thing in the crowd. With growing fear and distress the sheep ran about more clumsily and became a source of amusement to the onlookers, who laughed and jeered at it. At last it was caught by its two gaolers, and as they carried it away one of them, resenting its struggles, gave it a great cuff in the face. At that I felt exasperated. I went up to the men and said:

Don't you know your own business? You have this creature absolutely in your power. If you were holding it properly it would be still. You are taking it to be killed, you are doing your job badly to hurt and insult it besides.

The men seemed ashamed, they adjusted their hold more efficiently and the crowd slunk away. From my babyhood I have felt a burning indignation against unkindness to animals, and in their defence I have sometimes acted with a courage not natural to me. But on seeing

19

this sheep it seemed to reveal to me for the first time the position of women throughout the world. I realised how often women are held in contempt as beings outside the pale of human dignity, excluded or confined, laughed at and insulted because of conditions in themselves for which they are not responsible, but which are due to fundamental injustices with regard to them, and to the mistakes of a civilisation in the shaping of which they have had no free share. I was ashamed to remember that although my sympathy had been spontaneous with regard to the wrongs of animals, of children, of men and women who belonged to down-trodden races or classes of society, yet that hitherto I had been blind to the sufferings peculiar to women as such, which are endured by women of every class, every race, every nationality, and that although nearly all the great thinkers and teachers of humanity have preached sex-equality, women have no champions among the various accepted political or moral laws which serve to mould public opinion of the present day.

Nothing could have exceeded the patience, the considerate sympathy even, with which both Annie Kenney and Mrs. Lawrence endured my arguments, arguments, as I now realise them to have been, without any genuine element, stereotyped and shallow. Before we parted, Mrs. Lawrence said to me, and it was the only one of her remarks which savoured in the least of the contempt which my attitude at that time so richly deserved, "You are sufficiently interested in our policy to criticise it, will you be sufficiently interested to study its cause and read up our case? "

For two months I "read up" the subject as I had never read in my life before; I took in the weekly paper *Votes for Women*, the only publication which gave events as they happened, not as they were supposed to happen. I attended as many meetings as I could, and the breakfasts of released suffrage prisoners, whereat the spirit behind this movement, its driving force, seemed best exemplified. Above all, I watched current politics from a different point of view. I still held back from being converted, I criticised and argued at every turn, over every fresh demonstration of the W.S.P.U., but I began to realise of what stuff the workers in the movement were made; what price they paid for their services so gladly given; how far removed they were from any taint of self-glorification, and how amazingly they played the game of incessantly advertising the Cause without ever developing the curse of self-advertisement. I have never been amongst people of any sort who were so entirely free from self-consciousness, self-seeking and

20

self-vaunting.

At this juncture of my conversion I was much concerned with the arguments of Anti-Suffragists. I wrote a pamphlet to refute their points of view, as generally presented in newspapers and magazines. I was always, as it were, stopping on my road to combat their attitude. It was only after considerably longer experience that I realised the waste of energy entailed by this process, since the practical opposition which blocks the way to the legal removal of sex disability is not due to those men or women who have courage to publicly record their opposition, but to those who take shelter in verbally advocating the cause, while at the same time opposing any effective move for its achievement. Anti-suffrage arguments or agitations should, of course, be met whenever they present themselves, but it soon became clear to me that in private intercourse many people put them forward without any conviction, merely as a way of opening the conversation, and while at heart much more interested in the positive than the negative side of the question.

The same is true of public audiences. The assertive claim to the value of voting rights for men, wherever these are denied, is perennially educating the public to our contention; one has but to catch them "at it" to illustrate the claim of women. The drawbacks resulting from laws and customs based on sex bias are also constantly put forward by Anti-Suffragist men themselves, when they are not considering the possible infringement of their own monopolies. Lord Cromer has headed the agitation against freedom for women in Great Britain. When he was responsible for the welfare of Egypt, he wrote, concerning the Prophet Mahomet:

> Unfortunately the great Arabian reformer of the seventh century was driven by the necessities of his position to do more than found a religion. He endeavoured to found a social system. The reasons why Islam as a social system has been a complete failure are manifold. First and foremost Islam keeps women in a position of marked inferiority."

He quotes Stanley Lane Poole in corroboration:

> The degradation of women in the East is a canker that begins its destructive work early in childhood, and has eaten into the whole system of Islam.

Lord Cromer then draws conclusions worthy of the most ardent Suffragette:

Look now to the consequences which result from the degradation of women in Mahomedan countries. It cannot be doubted that the seclusion of women exercises a baneful effect on Eastern society. The arguments on this subject are indeed so commonplace that it is unnecessary to dwell on them. It will be sufficient to say that seclusion, by confining the sphere of women's interest to a very limited horizon, cramps the intellect and withers the mental development of one-half of the population in Moslem countries. . . . Moreover, inasmuch as women, in their capacities of wives and mothers exercise a great influence over the characters of their husbands and sons, it is obvious that the seclusion of women must produce a deteriorating effect on the male population, in whose presumed interests the custom was originally established, and is still maintained (*Modern Egypt*, Vol. II., chapter entitled "Dwellers in Egypt").

The contention of woman Suffragists could not be more reasonably presented. Add to this the belief of Englishmen in the power of the vote to lift from degradation and to widen the outlook of citizens; their attitude towards rebellions on behalf of constitutional rights by Russians, Turks, Persians, and Uitlanders of South Africa; the principles of every constitution in which Britishers have had a hand, notably in Australasia and South Africa, and the case is complete. To meet the Anti-Woman Suffragist arguments, it is only necessary to quote their own utterances.

My own researches had shown me not only the grievous harm to women from the inequalities of law and custom with regard to them, but that in many matters concerning men, and in practically all questions relating to children, the help of women was needed with an urgency that would no longer justify delay. I learnt that before resorting to militancy the women's organisations had for many years past succeeded in obtaining a majority of supporters in the House of Commons, and the backing of leading men of both parties. It was startling to realise that the professed advocacy of such men as Lord Beacons field, the late Lord Salisbury and Mr. Arthur Balfour had not moved the Conservative party in any way to assist their cause.

When the Liberal Government was returned to power in 1906, under the leadership of Sir Henry Campbell Bannerman, he himself was a declared Suffragist, as were all but a few of the men of most influence in his Cabinet, including Mr. Birrell, Mr. Buxton, Mr. John Morley and Mr. John Burns. Sir Edward Grey and Mr. Haldane had themselves introduced a Woman Suffrage Bill in 1889. Mr. Lloyd George, Mr. Runciman and Mr. Winston Churchill, who joined the Cabinet in 1908, were strong verbal advocates of votes for women. The women had tried repeatedly, and always in vain, every peaceable means open to them of influencing successive governments. Processions and petitions were absolutely useless. I saw the extreme need of their position, the ineffectiveness of every method hitherto adopted to persuade these professed Suffragists to put their theories into practice. But I still held aloof from completely backing their militant action owing to mistrustfulness bred of ignorance as to its true nature.

After six weeks I reached the stage when I had little left to say against the movement and my enthusiasm for the workers in it was considerable, but on the whole my attitude was of a negative order. I was still not prepared to back my theoretic approval by action when, on October 13, Mrs. Pankhurst, Mrs. Drummond and Christabel Pankhurst were arrested for issuing the famous handbill calling upon the people of London to witness the women's deputation to the prime minister and to help them "rush" the House of Commons.

At a crowded meeting at the Queen's Hall the previous day, Monday, October 12, the leaders announced that a warrant had been served upon them and that at any moment the police might come in and arrest them on the platform. The meeting was enthusiastically in their favour and the announcement caused an outburst of indignation. This, however, was instantly suppressed by the leaders, who explained that they were under a compact with the managers of the hall never to use these weekly meetings for any insubordinate demonstrations; that if the police arrived and proceeded to arrest them they would only be carrying out their orders; that if this happened, no interference, not a murmur of resentment must come from the audience. After a few moments they settled down under this decree with reluctant but strikingly obedient resignation.

Before long the police were announced to be at the door. After some moments of interchanging messages with the leaders on the platform, during which the suspense in the hall was tremendously taut, the police left saying that the women arrested would have to report themselves at Bow Street the following morning. The next day, Tuesday, October 13, I called at the W.S.P.U. offices in Clement's Inn to offer my sympathy. I regretted that I was still not sufficiently in

23

agreement with their militant policy to join the deputation, but inquired whether there were any lesser services which I could render them. I was asked to try and approach the Home Secretary with a view to securing 1st Division treatment for the prisoners as political offenders instead of ranking them, as hitherto, with criminals in the 2nd and 3rd Divisions. From the first I had been in sympathy with this demand. To publicly maintain that the Suffragists, even if their breaking of the law were proved, had anything in common with the ordinary transgressor for selfish ends, appeared to me ludicrous as well as tyrannous on the part of the government.

I therefore willingly undertook the task, although I was convinced that my efforts would meet with no immediate success. I had already grasped this much of the spirit of the militants that rightness of aim is the factor controlling their actions; likeliness of achievement, in so far as this depends not on themselves but on their opponents, is not a matter to be considered. Looking back at the advance of their cause since militant action began in October, 1905, it seems to me that its amazing rapidity has been chiefly due to the unswerving carrying out of this principle. At every stage the militants selected a line of conduct, not in itself rebellious, but on the contrary, morally and constitutionally in accordance with accepted opinion and law.

It has been the ignoring or deliberate repression of their lawful claims which produced disturbances. The unreasoned punishments which followed in no way altered the women's need nor their determined claim for legal redress. The sufferings of their comrades merely heaped fuel on the fires of their enthusiasm and inevitably exposed the reactionary nature of the government's attitude towards them. I did not obtain 1st Division treatment for the prisoners, but my observations during that memorable day made me a complete convert to the policy of militancy.

From about 4 in the afternoon to 11.30 at night I was incessantly on the move between Clement's Inn, the House of Commons, Bow Street Police Station and the private residence of the magistrate. I had ample opportunity of noticing the nature of the crowd summoned by the famous handbill and of studying the attitude of mind of the authorities, of the Home Office, the magistrate, and of the police towards our movement. The facts which I noted that day as a spectator were typical, and corroborated afterwards in every respect when it came to my own experience. The decisions of the government as expressed through the Home Office were pre-determined and detached from any consideration of the political demand which was the root cause of the women's rebellion.

The magistrate's attitude was obviously affected, whether directly or indirectly, by the government's lead. The political nature of the offences of which our t prisoners were accused was not admitted; their purely nominal crimes were nevertheless punished with a severity that was unheard of had they been judged as ordinary disturbers of the peace. It was clear that the political motive of their actions was recognised sufficiently to justify the authorities in assuming that these actions would be continuous, an example to others, and a dangerous appeal from an organised body, but the reason was ignored when there was question of an inquiry into the political motive itself. The police showed a much more straightforward and impartial attitude whenever the conduct of our case was left entirely in their hands. They never for a moment looked upon the suffrage prisoners as ordinary rowdies, they realised that our motives were political and our actions peaceable, but that our appeals were met in a quite different spirit from those of other political agitators.

The police, of course, in turn came under the influence of those in authority over them, and when under orders would knock us about in the streets, and accuse us in the courts, according to the requirements imposed upon them. Under this pressure, individual policemen would occasionally act with brutality and unfairness, but in the main their treatment of Suffragists was in striking contrast to that of the magistrates, the Home Office and the government. A great number of police constables are better versed in the suffrage question and the woman question generally than most politicians. They have been obliged to attend our meetings. They know both the political and moral ethics of our policy. I have heard more intelligent reasoning about votes for women from policemen (both when my identity was known to them and when it was not) than has issued, with but rare exceptions, from the House of Commons.

During the afternoon and evening of this day I had my first experience of a suffrage crowd, immense in numbers, embracing every shade of opinion on the question, from enthusiasm in favour to contemptuous or angry hostility, largely interspersed with curiosity-mongers who were fascinated by the fight although without interest for its cause. There were men and women of all classes, but rowdyism was plainly not there, and from that day forward I was convinced of the fact, self-evident enough in all conscience, that the women never appealed to hooliganism and that they had nothing to gain from and nothing to offer to that element in the mob. The women, and the men too, who fight in this cause, or assist it ever so remotely, have never been and never will be of a self-seeking type, nor are they lovers of disturbance for its own sake.

I first of all tried to interview the Home Secretary, Mr. Herbert Gladstone, (afterwards Lord Gladstone), at the House of Commons. I did not see him, but a friendly member of Parliament acted as messenger boy between us. I asked:

(1) Would he use his powers to ensure that the three prisoners should be sentenced to the 1st Division, and not to the 2nd Division as though they were common criminals, which obviously they were not?

Reply: As the prisoners were not yet arrested he could not possibly adjudicate on the question of their sentences.

(2) If I returned at six o'clock, the hour when they were to surrender to the summons, would he then give me an answer?

Reply: He had not the power, the question rested with the police-court authorities; he had determined never to interfere with sentences.

(3) Would he give me a permit or some sort of facilities to approach the magistrate?

My messenger told me that it would be useless to put this question, that Mr. Gladstone was in a state of great anger over the whole proceedings, and that, even if he had the power, nothing would induce him to help the Suffragettes to 1st Division treatment. I then went to Bow Street Police Court. The crowds were dense in Parliament Square, Parliament Street, and Trafalgar Square, but extremely orderly.

When I reached Bow Street it was past six o'clock and the magistrate had left. On inquiring where I could find him, I was ushered into an inner room before a superintendent who wore a flat cap, not the usual policeman's helmet. He was very civil, but told me it was against the rules to give the private addresses of magistrates and that Mr. Curtis Bennett would not be back until ten o'clock the following morning for the court. I put various other questions. Though offering no practical assistance the answers led me to realise a strangely unexpected atmosphere of sympathy, and after a few moments hesitation I found myself telling this superintendent the full purport of my mission.

To my intense surprise he not only expressed much approval, but burst out with a torrent of abuse against the government—

Why to goodness couldn't the prime minister receive the women's deputation same as any other? The brunt of the whole business falls on us, and it's the beastliest job we've ever had.

Then he added:

The prisoners are here now, in the cells, would you like to see them?

I felt almost overwhelmed that so unworthy and half-hearted a follower as myself should be the one to have this grand opportunity, but, of course, I availed myself of it without a moment's hesitation. I was shown through a series of passages and up a flight of stairs, where a wardress was in charge. This October day was damp and foggy with the first sense of autumn chill, but as I was led on towards the cells the atmosphere became perceptibly damper and colder at every step, as in a vault. I realised for the first time the actual meaning of the word *"puanteur,"* which haunts the pages of Dostoievsky's account of his imprisonments, the smell, as it were, of deadness pervading, I should imagine, every building, however cleanly washed, which is built and used to incarcerate human beings solely for punitive purposes. I had never seen Mrs. Pankhurst except on a public platform at moments when she was surrounded by public enthusiasm and personal devotion, such as are rarely accorded even to great leaders.

My critical faculty is easily aroused by success, and although I recognised the single-mindedness of her aims, the uprightness of her character, the vigour of her intellect and convincing oratorical gifts, the charm of her personality and, above all, the magnificent power of her leadership, yet I had hitherto not felt drawn to this remarkable woman. It was with no sense of hero-worship that in reply to the wardress' friendly question, "Which of the ladies do you wish to see?" I answered, "Mrs. Pankhurst." She went to a cell door, many of which lined one side of a passage as the horse-boxes of a stable, and drew aside the shutter of a small grating. I looked through into a land of animal's den, dimly lit and furnished only with a bare wooden bench running along the side of the wall, and terminating in a sanitary convenience. Standing erect as she moved towards the grating, was a

27

woman whose appearance struck awe into every fibre of my being. A splendour of defiance and indignation pervaded her face, yet she was controlled and her attitude conveyed no suggestion of personal grievance.

From that moment I recognised in her, and I have held the vision undimmed ever since, the guardian protector of this amazing woman's movement, conscious not only of the thousands who follow her lead to-day, but of the martyred generations of the past and of the women of the future whose welfare depends upon the path hewn out for them today. I seemed to grasp prophetically and all at once the characteristic qualities which I learnt later on by closer observation and experience. I saw that the quality of sternness, which presented so unyielding a front to every opponent and every obstacle, drew its force from deep fountains of understanding, of sympathy and of love. While she most perfectly fulfilled her mission of pioneer, and shirked none of the responsibilities accruing to the lead, yet the efficiency and glamour attending the fulfilment of that mission were due to her recognition of the elements behind her, as an arrow-head derives its force from the construction of the whole weapon.

The seemingly miraculous power of leadership with which the controllers of this militant movement are gifted is due to the fact that they too are fellow servants of a cause which they recognise is of infinitely greater importance than themselves or any other individual, they share with the humblest member of the rank and file the sense of loyalty and bond-allegiance to a common ideal—the welfare of women throughout the world.

I was advised by Mrs. Pankhurst how to turn my services to the best account and not to mind about the 1st Division, as they themselves could plead it in court, but to get them released for that night or they would not be able to plead properly, from fatigue. After a fruitless search of some hours for the magistrate in the wilds of West Kensington and a return to the office at Clement's Inn for further instructions, I at last ran my quarry to ground somewhere near Olympia. The magistrate, Mr. Curtis Bennett, (afterwards Sir Curtis Bennett, who since died in 1913), received me courteously, but his face promptly assumed an official-defensive expression on learning my quest. If I had come to ask him about the trial next day he must request me not to proceed, since he must keep his mind unbiased. I explained that I was altogether new to the rules of the game which he had at his fingers' ends. That, as I was ignorant which questions I might or might not put to him, it would be best for me to unburden myself and for him to select which of my demands he could answer.

He saw the reason of this and kindly consented to the arrangement. In reply, he could make no statement as to which Division he would sentence the prisoners, nor could they be let out on bail that night, because of the late hour at which they had responded to the summonses. As to taking them food and bedding, that was a matter for the police to decide, it was beyond his jurisdiction. I was thankful to hear this, knowing that the police were not likely to offer objections when matters were left solely to their care. I went back to Mrs. Pethick Lawrence, and in a few minutes we had taken bedding and rugs and were off to the police station at Bow Street. We found that a Member of Parliament, Mr. James Murray, had visited our friends and ordered everything they wanted from an hotel, making them as comfortable as possible for the night.

The next day their trial took place. After the evidence of the police had been taken, Christabel Pankhurst asked for an adjournment, in order to take legal advice and to prepare a defence. This was granted for one week. During the interval, Christabel secured the attendance of Mr. Lloyd George, Chancellor of the Exchequer, and of Mr. Herbert Gladstone, Home Secretary, as witnesses for the defence. The adjourned hearing of the case on October 21 lasted from 10.30 to 7.30 at night, with only two short intervals. The trial was immensely impressive, the three figures stood up at different times, and it was obvious to all who listened to the case that they were fighting against evil and were in all things most essentially good, so that one was awed by them. When the two members of the Cabinet gave evidence, the futility of the part they played was most obvious and they presented an appearance that was petty and contemptible to the last degree.

There were a great many other witnesses, of whom I was one, in support of the contention that the crowd on the evening of October 13 was an orderly one, and that no violence was done. At 7.30 Christabel Pankhurst said she had still fifty witnesses to call, and the case was adjourned to Saturday, October 24. It was owing to Mrs. Pankhurst's speech on this occasion that I felt taken hold of by the movement. Every sentence of it seemed to be true, dignified, strong, entirely respectful. This passage I more especially remember:

You know that women have tried to do something to come to the aid of their own sex. . . . I was in the hospital at Holloway, and when I was there I heard from one of the beds near me the moans of a woman who was in the pangs of childbirth. I should like you to realise how women feel at helpless little infants breathing their first breath in the atmosphere of a prison. We believe that if we get the vote we will find some more humane way of dealing with women than that.

Mrs. Drummond made me feel faith in the woman's movement, her type was most lovable, full of daring for the enemies of woman, full of patience in working for them, full of the most noble kind of humility in her reverence for them.

Christabel Pankhurst was the sunrise of the woman's movement, I cannot describe her in any other way. The glow of her great vitality and the joy of her being took hold of the movement and made it gladness. Yet, her nature being so essentially a woman's, there was a vein of tenderness throughout her speech, and her strength lay in her steadfast, resourceful and brilliant intellect.

With the exception of declining to give a pledge to keep the peace for twelve months, a pledge which these women were quite unable to accept, they had been guilty of no offence. Mrs. Pankhurst and Mrs. Drummond were each sentenced to three months' imprisonment, and Christabel Pankhurst to ten weeks' (two and a half months) imprisonment. It was like darkness when these three were in prison. Mrs. Pethick Lawrence and Sylvia Pankhurst, Christabel's sister, kept the weekly meetings going at the Queen's Hall in a splendid way. Sylvia is an artist by profession and an artist at heart, but whenever the women's movement wants her she is there for its bidding. She looked all that is most modest and humble, but speaking seemed to come as a second nature to her as to every one of the Pankhursts, and at times I could not have believed, but for having heard and seen, the splendid political speech which came from that young girl. During this time I lived in the country and seldom came to London. I needed no converting now and my only wish was to convince my mother.

CHAPTER 3: A DEPUTATION TO THE PRIME MINISTER

Throughout this month of January, 1909, I became convinced that I should be justified in offering myself as a member of the next deputation to the prime minister to demand the removal of women's disabilities to the Parliamentary franchise. I became a member of the Women's Social and Political Union, and on January 28 I wrote to Mrs. Pethick Lawrence offering myself for the deputation. I did not tell anybody but her of my decision. On the 30th I received her answer, accepting my offer.

On February 24 I went up to London from Homewood, without telling mother of the plan and actually without saying goodbye to her, as she went out to the village before I started. I wrote her the following letter at King's Cross Station, but did not post it till later in the day:—

Wednesday, February 24, 1909.

My Angel Mother,—I don't know whether I shall post this to you or see you first. I want to have a letter ready.

Don't be startled or afraid. I have something to tell you which—with the help of recent presentments—you, I know, are half expecting to hear.

If you ever see this letter it will mean that after joining the deputation I have been arrested and shall not see you again until I have been to Holloway. For months I have been planning this letter to you, but now that the time has come, it is not any easier to write for that. Of course, my hope has been all along that I should be able to take you into my confidence, that I should have the perhaps all-undeserved yet heaven-like joy of knowing that though you could not share all my views, yet that you would understand why I held them, and, granted these, you would further understand my action and the great sacrifice which I know it means to you.

My darling Muddy, you will never know, I trust, the pain it is to have to do this thing without your sympathy and help—with, on the contrary, the certainty that it shocks you and hurts you and makes you suffer in numberless ways. Hardly a day has passed but what I have tried to feel my way with you, tried to convert you—not to my theoretic views, difference there does not matter, but to my intended conduct in connection with them. Every day I have failed. If I decided to do this thing, absolute secrecy was necessary, for, the whole of these police regulations being arbitrarily ordered and special to the case, they would never arrest me, not, I mean, unless I really broke the law, if they knew who I was.

Unless I had your sympathy and understanding, it was, of course, hopeless to count on your secrecy. I had two alternatives, to give up the plan, or to keep it and deceive you about it. I chose this last. For your sake I have tried never to tell you an actual lie in words. I have not done this, and that is, perhaps, why you have your suspicions. But to my conscience that is no easier. It was my intention to deceive you, and I have deceived you, and, for all practical purposes, successfully. Once the intention is to deceive, it seems to me not to make any difference how it is done.

You will be angry. If it could be only that. But you will be hurt through and through. As I write the words their meaning is acute in my mind and heart. You will hardly care to know, but I must tell you what has decided me to take this torturing step. Prisons, as you know, have been my hobby. What maternity there lurks in me has for years past been gradually awakening over the fate of prisoners, the deliberate, cruel harm that is done to them, their souls and bodies, the ignorant, exasperating waste of good opportunities in connection with them, till now the thought of them, the yearning after them, turns in me and tugs at me as vitally and irrepressibly as ever a physical child can call upon its mother.

The moment I got near the Suffragettes the way to this child of mine seemed easy and straight. But I knew the temptation to think this must make me doubly sure of my ground. I have felt from the first that I could not take this woman's movement merely as an excuse for Holloway. I have waited till my conviction was genuine and deep at every point, and till the opportunity occurred for facing the police regulations in a way possible to my whole nature, temperament, conscience. There are several other things which the Suffragettes do, which I would not and could not do.

I finally made up my mind in about the middle of January, and soon after wrote to Mrs. Pethick Lawrence. Enclosed is her answer. I had not recently been seeing them, or going to meetings, or in any way specially communicating with them. I took the decision entirely on myself, in no way consulted her nor asked her advice; even had they not accepted me in the deputation I should have joined outside.

About the physical discomforts part of Holloway, don't be distressed for that. These are already nothing to what they were. And I am such a muff, what remains of hardship will be wholesome for me—really 'reformatory' for me as imprisonment seldom is to others. If I could only know that you will help me face it, it would be nothing to me. It's my journeying after the hobby that sucks up my soul like a tide, my Nile sources, my Thibet, my Ruvenzori. If you, my splendid Mother, will only help me in spirit that the little spark of Sven Hedin shall not fail in me. I am no hero, but the thought of other travellers' much worse privations on that road will, I believe, fizzle up my flimsy body enough for what is necessary, and if only I knew you were helping me in your heart I should not, could not, fail. Muddy darling.

You can't forgive me now, but perhaps you will some day. Whatever you feel towards me, whatever I do, I shall still be always

Your most loving and devoted

Con.

The account papers, tradesmen addresses, wages paper, are in the lift-up place of desk on dining-room writing table. I expect I shall be away from you a month. The others will cling round you. If I were going a trip abroad you would not resent the separation. In my little warm cupboard nest in Holloway my only thought of the outer world will be of you. I shall try anyhow to get back to you tonight.

Con.

I went to 4, Clement's Inn, lunched there with Mrs. Pethick Lawrence, Christabel, Mrs. Pankhurst and Mrs. Tuke; Miss Neal came too. She kindly undertook to post my letter to mother and buy me a brush and comb and toothbrush in case we should be sent to the 1st Division.

I had a cracking headache and felt quite dazed. They kindly put me to lie down in the upstairs rest room *boudoir*, where Mrs. Pankhurst and Christabel had remained hidden from the police on October 14, 1908.

At about six o'clock we had supper. I ate next to nothing. Miss Elsa Gye, who had been summoned by telegraph to come and assist me through the Deputation, was at supper. She was a delightful girl, young and fresh-looking. I had been told that she was just engaged to be married, and I felt it was horrible that she should risk weeks of imprisonment solely because of me.

I had disguised myself by doing my hair in an early-Victorian way, so that the police, if on the look out for me, should not recognise me and so be tempted not to arrest me; for people whose relatives might make a fuss effectively are considered awkward customers.

At about seven Miss Gye and I set out and hailed a taxi. I found I had left my ticket behind for the Caxton Hall Meeting. So I flew back to Clement's Inn to get it. It was a raw, cold night, but I had been advised to dispense with my muff and boa, as these, I was told, would almost certainly be torn to shreds "in the hustling"; this gave one a rather gruesome warning of what was to be expected from the handling of the police. We were each given a copy of the resolution which was to be put to the meeting. As we drove to Caxton Hall, it suddenly struck me that I had not sufficiently learnt up my part.

"What does one have to do?" I asked. "I suppose I must do something to show that I mean business."

"Oh, no," my companion answered, "you needn't bother about what you'll do. It will all be done *to* you. There is only one thing you must remember. It is our business to go forward, and whatever is said to you and whatever is done to you, you must on no account be turned back."

That seemed to me at the time, and has seemed to me ever since, to be the essence of our militant tactics. I afterwards heard it yet better summarised by Mrs. Pankhurst:

"Our demand is just and moderate. We press our cause reasonably and in a law-abiding spirit, but in such a way that we give the government but two alternatives—either to do us justice or to do us violence."

My companion also told me that if the police became too violent, I could cut matters short and ensure instant arrest by the semblance of making a speech or collecting a crowd round me for that purpose, since these offences constituted a breach of the peace. Miss Gye and I sat in the body of the hall, we had on the "Votes for Women" sashes and were to join the deputation unostentatiously as it left the building.

The appearance of the deputation on the platform was remarkable for the look of dignity and pathetic earnestness of the members, many of them white-haired, and one or two young and pretty girls.

★★★★★★

The deputation was composed of our leader Mrs. Pethick Lawrence, Miss Daisy Solomon, Mrs. Vans Agnew Corbett, Miss Una Dugdale, Miss Madeline Petre, Miss E. H. Chesshire, Mrs. Caprina Fahey, Miss M. Barnet, Miss Margaret Davies Colley, Miss Margaret E. Dodgers, Miss Mary Allen, Miss Ellen Pitman,

Miss Maud Freeman, Mrs. Katherine Richmond, Miss Mary Lethune, Miss M. Adair Roberts, Miss Leslie Lawless, Miss Caroline Townsend, Mrs. Tyson, Miss M. Tyson, Miss Ainsworth, Mrs. Lamartine Yates, Miss M. E. Thompson, Miss Helen Kirkpatrick Watts, Miss Kate Walsh, Miss Sara Carwin, Mrs. Saul Solomon, who was not eventually arrested, and Miss Elsa Gye and myself brought the number to twenty-nine.

★★★★★★

The speeches seemed to be very much to the point. I could hardly listen to them for the distracting thought of when my mother would hear about me and what she would think and feel; but I had no wish to shirk, and never for a moment did I doubt that I had done right.

Many friends had seen and not recognised me, at which I was delighted. Others did recognise me, and seeing I had the sash on, which meant the deputation, they looked immensely surprised.

Presently the deputation came down from the platform, formed up in couples, headed by Mrs. Pethick Lawrence, and marched out of the hall. Miss Gye and I joined in behind the sixth or seventh couple. We were thirty women in all. By this time I had a feeling of exhilaration that the moment for my own independent action had come at last. I had a vague notion that I should have to encounter physical difficulties, but since I had merely to meet them and endure them, knowing that I could lay no claim' to overcoming these by physical powers of which I was deficient, the way from that moment seemed plain and easy. I felt proud to be one of the active ones at last, to be the companion of these women in particular, whom I had watched on the platform, and to know that the deputation was headed by one of our leaders who had first revealed the woman's movement to me.

The following resolution was put to the meeting and carried with acclamation:

That this Parliament of women expresses its indignation that while every measure in the King's Speech vitally affects the interests of their sex, and while heavier financial burdens are to be laid upon woman tax-payers, the government have not included in the programme for the session a measure to confer the Parliamentary vote upon duly qualified women. The women here assembled call upon the government to introduce and carry into law this session a measure giving votes to women on the same terms as to men.

A deputation is hereby appointed, to whom is entrusted the duty of forthwith conveying this resolution to the prime minister at the House of Commons and eliciting his reply.

A copy was then handed to each member of the deputation.

Of all the undesirable possibilities before me, I dreaded most lest by some horrible twist of fate the leaders of the deputation should be refused admittance, and I, if recognised, should have the lonely privilege thrust upon me of being received. I had never made a regular speech, and two attempts I had made at narrating my experiences of the previous October to a village audience had not been reassuring. My own point of view was definite enough, but I did not feel equipped to speak for others. When deciding to go on the deputation I had, however, taken stock of my representative character and asked myself for which group of women I should stand, what was my atom's share in this movement if I did not strain after any vicarious office but merely added my own personal weight to the scale? Without doubt I myself was one of that numerous gang of upper class leisured class spinsters, unemployed, unpropertied, unendowed, uneducated, without equipment or training for public service, economically dependent entirely upon others, not masters of their own leisure, however oppressively abundant that might seem to the onlooker.

In a class where property runs with primogeniture, the first-born, if a female, is overlooked. In a class the whole status of which is based on property, on wealth to live at ease and in luxury, property is only dealt out to women, if at all, after male relatives have been served first, and then, as a rule, in much less proportion. Posts of honour and remuneration are barred to them in nearly all professions, in even those few they are allowed to enter. They remain almost invariably without honour of titles or lands or wealth, even where their services have been sought. Posts of government are exclusively for men, with the sole exception of the sovereign. Trained to luxury and untrained to remunerative work, they are for the most part dependents from childhood to the grave. A maiming subserviency is so conditional to their very existence that it becomes an aim in itself, an ideal. Driven through life with blinkers on, they are unresentful of the bridle, the rein and the whip, uncritical of the direction in which they are driven, unmindful of the result to others as well as to themselves of their maintainer's beliefs and policy, whatever they may be. The bride at the sacred ritual of her marriage festival hears from her husband the words:

With this ring I thee wed, with my body I thee worship, with all my worldly goods I thee endow.

She knows at the time and she learns yet more intimately as life goes on that those words have no practical bearing, and that at her husband's death the greater part of even that property which had been seemingly made over to her during his lifetime will pass from her hands at the wane of her lonely existence, when she needs it most, into those of her son or some more distant relative. The literal, practical, interpretation of that husband's vow—yes, of the vow even of good and well-intentioned husbands—most usually is:

With this ring I thee bind, with my body I thee control, with none of my worldly goods I thee endow.

As a widow more often than not she sinks, because of her financial position, to a social state out of touch with all her past life. But at least the wives, the widows, generally have children through whom their powers of service to their families and to the community in general are to a certain extent developed and recognised, and which give them a certain insight into the realities of existence. They also have known well-being and vicarious honour through their husbands. But to the single woman, the old maid of later years, the paralysing worship of incapacity dominates life, the chain of limitations and restrictions is but seldom broken, and never overcome save by exceptional force of character or ability. Even then how often it is only the beating of wings against unyielding and maiming bars; freedom, if attained, rendered useless by lack of preparation in the competition against trained and privileged beings of the male sex, and the vain ambition ends in a seeming mutiny, nothing more—a distortion, an abnormality, an untidiness of creation.

I could stand indeed for the superfluous spinster, but who would listen to a messenger from this mute array, who cares for the blind, the lamed, the maimed and the dumb? The fearful unnecessity of their disablement awakes no pity, no heart softens at thought of them, no politician would feel his conscience pricked by the narration of their grievances. A yoke so submitted to, so uselessly endured, can claim no reverence of martyrdom. But before condemning those who submit to it, I wish that our critics could realise what it means to be born under this yoke and then try to shake it off.

37

It is easy to see that if women are to appeal effectively to a modern parliament for the rights of liberty and representation which so long have been recognised among men, it must be through the working women, the breadwinning woman. Her situation is easily comparable to that of the working-class man who quite recently has had himself to fight in order to win his denied claim to freedom, a fact which he, and others for him, still remember. The aristocracy, the landed proprietor, the middleclass trader, each in turn was driven to claim and fight for these same rights. But their struggle was of long ago, their security in this right has remained unshaken for so many generations that they have clean forgotten what it would mean to be without it.

It is by the side of the most recent victors that women must put in their claim. With this class, the working-class women, though at all times at one with them in point of sympathy from theoretic understanding of their troubles and needs, I was not in direct touch and had no first-hand experiences that I could share with them. I read the petitions of factory workers, of the sweated home workers, of the professions—teachers, nurses, medical women—with respect and whole-hearted sympathy, but how could I stand for them when I was not equipped to represent them?

This was my state of mind until, walking from Holloway to the City in one of our Suffragette processions, I heard for the first time with my own ears the well-worn taunt "Go home and do your washing." This awoke in me a magic response. Since the days of my earliest childhood washing had held great charm for me, and as a result I had revered the washers exceptionally. In my youth, the pursuit was associated exclusively with laundry-workers, but in later years I realised that, except in that small proportion of houses where servants are kept, every woman is a laundry-maid, and that in every house throughout the land, or indeed throughout the world, the cleaning and the washing are done mainly by women, by wives and mothers, their girl children or women servants. Washing, the making clean that which had been dirty, and making the crumpled and uncomfortable things smooth, was my hobby. I was an amateur scrubber and laundry-woman in the same spirit as other unemployed females dabble in water-colour drawings or hand embroidery.

But much as I personally enjoyed occasional experimenting in the craft, it was easy to imagine how irksome the occupation might become if one were driven to it week by week with no release, under unsuitable conditions, without the necessary equipment, in a small house or single room, surrounded by children, with a stinted water supply, inadequate firing utensils, a weary body and a mind distraught as to how to exist from day to day. From the moment I heard that "washing" taunt in the street, I have had eyes for the work of the washers. If there is one single industry highly deserving of recognition throughout the world of human existence and of representation under parliamentary systems, it surely is that of the washers, the renewers week by week, the makers clean.

I determined, if I should find myself the solitary representative of the Deputation and its untrained spokeswoman, I should point to the collars and shirt fronts of the gentlemen who received me and claim the freedom of citizenship for the washers. As I stepped out from Caxton Hall, through the grime of a foggy February evening, I caught sight of white collars here and there in the crowd, like little flashing code-signals beckoning to us across the darkness. The gnarled hands, the bent backs, the tear-dimmed eyes of those that had washed them white seemed to cry out, "Remember us. Don't be afraid to speak for us if you get through to the presence of those who know nothing, heed nothing of our toil."

I said in my heart, "I shall remember, and I shall not be afraid in their presence." We had scarcely stepped into the street before we found ourselves hedged in by a Λ shaped avenue of police, narrowing as we advanced. They asked no questions, said nothing, but proceeded to close upon us from either side. My companion and I kept together. Very soon all breath seemed to have been pressed out of my body, but remembering the order of the day, "Don't be turned back," I tried to hold my ground even when advance was out of the question. Miss Gye, however, soon realised the situation and pulled me back, saying, "We are not yet in Parliament Square; we must manage to get there somehow; let's try another way."

The police had forced themselves between the ranks of the Deputation, keeping them apart and trying also to sever the couples, but Miss Gye and I managed to regain hold of each other. I had not been able to reconnoitre in the morning as I had intended. The whereabouts of Caxton Hall was unknown to me, and in the darkness I felt quite at sea as regards direction. We soon got clear of the police and found ourselves in a friendly crowd who half hindered, half pushed, us along. But I was already so incapacitated by breathlessness I could not lift my chest and head.

I had repeatedly to stop, and, but for the kindly assistance of my companion and an unknown man and woman of the crowd, I should have been unable to get any further. The main body of the deputation had made for the strangers' entrance of the House of Commons, near the House of Lords. I saw none of them again until we met in the police station. In Parliament Square we soon became entangled in a thick crowd, some of them friendly, as many not, the great bulk curiosity-mongers. Miss Gye and I were, of course, recognisable as members of the deputation by our sashes, and though at first whenever the police or the crowd pushed us apart she managed to return to me, we eventually got completely separated and lost sight of each other. My two stranger friends in the crowd, however, not being marked by badges were always returning to my help.

The occasion most literally turned out to be one for "*deeds, not words.*" Being doubled up for want of breath, I could scarcely see where I was going, but my instinct led me to avoid the police in every way that I could. They were placed about in twos and threes in no apparent special formation, but now and then one came to a whole line of them, standing shoulder to shoulder. I was during most of the time physically incapable of speech. I only twice was able to express myself in words, on both occasions when I was lifted off my feet and relieved of the toil of dragging my own body. First when the crowd wedged me up against a policeman, I said to him: "I know you are only doing your duty and I am doing mine." His only answer was to seize me with 1 both his hands round the ribs, squeeze the remaining breath out of my body and, lifting me completely into the air, throw me with all his strength.

Thanks to the crowd I did not reach the ground; several of my companions in more isolated parts of the square were thrown repeatedly on to the pavement. Another time a policeman turned me round and, holding my arms behind me, drove me ahead of him for several yards at a great pace. So that his violence would not land me on to my face I exerted what pressure I could to steady my feet. No doubt this looked very "violent" on my part to some of the crowd who jeered and booed. I said to them, in gasps:

You ask women to behave in a womanly way; do you think this is treating them in a manly way?

Twice again I was thrown as before described. I offered no resistance to this whatever, and being of light weight for my size, I feared that I was becoming a specially desirable victim for the experts in this line. Each time I was thrown to a greater distance and the concussion on reaching the ground was painful and straining, though in each case the crowd acted for me as sort of buffers. When seized for the throw there is also a feeling of wrenching throughout the body. But I gained in the direction of the House nevertheless, always assisted by the crowd. The stranger woman in particular, a German lady who was tall, well-built, and of considerable strength, had managed to keep near me. Three times, after each of the "throws," she came to my help and warded off the crowd while I leant up against some railings, or against her shoulder to recover my breath.

Several times I said to her, "I can't go on; I simply can't go on."

She answered, "Wait for a little, you will be all right presently."

At the time and ever since I have felt most inexpressibly grateful to this stranger friend, I was goaded on most of all, perhaps, by the fear that I should be taken off by an ambulance—I heard that some were about—and, if so, that all I had achieved so far would have to be faced again, probably with renewed difficulty. Flashes of vivid light and the sound of a slight muffled explosion came about from time to time. I did not know what these were, they added to the sense of incomprehensibleness and general confusion. It was only towards the end of the day I realised that they were the newspaper photographers' flashlights. The irony of their attentions seemed great.

It was cheering to find that in spite of everything I had gained ground and was quite near to the House. The police were now far less numerous, standing only in small groups of twos and threes. Several of these to my surprise let me pass quite close by them unmolested. The prospect of actually entering the House seemed now not unattainable. My utterly dishevelled condition, my inability for want of breath to stand upright or to string more than two words together at a time, should have enhanced the nightmare of possibly being admitted to the presence of the prime minister. But strange to say that fear had left me. The instinct for achievement engendered by the rebuffs of the police, the indignation aroused by the fact that such treatment of a deputation of voteless citizens had been deliberately ordered and sanctioned by the government, had for the moment cured all fears as to my personal inadequacy as a spokesman.

I found myself at the gates of the members' entrance. No crowd was near and only two policemen stood, ordinary wise, at either side of the gate. They did not seem to be noticing me. I straightened my back to assume as much of a normal appearance as possible. I passed through the gate. At this the policeman nearest to me turned and seized my arm. Expecting to be thrown as before, I tried to hold my ground and said, "Please let me pass," or words to that effect. Another policeman promptly took me by the other arm and I was led off at a great pace. The effort to try and realise what was happening seemed to use up the last remnant of physical power at my disposal. I supposed I was being led away, as I had been warned was sometimes done as a means of disheartening the women, to some distant and lonely street.

But there was nothing of roughness or insult in the attitude of the police who held me. I thought perhaps I had fainted or fallen without knowing it and that they were ambulance men. I felt unable to cope with the problem, my eyes shut and my head fell forward. We seemed to be going a long way. "How shall I ever get back from here," I wondered. Presently there was an alteration in the sounds of our footsteps and in the gestures of the men. I opened my eyes and looked up. Close in front of me, over a doorway, was a blue lamp with the words "Police Station" printed upon it. I knew then that I had been arrested. The discovery was positively life-giving. To think that it was over, that the struggle would not have to begin all over again! I was able to lift my head and walk fairly easily; the crushing sense of failure was gone.

When anticipating events, and trying to prepare myself for the various stages of the ordeal before me, I had supposed that one of the worst moments would be this of being actually "had up," when I should find myself in the police station and know the first step towards prison had been taken; that there could be no going back. When it came to actual experience, Cannon Row police station had all the attractions of a harbour after a storm. From the moment I set foot inside this domain of the police nothing could exceed their courtesy and even sympathy. In a large, nondescript kind of waiting room I was taken up to a table at which a policeman sat making entries in a ledger. I was asked my name, address, age, vocation, etc. I wondered whether I was the only one that had been arrested, but presently two more of the deputation came in. The delight at seeing again some of my companions was very great; it was only then I fully realised how the isolation from the others had added to the toil and gruesomeness of the struggle in Parliament Square.

We were taken up to a large sort of club room, in which there were billiard tables. Several of the deputation were already there. We were eager, of course, to hear each other's experiences. I quickly realised that I had had an unusually good time of it. Several of them had been thrown on to the ground, some kicked, one had had her thumb dislocated, another had a sprained ankle. One had her face streaming with blood from a blow on the nose. Before long Mrs. Pethick Lawrence joined us. It was a curious sensation on seeing her, of mingled delight that she was with us again, and indignation that a woman such as she is should have been arrested. The word quickly went round that we were to conceal as best we might our various injuries. It was no part of our policy to get the police into trouble. Except where they were given definite orders to the contrary, they did their best for us, and whenever they themselves controlled the situation their good will towards us was most marked. I remember that the most difficult thing to disguise was the wounded nose of Miss Dugdale, when a policeman came up to inquire whether any were hurt or if a doctor were wanted for us.

It was here, at Cannon Row, that I first tasted the delights of that full, unfetterd companionship which is among the greatest immediate rewards of those who work actively in this cause. No drudgery of preliminary acquaintanceship has to be got through, no misdoubting inquiries as to kindred temperaments or interests. The sense of unity and mutual confidence is complete and begins from the first unhesitatingly. It was most noticeable, as it had been to me before when a mere looker-on, that this unity, so far from tending to produce uniformity of type, had the very opposite effect, it enhanced individuality. One felt like so many different bolts and cranks and wheels of a machine, each bringing a different quality to serve a different purpose for the smooth working of the whole.

For the first time in my life I felt of some use; since we all were so different from each other, it seemed we could each contribute something to the general solidarity of experience of. opinion, of conduct.

The throwing about had brought on an aggressive cough which at first checked my ardour to brisk up with my companions. I found refuge in a distant bow window where there was a seat, and where I managed to allay the worst of my cough. Presently a wardress appeared. I asked her if we might have a glass of water for myself and one other woman who had a badly hurt ankle. She was most kind and quickly brought several glasses. I wrote a letter to my mother, reassuring her as to our having got through all right, assuming that some account of the way the women had been treated would appear in the press the next morning, and knowing how great would be her anxiety in consequence. As I recovered from the excessive spasms of the cough, I was able to talk to some of my companions. I felt, for about the fiftieth time since I had come in touch with the W.S.P.U., ashamed of myself in their presence. They were drawn from many different grades of society.

Several were women of considerable intellectual gifts, a good many were from the leisured class, some belonged to the working class. Most of them could look back on lives of much more useful service to the community than I could boast, many had made sacrifices greater than my own to join the deputation, several were running much graver risk, physically, in facing the hardship of prison than I incurred. Some had to face a situation in their homes more distressing even than my own. My little share of difficulty and sacrifice, of risk and dread, which had completely filled my horizon for so many weeks, seemed insignificant enough now. Time passed very slowly, but rather from intensity of interest, acuteness of minute observation, than from boredom. We were to be detained until the House of Commons rose. At last at about eleven the light in the Clock Tower went out and our good friend, Mr. Pethick Lawrence, appeared and bailed us out for the night. One by one we again passed before a seated head constable and his book, and were handed an official paper requiring us to appear at Bow Street the next morning.

I had made no arrangements as to where I should spend the night, my chief concern having been to keep secret my share in the day's proceedings till they were over. I felt stunned and cold as ice. I was in a sense, of course, satisfied and glad that, at least, I had shared what the other women had endured, but for the first time during that day it had come before me forcibly that, not only the government, but the general public too were to a great extent responsible for the official treatment of the deputation. I shuddered when I remembered the crowd of curiosity mongers, most of them "respectable" looking people who had treated the whole thing as a kind of cock-fight, and who took sides with the baiters or the baited, according to their apparent likeliness of victory. It was revolting, the kind of thing I could not have believed of a London crowd unless I had myself witnessed it. It made me feel ashamed to the marrow of my bones.

★★★★★★

I met a lady, Winifred, Lady Arran, in July, 1911, who told me that she had been in Parliament Square and had seen our Deputation. She saw and recognised me. "But," she said, "you seemed not to realise that all the men in the crowd were for you."

44

★★★★★★

I took a four-wheeler and made for my youngest sister's house in Bloomsbury Square. On the way, by as it seemed a strange coincidence, I passed my eldest sister, who was just emerging from a theatre with a friend. I stopped and spoke to her. She apparently did not notice my dishevelled condition or suspect that I had been with the deputation. She told me that she too was staying in Bloomsbury Square. Arrived there, I found my hostess in bed. I asked her if she could put me up.

"You've been with the deputation?" she asked.

"Yes."

"You've not been arrested yourself?"

"Yes."

Her look of mingled sympathy and satisfaction was life-giving, I shall never forget it. Both my sisters were immensely kind and helpful. The house was full, and I shared a bed with my eldest sister. All night she kept her strong arm round my heart and steadied my throbbing body which, owing to the attentions of the police, continued to shake all night. Several times in the night my sister said with great distress, "Oh! Con, you arc not fit to go to prison;" but she, of course, was thinking only of the physical side of things. We were able to discuss what best could be done to comfort Mother. Neither of my sisters ever tried to persuade me to take advantage of any possible way out from imprisonment if it should be offered at the trial. They knew my decision could only have been taken after deep and prolonged consideration and for reasons good enough in my estimation to outweigh all those against.

CHAPTER 4: POLICE COURT TRIAL

In the morning we telephoned to mother, supposing she would have received my letter, telling her of the trial at Bow Street that morning, but begging her not to come up for it unless she specially wished to do so. This telephone message was, unfortunately, the first news that reached her of my arrest, and was a great shock to her. She could not have caught a train that would have brought her in time to Bow Street; my eldest sister, Betty Balfour, and my eldest brother, Vic, went down to her later in the day. I felt happier than I had done for a long time. I knew that the first news would be the worst to her, that had now reached her, all else would seem unimportant in comparison; the most difficult, most dreaded part of my job was over. I felt less ill in health than the day before, only played out. My one anxiety was lest I should break down physically and be dismissed from the prison at once "on medical grounds." The wish to avoid this contingency was about as stimulating a tonic as could be desired. It had exactly the same happy effect upon me as some people seem to derive from a glass of brandy.

My sister, Betty Balfour, drove with me in a hansom to Bow Street. A considerable crowd was waiting outside the police station; we elbowed our way through them with great difficulty and only by the help of the police, to whom we appealed to ease matters "for one of the accused." I felt dazed with the press of people. Before long I found myself in a sort of loose-box guard-room, or wide passage, where all my fellow criminals and many of their friends were assembled. Many of my personal friends were there and most heart-gladdeningly kind to me. I had concocted a short speech, explaining the reasons of my action. I was told it was not very likely that the magistrate would allow me to deliver it; my friends kindly helped me to condense it as much as possible. It consisted of about four short paragraphs, sentences bearing on the reasonableness, justice and urgency of our demand. I remember nothing of it but these words:

I have been more proud to stand by my friends in their trouble than I have ever been of anything in my life before.

Presently there was a roll call and we were all told off to the various policemen who had taken us prisoners. I had been so exhausted at the moment of my capture the night before that I had not realised what sort of a human being underlay the helmet and uniform responsible for my arrest. In the morning I saw that he was a particularly pleasant-spoken and obliging man, who seemed to understand all about it from our point of view. He explained what I had to do. We were first congregated in a sort of waiting-room with a wooden bench round the wall, and then, as our time drew near, we were called out into a narrow passage where the particular policemen who were charging us stood facing us against the opposite wall. It looked as if we were *vis à vis* partners waiting for a country dance to strike up. We went into the court as our names were called. I was thankful that I knew a little of the hang of the business from having been present at the trial of Mrs. Pankhurst, Christabel Pankhurst and Mrs. Drummond.

It is the absolutely unknown element in these kinds of ceremonies that adds considerably to their fearfulness. My name came rather early on the list. I was thankful that at least this time I had not to go into the awe-inspiring witness-box. Sir Albert de Rützen was the magistrate; he seemed old for the work. His manner throughout was querulous rather than dignified. The feeling of publicity and exposure struck me as completely odious; I was extremely nervous and rather dazed. I remember thinking, "If I feel like this, what must it be for the ordinary prisoners, whether guilty or not, who, day after day, file into this court?"

I had a vague sense that friends were present amongst the crowd at the back of the court, but the mechanism of the official proceedings and the individuals who worked it seemed all at enmity with us—all, that is, except my partner the policeman. His look, manner and voice were so friendly that the set phrases in which he told of my conduct in Parliament Square and consequent arrest had a strangely incongruous and unreal ring about them. Not that he accused me of anything very terrible. He reported that I had pushed past him exclaiming, "I must see Mr. Asquith, I must get to Mr. Asquith." I had never said anything of the kind, but no doubt, in the policeman's estimation, this was a remark in keeping with my actions, and he thought it most probable that I had said words to that effect. I did not comment on the charge. It seemed all to be known and settled beforehand, and the processes which had to be got through seemed more or less farcical and unreal. When allowed to speak, I managed hastily to blurt out some of my speech, but I felt that nobody listened.

The sentence was one month, with the alternative of being bound over to "keep the peace." I was immensely relieved that there was no fine. At the same time the length of the sentence was a surprise and somewhat of a shock, although I had prepared myself for it. It seemed hardly believable that what I had done was really considered worthy of four weeks in prison. I must, nevertheless, have heard, though the fact did not penetrate into my mind, that Miss Joachim and several others had, less than a year ago, been given three months for this crime of going on a deputation—they, like myself, were first offenders.

On leaving the court we were taken downstairs to the cells. Four or five of us were put together. I was in one with Miss Daisy Solomon, Miss Elsa Gye, my guide and friend of the day before, Miss Dugdale and a sympathetic young girl unknown to me. These cells are narrow compartments, unfurnished, except for a wide wooden bench running the entire length of one wall and terminating in a lavatory seat. This was unconcealed and without any means of drawing water from within the cell. It was periodically flushed with water by a pulley communicating with all the cells from outside. The door had a small grating of iron bars, through which one could look and speak to people outside. Many of our friends came by in the passage and spoke to us through this grille. They also brought us some sandwiches and fruit—very acceptable. This was the worst moment for the friends, and several mothers who came to say goodbye to their daughters must have left feeling very miserable. I felt thankful that my mother was not there. For me, it seemed the best moment for many a long day.

My part was over, so far as initiative and activities were concerned, the rest required only enduring, always a much easier job to my lazy temperament. My sisters and youngest brother came to bid me goodbye. Some other friends came and said "Well done," or words of that kind. Christabel Pankhurst came. She said "Thank you," and seemed grateful for my share in the day's work. This was a most unlooked-for honour and joy, from that moment I felt a very privileged and happy person. The sound of her voice and the look in her eyes remained stamped upon my mind, and played the part of a sort of talisman of consolation whenever the trials of my imprisonment weighed upon my spirits.

As for the physical hardships of prison, these had been the first items to be measured and prepared for when deciding to go on the deputation; of all the anticipatory difficulties they had been the least, and it was a comfort to think that now, before long, one would know the worst in this respect. I felt considerably exhausted still from the battering about the day before, and I had a craving to be alone. Unlimited hours of "solitary confinement" were the most desirable paradise I could vision to myself.

It was a time of longer waiting than I had ever thought a single day could contain. Already one began to taste that peculiar feature, most markedly characteristic of the whole of prison life, that of being in ignorance of what is going on outside your cell, of why you are being kept there, and of what will happen to you when the keys jangle, bolts rattle, the door is thrown open and you are ordered out. We passed the time recommending to each other various dodges of how to keep in touch while in prison. Knocks on the cell walls with a brush or boot, and at the hour when the wardresses went to meals it was said to be possible to communicate by speaking on the hot water pipe, which runs through all the cells, at the point where it touches the wall. We were to maintain the right to talk to each other at associated labour. Mrs. Pankhurst had obtained the right to speak to her daughter when they were in prison together. Otherwise the silence rule, at all other times we were told, was very rigidly enforced. I showed my companions some leg and arm exercises which I urged them to do, so as to counteract the want of exercise and general stagnation of life which makes so many people ill in prison.

We had great fun over this. We were all able to send messages and little scraps of letters to our relations. I was distressed that the stranger girl seemed to have no friends, and no one came to the grille to ask for her. It spoilt the pleasure of our visitors. She seemed of a very retiring and unassertive nature, and I did not like to make inquiries as to how we could help her communicate with her friends for fear that she had none. Happily, just before the passage was cleared of all visitors, three kind-looking women came to the window and she sprang up. They were her friends.

The courtesy of the police continued, and Christabel Pankhurst and a few others were allowed to remain talking to us for some time after the general public had been sent out of the passage communicating with the cells.

Knowing that we had yet a long day before us, we in turns took advantage of the lavatory end of the cell, the others mounting guard in a group round the grating to ensure privacy. This was my first experience of the publicity attending this process throughout prison life. It is, without doubt, one of the greatest trials to the better-educated prisoner; my sympathy went out especially to the younger members of our deputation and to all young prisoners.

At about 2.30 there came a jangling of keys, rattling of bolts, and the cell doors were thrown open. We came out and lined up in the passage outside, and our names were called out in the order of our arrest. There were again some delays and waiting in different passages. One seemed to be dealt with much like goods at a custom house, certain facts about one being recurringly inquired after, investigated, noted in a book, and the goods then passed on for the same process to take place elsewhere. Eventually we filed out into a courtyard where the prison van, "Black Maria," as the hull of a great dead ship, awaited her cargo.

The grim appearance of that celebrated vehicle had always been a signal to me, when passing it in the street, for having to repress an instinct to follow it, an awed reverence for the distressful plight of those inside it, an almost maddening craving to know what had been the cause of their law-breaking, the nature of their crimes, how far their present degradation could morally uplift them, what was happening to their human belongings, what would happen to themselves when they were once more free, whether indignation, revolt, dull indifference, remorse, or the harrowingly abject penitence so frequent in suffering beings was uppermost in their minds. Now I myself was one of the criminals. I should know the sensations from actual experience, literally from within.

Of course I in no sense regarded myself as a criminal, and was aware of a detached spectator's commentary running through my mind all the while. It suddenly struck me, perhaps, after all, this is a sensation common to many criminals. A good number of them no doubt either know they have not, or think they have not, committed the offence for which they are condemned. Many, while admitting their acts, probably have a moral standard with regard to them quite different from that which controls the law. Others, perhaps, like myself, think their acts were entirely justified and right; some, again, would feel consciously and aggressively at war with all recognised standards.

I had several times seen men arrested and male prisoners in the streets, travelling, outside prisons and police courts, but I had never seen any women prisoners. Suddenly the picture of them and of women's crimes came into my mind with a rush. Who were the women who, day by day, trod the very stones on which my feet now stood, whose eyes would look up, a few minutes after mine, to the terrifying form of Black Maria? How and why had they broken the law, in what way were they enemies of Society? The impress of their feet seemed to be one with mine, and up from that criminals' pavement their mind seemed to get into my own. Child burdened women who were left without money, without the means or opportunity or physical power to earn it, who had stolen in order to save their lives and that of their children,—thieves!

Women who from their childhood had been trained to physical shame, women who at their first adolescence had borne children by their own fathers under circumstances when resistance was inconceivable. Women who had been seduced by their employers. Women deceived and deserted by their friends and lovers. Women employed by their own parents for wage-earning prostitution. Women reduced to cruelty after being for years the unconsulted churning mills for producing in degradation and want and physical suffering the incessant annual babies of an undesired family. Women who had been stolen in their bloom and imprisoned for purposes of immoral gain.

If amongst such women, such criminals, there are many who are professionally thieves, prostitutes "by choice," immoral "past redemption" as it is called, sodden with drink, undermined by drug taking, their maternity transformed into cruelty, their brains worn to madness, what cause is there for surprise or reproach, and what hope is there of cure by imprisonment? Before they took to these muddy lanes have they not been driven out from the fair road? What was their training, what their choice from the start? Are not the doors of the professions and many trades still barred to them? Their right to work, a fair value for their work, is it not denied to them? When they undertake the burdensome but joyous labour of maternity, is there any security to them of physical respect and choice, of economic security, of rewardful honour and social influence? Where is the recognition of the woman's great service, how is she helped to render it suitably and efficiently; does the State, the race, the family, the individual, see to it that she has her reward?

I moved forward after the others. Black Maria looked like a sort of hearse with elephantiasis—warranted to carry many coffins concealed in her body and to bear them to as many graves. She fairly set one shuddering. To get inside her seemed a sort of living death, certainly, most literally, entry into another world. For a moment I hesitated and thought, "Suppose I refuse to get in?" The mere notion called up the forces arrayed against one and made me realise my utter helplessness. The gates, the bolts, locks and chains, the cells we had just left, the court and magistrate, the high walls all around, the enormous policemen on every hand. The one who stood at the open door of the van said, "Come along, please." His words were civil enough and linked one back to the normal outer world, but his voice and beckoning gesture were authoritative and the sense of physical power seemed to wedge one in. It was clear that henceforth all one's actions would be initiated and carried out without choice, solely by necessity of obedience.

The policeman who had special charge of us for the journey was a man of jovial disposition, and he cracked witticisms as he played his 'bus-conductor's part. We readily responded to his mood. An antidote was needed to the grimness of the proceedings, but the merriment was by no means all forced. As soon as I laid aside the remembrance of the real prisoners and limited the outlook to that of our own immediate experience, the comic element was rampant and seemed to dig one in the ribs, making me laugh with heartiness. We were all, it seemed, playing some ludicrous, babyish game, unsuited to our years, but all the more absurd for that.

The 'bus-conductor-policeman got inside; we followed him one by one into the narrow central gangway that forms the spinal marrow of Black Maria. On either side are tiny separate cells, like the compartments of a cupboard, the doors of which when opened completely obstruct the passage so that only one prisoner at a time can be admitted or released. On first getting in it seems quite dark, and the sensation of being rapidly pushed into a very small hole, squeezed back, the door shut and locked to the accompanying sound of banging and much jangling and turning of keys, is extremely disagreeable.

The cell contains a seat and is ventilated by a grating in the door, by groups of small holes on either side, in the floor at one's feet, and by a wire-netted ventilator running under the roof of the van, as in a 'bus. The cell was so small that my legs, which are long, had to be tucked up almost under my chin; I could imagine that in hot weather the want of air would be oppressive, but though the sense of being so closely confined was disagreeable, the draughts from the ventilators seemed to play upon one almost excessively and I felt very cold. When the cells were all filled the passage was duly packed with prisoners, standing one against the other like tinned sardines. As the van was not high enough to admit of standing upright, this must have been a most tiring position. Presently there was a final shutting and locking of the outer door, in which was a small grating window, as we know it from the outside. Then followed a rumbling jerk and Black Maria's great overcharged body began her long, jolting drive to Holloway. The sensation reminded me of a bathing machine when it sets out for the sea, but the noise and jolting and darkness were all greater in degree.

We tried to communicate with each other, to find out who was in which cell and who was standing in the passage. We started singing the Women's *Marseillaise* and other of our songs. Those in the passage managed to put a scarf with our colours through the ventilator under the coachman's seat, others passed a scarf through the grating window of the door at the opposite end. These feats were, of course, communicated to the whole Mariafull of us, and the news that the police were allowing the scarves to remain was greeted with much cheering. Possibly, the driver was unconscious of his magnanimous action, since the scarf end, I expect, flowed put somewhere near his feet. The colours every now and then were seen and loudly cheered by friends in the street. This woke in me an appreciation of the colours and understanding of their meaning in a way I had not grasped before.

There is so little need for symbolism in these days of print, newspapers, advertisements, etc., but our movement has had to combat all the conditions of an era of darkness, ignorance, and barbaric repression. When newspapers will not accept, publishers will not print, and booksellers will not sell the true facts concerning us, then a rapid means of irrepressible communication had to be sought through the symbolism of colours, purple, white and green—justice, purity, hope. Wherever you see them you know we are there, and you know our meaning.

I joined in the songs for as long as I could and in the counter-cheering whenever we had a cheer from the streets, but I soon withdrew into the luxury of my solitude. I was exhilarated and happy in mind, but my physical exhaustion was considerable. The physical tax of the Deputation and the nervous tax of the trial proceedings had strained my powers to their uttermost. At last I was alone with myself. The sense of release from the necessity of keeping up appearances, of having to put on a good front, was great. I wondered how often the occupants of my cell in that black hive must have felt the same after the anguish, suspense, complication of fears, connected with their trial. I noticed that if for a moment I entertained the idea of initiative, action, the wish to touch normal existence, to be and behave like an ordinary being, then the sense of subjection, of being buried alive was all but insufferable and might quickly drive one to the verge of insanity. But the physical exhaustion which leads to the craving for inanition, for solitude and privacy, turned that locked-up slice of the van into a welcome sanctuary.

After a long drive, for seemingly the better part of an hour, the sounds changed and Black Maria quivered over a courtyard pavement, filling us with expectations of arrival. The jolting and noise ceased, the doors were unlocked, one by one as we had been packed in we emerged again and were quickly ushered into Holloway Prison, through what seemed a back door in a yard surrounded by high walls. It made no particular impression upon me. It might have been another police court, less dingy and more clean.

CHAPTER 5: HOLLOWAY PRISON

When we arrived at the prison we formed up along a passage in the order of our arrest. We were taken in charge by two or three wardresses who, without a word or sign of greeting, went through the routine of taking our names, ages, sentences, etc. Then we were removed into waiting cells, three or four of us to each one. I found myself, to my joy, in a cell with our leader, Mrs. Pethick Lawrence, Miss Leslie Lawless and Mrs. Fahey, daughter of the great sculptor Gilbert. Strength came back into my bones with delight at being with Mrs. Lawrence. She having been in the prison before gave us various directions and advice. The cell was small and old, the walls and ceiling were dirty, the window of grained glass looked extremely dingy; but Mrs. Lawrence said that in all probability we should eventually be put into new and very clean cells. There was only one stool. Mrs. Lawrence had to sacrifice herself and sit on it, as we none of us would do so in her presence. We ranged ourselves at her feet on the floor, some of us leaning back against the wall. I was very happy to meet Mrs. Fahey, her father and mine had known one another; everything about her had the indication that she was a good woman and probably would become a great one.

I remember vaguely that conversation turned on to personal yarns as to how we had severally fared during the deputation, what had first brought us into the movement, the experiences of ex-prisoners. We were to try and claim associated labour and the right to speak to each other at that time. All other rules so far as we could grasp them were to be rigidly observed. If anything in the prison routine seemed to us unjust we were to petition the Home Secretary about it, or ask for an interview with the governor. If we were ill or felt that any part of the prison life was being seriously injurious to our health, we were to ask to see the doctor.

But my recollection of the two or three hours spent in this cell are vague and shadowy. I was at the end of my tether, and the craving to be alone overtopped everything else. Soon after we were inside a light was lit from without, and I noticed for the first time a curious aperture in the thick wall to the left of the door. A piece of grained glass near to the passage side of this hole, shielded the light which was lit from outside. The cell was thus lit up with rays as from a bull's eye lantern. These details interested me very much. I was fascinated in a grim sort of way by the "eye" in the door of which I had heard so much. An oval wedge-shaped indentation in the thick nail-studded door, at about the height of one's head, was finished off in the centre by a small circular bit of glass about the size of a large eyeglass. On the passage side of the door this was overlaid with a bit of wood which could be turned aside like the flap over a key-hole, for the warders and others to take a look at the prisoner, unobserved, whenever they chose.

Presently there was a rattling of keys, the lock turned with what seemed a thundering sound and the door burst open. I thought it must be some remarkable and unexpected event that had caused so much hurry and noise, a fire perhaps had broken out, but this was my first introduction to the prison door drill; the thunder and rattle and haste I was soon to learn were the invariable accompaniments of being visited for no matter what cause. The door was opened only a very little way. No face was to be seen, but a hand thrust in four tins of food and loaves of bread on to a little shelf in the corner of the cell nearest to the door. This was our supper—the last meal before the night. The little brown loaves looked appetising, and we were hungry. The kind of breakfast one eats before one's first "trial" is nothing sumptuous, and the sandwiches brought in by our friends made an excellent but not too substantial lunch. The slice of cold pressed meat lying at the bottom of a dirty-looking tin was not attractive, and the cocoa in a can of the same metal was positively repellent. We most of us ate some bread, one was bold enough to try the cocoa, no one sampled the meat. I thought I would keep my loaf as a sleeping draught for whenever bedtime came to this seemingly endless day.

Some time after supper had been let in upon us, the door was again opened and "Lytton" was summoned to an unknown presence. I was conducted to a room where a lady in a bonnet stood waiting to receive me. She was the matron. She told me in a civil and considerate manner that she had a letter for me from my mother which she had been allowed to give to me. I wondered if my mother were ill or inordinately distressed at my sentence. I had a great longing to take the letter, but I had prepared myself for special privileges being extended to me and I was determined not to profit by anything of the sort unless I could also secure it for my companions. I asked: "Is it not against prison rules that I should have the letter?"

She looked surprised, but promptly answered, "We make the rules as the occasion calls for, and you have been allowed to receive this letter."

"Will the other Suffrage prisoners also be allowed to receive letters?"

She hesitated, but eventually said decisively, "No."

"Then I am afraid I can't have this letter either."

In spite of my effort to conceal it, I think she saw or guessed my great desire to have the letter, for the look in her eyes became very kind and she pleaded with me to take the letter. I shook my head. Then she told me it was within the ordinary rules that she should read the letter to me. I hesitated for a moment; there might be something sacredly private in the letter and it seemed such desecration that strangers should know what my mother felt. Then I glanced at the envelope and realised that it had been officially opened and probably read already. So I agreed. The letter had been written under the agitation of the news about me and was not easily legible in places, so that the matron, although she did her best, could not decipher some passages, and the tension of deferred anxiety as to its contents made my mind and hearing dull from overstrain. As a result, I received the impression that my mother was more angry with me than was actually the case. She did not speak of being ill or broken down herself, and I felt I could bear everything but that; but the imagined degree of her disapproval shadowed the whole of my imprisonment without cause.

However, when I was handed the letter on my release and read it for myself, I found in it so much more sympathy than I expected that the rebound of joy made up for everything. My mother had sent it by her maid to London, telling her to deliver it into the hands of the governor with a covering letter to him asking him kindly to give it to me. She had thought out all this most considerately so that at least I might be reassured about herself, and be spared any unnecessary anxiety. The maid, on arriving at Holloway Prison, had sent my mother's card up to the governor as a passport to his presence and asking if she, the maid, might see him. He understood it to mean that mother herself was there, and he came rushing down the stairs in hot haste to greet her! Poor man, how relieved he must have been to find it was only her maid!

After the matron had finished reading the letter I, for the moment, forgot all wish to restrict my privileges into line with those of other Suffragettes. I asked, "Can I write an answer to this letter?"

"No."

"Nor send a message?"

The matron shook her head. On returning to my companions in the waiting cell I told them what had taken place. My mind was filled with thoughts of my mother and I remember no details until the door was again thrown open and a wardress told us to line up in the passage, preparatory to inspection by the medical officer. It was good to see the rest of the deputation once more. We were told to open our dresses and underclothes at the neck so that our chests might be examined.

There was some further waiting, during which time I was able to take note of the wardresses, several of whom were waiting about and superintending us while others came and went.

They were fine-looking women, young and vigorous, most of them had good figures and all of them had beautifully-kept hair which gave me a. deal of pleasure to look at. They wore uniforms more or less in the style of hospital nurses. Most of them wore dresses of dark blue cloth with nurse-like, small black bonnets and strings. Some had holland dresses with aprons, and black velvet bows on their heads. They held themselves very upright, and their general bearing brought to my mind certain types of the chaperon's bench at court balls.

I had made up my mind to ask the doctor for a few medical privileges. I dreaded lest he was coming round to inspect and question us as we stood in the passage, or that we should have to go before some "board" or "committee" of men. To my relief I found that we were being shown into a room singly, and when it came to my turn I found there only one individual, a young man sitting at a table with a big book in front of him. I stood beside him and answered his questions with regard to my age, whether I was married or single, what illnesses I had had, etc. He then tapped my lungs and examined my heart with a stethoscope. An infancy and youth of chronic rheumatism had affected my heart, and the treatment I had received as member of the deputation had taxed it severely.

Moreover, the news of my mother's distress, the prison sounds of keys and bolts, the look of the cells, and my fears lest the doctor should take alarm at my flimsy physique and order my dismissal from the prison, each added considerably to my agitation of that moment. The doctor's impassive face and manner changed to one of concerned inquiry after testing my heart. He asked many questions, and seemed with difficulty to believe when I told him that strict vegetarianism had cured my chronic rheumatism and that it was six years since I had anything of an attack. I asked to be allowed flannel underclothing and vegetarian food. It was a new and strange experience to be so closely examined by a doctor and not to learn anything of his verdict. I longed to ask him "What are you going to report about me?" but I knew that I could do nothing if he should answer "Dismiss you," and I was anxious to end the interview as soon as possible.

After the medical examination we were soon taken off, separately, to the changing room. Here my trinkets, money, watch, the combs in my hair, and everything in my pocket were taken from me and a list made, which I had to sign. I had a great longing to keep my hand-kerchiefs. A wardress sitting at a desk with a large book on it asked a further string of questions as to age, name, address, place of birth, previous convictions. As I gave "Vienna, Austria," for the place of my birth, my father having been in the diplomatic service, I thought how impossible it would have seemed had some seer foretold, at the time of my birth in an official residence, that I was destined to be imprisoned in Holloway as a common criminal.

A description of the prisoner's personal appearance was also en-tered in the book. It was a comic moment when the wardress looked up with her head on one side, as any portrait painter might do, to investigate the colour of one's hair and eyes. During all these processes I had a first opportunity of noticing the manner of the wardresses which so many Suffragette friends had described to me, but which had conveyed no clear impression to my mind. I noticed that there was no inflection in the voice when speaking to prisoners, nor did the wardresses look at them when addressing them.

As a prisoner, it was almost impossible to look in the eyes of my keepers, they seemed to fear that direct means of communication; it was as if the wardresses wore a mask, and withdrew as much as pos-sible all expression of their own personality or recognition of it in the prisoner. At first, the impression received was as of something farcical. I remember that it amused me immensely and absorbed my attention with a sort of fascinated curiosity. But this soon went off, and made way for a chilling, deadening impression. When later on I saw it ap-plied to the ordinary prisoner, to my companions, to our leader, Mrs. Pethick Lawrence, it aroused in me a feeling of indignation and strong resentment. One corner of this room was divided off by a curtain. I was told to go behind it and take off my clothes. As I removed them one by one I wondered what would have been my experiences by the time I should see them again. I was handed a cotton chemise, wool-len stockings and a petticoat. In this queer get-up I was taken to be weighed and then shown to a bath.

The bath compartments were close together in a passage, like stalls in a stable, each one only just large enough to contain the bath and a few inches of standing room at one end. The door was of the cowshed order, about three feet deep, space above and below, and without a fastening. As I was ushered into one of these, an ordinary 3rd Division prisoner handed me a bundle of clothes and a pair of laced shoes. She had a charming, sympathetic face, and I never shall forget the look of deep kindness in her eyes and in her voice as she whispered to me, "If the shoes are too small, ask the officer and she'll let you have a larger pair." My tired body, my very soul, seemed to bask in comfort at her words. I looked and nodded my thanks to her, afraid to speak, for I had been warned how we might get the prisoners into trouble by breaking the silence rule with them.

"So this is the bath of evil fame," I thought, as I put down the bundle of clothes on the floor and pulled the cowshed door after me. For the most part, whatever bit of prison life I had heard about as specially objectionable seemed to me less bad than I had expected, and being prepared I was forearmed to put up with it without grumbling. But the much-abused, dirty bath which had been so often described by our prisoners, surpassed all expectations. The paint was blistered and broken to a surface of mottled unevenness in a way to gather the scum from the water into a thousand crevices every time the bath was used. Whatever the original colour of the paint might have been, it was now of a dull mud colour, sufficiently dirty-looking to arouse every sort of suspicion, but not dark enough to conceal the marks of the scum most recently added to the crevices.

A large but well-worn scrubbing brush was the only washing appliance, whether for the purpose of scrubbing the bath or the bather was not stated, probably it was used indiscriminately for both. I had been given a small towel of oatmeal coloured coarse linen striped with red, and a piece of soap wrapped up in a rag of white flannelette. The water was clean and delightfully hot. I tried to concentrate my mind on these two great merits and to raise a sense of present luxury by remembering that this was the last bath I should be able to indulge in for a week. The soap had a smell of disinfectant like dog soap, clean and hygienic enough, no doubt, but under the circumstances a disagreeable reminder of its anti-verminous properties.

The towel, which at first sight seemed ludicrously small and inadequate for the purpose of drying a body so large as mine, disclosed with use an almost miraculous faculty for not absorbing moisture. It left one to dry by dint of friction; my admiration for this towel grew even greater on closer acquaintance with it. Then came the moment for the clothes. They certainly looked a most repellent heap, and it was some time before I recognised their respective uses, and could decide in what order to put them on. I was pleased to see that the flannel garments promised by the doctor were there. Some of my companions, although they asked for and received permission for the same privilege, did not get any flannel clothes until the second week, and some not through the whole term of their imprisonment.

Warmth being my first consideration I started off with a low-necked flannel shirt without sleeves. It was patched in many places, the patches being so coarsely joined that one could easily trace their pattern from sensation while wearing it. The flannel was of numerous shades of yellow and grey, stained in many places, and freely marked with the broad arrow stamped on in black ink. The original cut of the shirt had evidently been nondescript. It was very short, reaching barely below the hips and low at the neck, and the patches set in at random had added variety and counter design in many directions. It looked like the production of a maniac. For propaganda purposes it was an absolutely priceless garment and I determined that, if possible, it should accompany me out of prison, for the enlightenment of those critics who are appalled, at the leniency of the prison treatment of Suffragettes.

Next I put on a chemise of unbleached, coarse cotton, striped with red, fairly high at the neck, but without sleeves. This however, was long to the knees and from its ample voluminous width was one of the most warmth producing of the garments. A pair of stays made without bones but exceedingly stiff and straight in shape. They had no fastenings and had to be laced up each time; the lace had no metal tag so that it was a slow process. These stays were so unyielding that I found it impossible to tie my petticoats around the sheer precipice of their make, and the very next day I had the courage to dispense with them. Flannel drawers, short like footballing "shorts," *ditto* of unbleached cotton. A very short flannel petticoat. An old-fashioned under-petticoat of coarse, linseed-coloured material, thickly pleated into a cotton band at the waist—it stuck out almost like a crinoline.

Then came the dress, skirt of dark green serge, pleated in same way as the petticoat and tied with black tape strings, the shirt of same material fastened by a single button at the neck; this was the only garment with long sleeves. A blue check apron which tied in the shirt and gave a very neat appearance. Finally, a small Dutch cap of starched white calico, tied under the chin with tapes. These caps are full of stains, from hairpin rust, etc., when seen from within, but outwardly they have an extremely clean and attractive appearance, redeeming the degraded look of the dress and decidedly becoming to many of the women. They pleased me immensely from the first and were a constant joy to my eyes in all my imprisonments.

Two check dusters were supplied, one as a handkerchief to hang from the apron string, one to be folded diagonally and worn round the neck, under the serge shirt. I always have thought this the most comfortable neck covering imaginable and the short time it takes to put on was a daily renewed pleasure compared to the complicated neck apparatus of more civilised modern garments with their innumerable hooks and eyes, pins, brooches, etc. The drawback to this duster-necktie was that it was identical with the handkerchief-duster, and, as they were changed from week to week, there was no means of knowing whether one's neckerchief of one week had not been the nose kerchief of another prisoner on previous occasions, As the clothes came from the laundry with many stains, unironed, unmangled, and looking in many respects as if they had not been washed, this detail of the handkerchiefs remained throughout my time in prison one of the most trying of the physical and minor disagreeables.

All the clothes were marked with the broad arrow, if light in colour they were marked with black ink or some kind of tar-like sticky substance; if the clothes were dark, as the petticoat and dress, then with whiting. The stockings were of thick, rough wool, most irritating to the skin but warm. I never had a pair that were long enough to cover my knees, and as the drawers stopped short of the knees in the opposite direction I had the chance of sampling the knee part of a Highlander's dress. I thought it very uncomfortable.

Woollen strips were given for garters; I thought these practical and hygienic. Last of all I turned to the shoes. They were immensely heavy and looked large enough for a giant, they were new and exceedingly stiff. After a great struggle I managed to get them on, but they were so uncomfortable that I remembered the advice of the kind woman and took them off again. I supposed that now would be my only chance of asking for another pair, and, although I never have been able to muster much courage in facing rebuffs, I had an impression that I should not grow any bolder as prison life went on.

It is comparatively easy to plead or protest on behalf of some general principle, but to do so for personal advantage was a more effortful business, and yet it seemed foolish to go in for needless discomforts when a remedy had been almost officially suggested. I gathered up my soap and towel and put my head over the cowshed door to inquire if I might come out. My eyes fell on a prisoner waiting in the passage. She was of the 2nd Division, for she wore a green dress; those of the 3rd Division wear brown. Her face had a genial expression and broke into a radiant smile as our eyes met. I thought I had never seen a more attractive-looking being. In spite of the subservient humility which the prison uniform conveys, the look of self-mastery and consequent dignity was prominently expressed in every line of her face and of her whole form. I felt drawn to her by a feeling of mixed curiosity and sympathy and determined to communicate with her if possible.

It never occurred to me that she was a Suffragette. She was Mrs. Pethick Lawrence, as the smile in her eyes betrayed before many moments had passed. My delight at recognising her was quickly succeeded by an almost irrepressible wave of indignant feeling that she should be subjected to these outward symbols of criminality and shame. However little they were able to degrade her, the authorities had sentenced her to wear them with that intent. The futility and injustice of their action seemed to me at that moment about on a par with each other.

A wardress told me I might come out. I picked up my shoes and went with them in my hand to an "officer" who seemed to be the most authoritative person present. I said to her, "I find these shoes are rather small for me. Could you kindly let me have a bigger pair?" She seemed not to have heard what I said, did not look my way, but shouted past me into the air, speaking in a loud voice, very rapidly, and without any variety of intonation in a way that sounded strange and unnatural, as if she were proclaiming an edict written by another person:

It's—no—good—complaining—about—those; they're—the—largest—size—in—stock; you—can't—have—any—others—so—you'd—better—make—the—best—of—them.

As soon as I realised that she was answering me I felt very curious and interested. "So that is what it means," I thought, "being in prison."

It required no flight of the imagination, no tags of theory, to understand what the effect of this manner would be on an ordinary prisoner.

Mrs. Lawrence and I waited together in the passage. Presently a wardress came up to us with a paper in her hand and began reading out the prison rules, which we were told had to be strictly observed under pain of punishment. There were a great many dealing with a variety of subjects. She read very fast like a wooden automaton, as if she herself were weary of this too frequent job. Although I had heard of many of the rules before from previous prisoners, I could with difficulty catch the drift, and it struck me how little the ordinary prisoner would be able to glean from this hurried reading of rules absolutely new to her, framed in official language often far beyond her comprehension.

We were then led off through various corridors, taken out of doors and into another building, weighed a second time, and taken up a staircase. At the top we were told to remove our shoes and carry them in our hands. In the passage there were cells with locked gates that looked very grim, and locked doors behind them. One door opposite the stairs was open and the gate only closed. This was unlocked for us and we were ushered into a large high room. A fire burned brightly at one end and beds were ranged on either side of the walls. It was evidently a hospital ward. We were shown to the beds nearest the fireplace, on either side of it, and told they would be ours.

Mrs. Lawrence came over to me and whispered, "They have put us in hospital." The one thing on which my hopes had centred throughout that seemingly eternal day was the prospect of being completely alone at the end of it. Now that was not to be. For the first time I was taken unawares, had made no preparation for the contingency; I felt quite unnerved and could have sobbed like a child. The fact that I was to remain with Mrs. Lawrence was my only consolation.

The ward was large and high, with big windows of grained glass at either end, opened at the top by pulleys so that one could not see out, but the ventilation was perfect. There were grating ventilators as well as the windows. It was well warmed by hot pipes running the length of one wall and by a large coal fire. The furnishings of the fire-place were both comic and grimly suggestive. A cage of thick iron bars covered it, from the mantelpiece to the floor, the cage had a central gate fastened by a padlock and inside this prison was a poker chained to the side of the grate, as if it could not be trusted not to run away and escape through the iron bars of the cage.

I looked round to see how much of lunacy, or violent criminality, such as were suggested by these precautions, was represented amongst the present inmates. There were ten beds in all, but only four or five occupants; most of them were already in bed—one looked extremely ill. A wardress, like a nurse, in a holland gown, came in accompanied by a 3rd Division prisoner carrying a wicker tray fitted with bottles containing drugs—the "poison-basket" I called it; it returned regularly twice a day. A dark-looking mixture was poured into a little cup and handed to me. I explained that I never took drugs and begged to be excused.

You've got to swallow that tonight—those are my orders, there's no choice about it. You can ask the medical officer about it tomorrow.

I supposed that responsibility for my refusal would fall upon the wardress, so I drank it down.

We were given slippers to replace the coarse nailed shoes which were not allowed to be worn in hospital on account of the polished wooden floor. The slippers were of yellow leather, blackened by much use. They were extremely dirty, both outside and in, and I made up my mind never to wear them without the protection of a stocking. Mine were not a pair, each one had an independence of size and shape which seemed to endow them with almost human personality; but they were comfortable, and I grew strangely fond of them before the end of my time. Our beds were already made; we were each brought a night-gown of coarse, unbleached calico striped with an occasional red line and marked at intervals with the broad arrow in tar-like ink; it had long sleeves. We were also provided with a short, grey flannel dressing-gown and a small tooth-brush.

We were told to undress and to tie up our day clothes in our aprons, all but the caps; these being both white and starched were treated with the utmost reverence. I discovered that this arrangement was most detrimental to the appearance of the apron the next day. Some prison rules, however trivial and apparently unimportant, are rigidly enforced, others after the first instructions are never referred to again. This was one of those, luckily, for an appearance of neatness in the prisoners depends entirely upon the cap and apron. I soon ventured upon a different plan of damping the apron over night, folding it evenly as for ironing and binding it tightly round the heating pipe whenever I could secure a share of that much sought-after luxury, for the pipe was not on my side of the ward. This device was successful to the point of giving me a ludicrous amount of pleasure.

When the clothes were dealt out from the laundry once a week they looked as if they had been washed in cold water by a child, but the hot-pipe dodge soon gave them quite a presentable look. In the free world I am accustomed to sleep in flannel sheets, woollen underclothes, and a hot bottle, also with two flannel pillows. The prison equipment was, of course, not of that order. I took off the dress, stiff petticoat, stays and neckerchief, but kept on all the rest of the day clothing and wore it under my night-gown. I also kept on the nightgown in the day time, as it was the only under-garment with long sleeves. This flagrant break of the regulations on my part was either not observed or was winked at by the authorities while I remained in hospital.

The bedsteads were of iron, the bedding much more luxurious than I had expected—two mattresses, a pillow, three blankets and calico sheets, unbleached, with red stripes, and marked frequently with the broad arrow, as was the rest of the bedding. My sheet, where turned over at the head, had a large stain, as if oil had been dropped upon it. The stain was dry, but, nevertheless, extremely objectionable to look at. I remade the bed, putting the other end qf the sheet at the top, only to find that the stains were everywhere. I seem to have been specially unfortunate in my outfit on arrival, for both this sheet and my flannel shirt were more revolting in appearance than anything I saw again in the whole course of my imprisonments.

In one respect I was lucky. My dress skirt, though painted here and there with the broad arrow and not new, was yet quite clean and of a convenient length; some of us had to submit to a skirt that touched the ground, an undesirable length in a place where dust abounds abnormally and no clothes brush is available, or else so short that the legs were disagreeably exposed and gave the appearance of a child's dress. My dress shirt was quite new, had evidently not been worn before, a luxury which I much appreciated, since the sleeves were worn next to the skin and it was made of non-washing material.

At each end of the bed was a small iron shelf. At the head were kept a pint mug for water, toothbrush, soap, towel, brush and comb.

On the shelf at the foot were a Bible, prayer book, hymn book, small devotional book, called *The Narrow Way*, and an instructive book on domestic hygiene, *A Perfect Home and How To Keep It*. This contained two chapters on the necessity of perfect ventilation in sleeping rooms, the want of which gave rise to ceaseless complaints from the Suffragettes in the cells, and the attempt to instruct prisoners by means of a book, while denying them the primal need therein declared to be essential, seemed a cruel as well as a rather ludicrous form of sarcasm. We proceeded to undress.

I took down my hair, which in those days I wore puffed out round the head by means of fluffing the inner hair. The hairbrush was of the size and shape of a small shoe brush, black and with black bristles which, in this particular brush of mine, were almost worn away. The comb was like a doll's comb, exactly the size of my first finger. Though my hair was not particularly abundant, I struggled in vain for the first two days to get it completely disentangled with these utterly inadequate tools. There were no looking glasses anywhere in the prison except, so I heard it rumoured, in the doctor's room, but I never saw it when there. I did not attempt to dress my hair, but did it up in a tight "bun" at the back of my head. This not only seemed to me most suitable for the prison cap and dress, but also I had an eye to seizing the advantages of the prison life.

If one was not to have the comforts and luxuries of free, civilised existence, I thought one had better shed as many as possible of its burdens; I have always ranked hair dressing as one of these. Some ex-prisoners had told me that the hair pins we took into prison in our hair would have to suffice us till our release. Others said that more could be obtained for the asking. I very soon found out that asking for extras of this kind generally produced a refusal and often something of a scolding as well, so that I limited my requests to those which would, I thought, be of general advantage to others as well as to myself. I never saw any hair pins being given out, and by the day of my release my own supply had fallen to three. Despite this lazy decision on my part I had the greatest admiration for those prisoners who took a contrary view and who in the teeth of difficulties, such as no looking glass, an ever-diminishing supply of hair pins, and the brush and comb as described, yet managed to produce elaborately dressed heads of hair.

Amongst the Suffragettes, a large proportion of them had remarkably beautiful and abundant hair, which when, towards the end of my sentence, I saw them in the exercise yard gave me an immense amount of pleasure. Some of these managed to dress their hair in puffed out and fashionable ways. Amongst the ordinary prisoners I remember one in particular who, in the way of hair dressing, excited my admiration almost to the point of awe. She could boast of no good looks, her face and her hair were of almost the same shade of pale sand-colour. Through all the week-days, whenever I saw her, a generous portion of her front hair was rolled up with bits of the thin, brown toilet paper, of which a practically unlimited supply is served out to each prisoner, and which is put to a great variety of uses.

On Sunday morning the curl papers were there as usual, but on Sunday afternoon the bond-hair was made free and a glory of frizzled hair encircled and brightened her poor, tired face. This adherence to outer-world Sabbatarian tradition and conformity to the requirements of orthodox public opinion had a meaning, an artistic and moral expression almost, in prison, such as they lack when occurring in ordinary life. The good-will and neighbourliness of which, no doubt, they were the outward symbol, had met with their reward, for this woman was allowed a share in some of the more privileged duties of the prison service.

I felt very tired as I laid down in the bed, but my brain was screwed to a pitch of nervous excitement that drove away all possibility of sleep. The bed and pillow were stonily hard. My pulses beat against the pillow; the stuffing of it gave back a sort of rattling echo to every beat. A naked gas jet immediately in front of my eyes was alight all night. At a long table underneath it sat a wardress reading or sewing at her own clothes. One of the patients in a bed next but one to mine seemed to be very ill. She tossed and turned continually, as if in a high fever, and her voice sounded parched as she coughed or called out in a half delirious sleep. My distress for her grew as I watched her. The wardress took not the smallest notice of her. I kept on scheming as to how I could help her, but my courage repeatedly failed me. At last I could bear it no longer. I went up to her bed and whispered, "Is there anything I can do for you?"

She answered, "I should like a little water."

I took the pint mug of white earthenware from the shelf behind her. It was empty; I took it to the wardress. "May I get that patient some water?" I asked. She nodded assent.

I went to a washing-stand with two jugs and basins on it that stood against the wall opposite the entrance door. The wardress beckoned to me and pointed towards another door which led to a small vestibule giving on to a sink and lavatory. This door was kept locked in the day time, but now it was open, another door leading from the vestibule to the landing being locked at night. I drew some fresh water from the tap. The water in Holloway seemed to be like mountain water, better than any I have ever tasted in a town—I suppose because the dry air in prison combined with much dust makes one very thirsty.

The prisoner thanked me most gratifyingly and told me she was very ill with influenza. I ventured to whisper before leaving her, "Are you a Suffragette?"

"Rather," came the prompt reply, and her face brightened at the word.

She was a nurse. Miss Povey, of the Freedom League. The wardress herself had a hard, hacking, bronchial cough, which must have hurt her a good deal. I longed to suggest various things to her to ease it, but

I had not the courage. Though I was immensely tired, all possibility of sleep seemed to go further and further from me, and I was too much on view for my thoughts to rest on my home and our people. Finally, I settled down to watching the wardress and the other prisoners, and wondering who they were and what their crimes. I had never seen many people in bed at night before. It was amusing to watch their various ways of lying and gestures, but none of them seemed to be really asleep, or only for very short spells at a time.

The wardress had meals brought to her, and there would be short snatches of whispered conversation with the wardress who brought them in. It seemed to me that it must be an appalling way of passing one's time. There was not the interest of a night nurse nor the excitement of a policeman on the beat. There was a large clock at one end of the ward above a swing door leading to a lavatory. It was an unexpected luxury to be able to watch the time.

CHAPTER 6: THE HOSPITAL

At about 5.15 a.m. the stillness of the prison was broken by many sounds. One of the unexpected things in prison life are the number of sounds one hears which one cannot interpret at the time, and which are never accounted for afterwards. One early morning sound, or rather wrenching noise, seemed to come from the ward or passages below our own, as if a giant iron fender, with the fire-irons loose and rattling within it, were being dragged from one end of the building to the other.

At home I am no early riser, and I had looked forward with most cowardly dread to the prison routine in this respect. The puritanical elements in my character, which hitherto had failed to drill the rest of me on this point, took on a triumphant air of sanctimonious glee with the expectation that a fundamental reform would be wrought in me by at least this portion of my punishment. But neither the fears of my vices nor the hopes of my virtues were realised. To rise at 5.30 requires no heroism, under any conditions, when you have been allowed to retire to rest at 6.30 or even earlier; but when in addition your bed is extremely uncomfortable, your pillow seems stuffed with thunder, you have with difficulty been able to keep warm, and when you have scarcely been able to sleep a wink all night, then the virtue necessary to make you rise early is nil.

At 5.30 punctually, a little 3rd Division prisoner, who slept in one of the infirmary cells along our passage, came in to clean the grate and fight the fire. She moved very quickly and did her work with precision and dexterity. She had a most attractive and lovable face, refined features and a beautiful expression. I wondered for what crime she had been sent to prison. She wore several stripes on her arm denoting good conduct during a protracted sentence.

Soon after this the wardress came near my bed and said it was time to get up. She told me to make my bed and gave me what she called a duster for the purpose of cleaning the iron bedstead. The duster was a strip of thick sail-cloth, which moved the dust but refused to absorb it. I dusted every part of the iron, turned the mattresses and remade the bed. A thin counterpane of blue check gave a rather pleasing finish. This had to be folded in a particular way at the foot of the bed so as to fall over the side in rectangular fashion. The wardress came up to show me how to do it.

It required a certain dodge which pleased me very much, as did all the other old-maidish fads of the kind in the prison routine. But I found that no two experts achieved this bed-cover fold in quite the same way. On that first morning several of the prisoners, two wardresses, and one of the overseeing wardresses ("officers" is the correct term) came up to my bed and refolded the corners of the bed cover, saying, "You haven't got that quite right," or "That's wrong; this is the way you should do it."

We took it in turns to wash. Hot water was brought by the 3rd Division servant of the ward in jugs. There were two crockery basins on the washing-stand, which stood against the wall in the centre of the ward. Such appointments seemed positively luxurious, but one detail was sorely lacking, and its absence marred all the rest—privacy.

When dressed a superintendent "officer" came into the ward. She looked extremely severe. She asked, "Had I dusted my bed thoroughly before I made it?"

"Yes."

"Had I turned up the movable half of the iron frame, and dusted it underneath?"

"No, I did not know there was a part that turned up."

She said that was wrong, that another morning I must be sure and do it, but she did not tell me to make the bed again. I was fortunate, for I heard afterwards that this same officer took hold of the bedclothes and threw them all off without explaining to their owner anything of what it was about.

Breakfast was brought in at about 6.30. The patients who were well enough to be out of bed laid the cloth and put out plates from a small cupboard hung on the wall near the door. Then a wardress and two 3rd Division prisoners carried in the hot milk and tea in large cans, loaves of bread, a small supply of butter and boiled eggs. The tea was ladled out from the cans with a long tin spoon and poured into the earthenware mugs. It looked as if it must make a great mess, but was always very skilfully done. The mugs and plates, I was pleased to notice, were made of leadless glaze. In ordinary life I have always considered hot boiled milk a very disagreeable drink, but that morning, after the long wide-awake night, it seemed to me positive nectar.

In hospital we were allowed white bread; it was of excellent quality, made of seconds flour. Tea and eggs are no part of my diet, so I was limited to the milk and bread and butter, but they were dealt out abundantly, all except the butter, which was fresh and of fairly good quality. Those of us who were well sat at the table all together and waited on the patients in bed. We were not supposed to talk to each other, but we were allowed to communicate to a certain extent in whispers. We were very much amused at each other's appearance in the strange clothes and cap.

After breakfast we cleared the table, the gate of the ward was unlocked and we carried the crockery to baskets on the floor in the passage. From there the 3rd Division prisoners took them and washed them out in the bath room cell next door. The hospital wardress had to stand at the gate all the time that we were doing this. Some wardresses allowed us sometimes to come and go freely; others, or the same wardresses on different days, would allow only one of us out of the ward at a time. This and all other rules of the kind would hardly ever be told to us in so many words, but suddenly the wardress would step out and block the way, laying her hand upon us without a word as if we were animals. This being handled when there is no occasion for it seems very insulting.

Like all these prison methods, it seemed curious and interesting when first done to oneself, but aroused a feeling of indignation when one saw it being done to others. It gave one the feeling of belonging to a race apart, something degraded and imbecile, despised not only for the particular crime one had committed but as an all-round inferior being. The moral influence of this kind of treatment is rubbed in afresh through every hour of prison life and has a bad moral influence on both prisoners and wardresses. It seemed, moreover, quite unnecessary.

After breakfast the chief wardress who had reproved us for not lifting up the movable section of the beds, beckoned me to her—"Take off your slippers. Bring your shoes; you have to go before the Senior Medical Officer." This made me anxious. I knew quite well that I was not in a state of ill-health to cause the release of an ordinary prisoner; I knew, too, that many suffrage prisoners had been kept in prison when much more seriously ill than I was. But I remembered the specially constructed rule which had sanctioned a letter being delivered to me, and I was on the look-out for more privileges of the kind. The wish was strong in me to have personal experience of the inflictions which a Liberal Government thought suitable to woman Suffragists, to share every incident of the treatment which my leaders and friends had suffered in our cause and to gain some experience of prison life from within for the sake of one day being equipped to work for prison reforms.

Outside the ward I was told to put on my shoes. I hated those shoes with the vigorous hatred of a child. The laces had no tags, my fingers were very cold, and being hurried up by the wardress made them the more awkward. I was given a cloak of green cloth and taken downstairs. The staircase was of stone and, with my feet encased in these thick unyielding shoes, I was afraid of slipping. I laid my hand on the banister to steady myself.

"If you must have hold of that rail, can't you use the uprights? Don't you see the top's polished, you'll soil it." This remark was made by the wardress who shouted past me with a sort of bark. At the foot of the stairs she pulled at my cloak, "Got it on inside out, is that how you mean to wear it?" This was said in the same voice, but I thought I caught something of a twinkle in her eye as if she were not without a sense of humour and would welcome an appeal to the same. I noted this for future experimenting, but was at the moment unable to take advantage of it. I felt mentally stunned, physically cowed, morally indignant, a blend of sensations which I think must be common to many prisoners. The doctor's room was a sort of office well lit by several large windows.

The Senior Medical Officer was a different man from the doctor who had inspected us the previous night. I had expected a struggle on the question of tonics, but to my delight he quickly agreed that I should survive without drugs. He spoke in an ordinary voice, his expression of face and the things he said were quite natural, he treated me as though I were an ordinary mortal. After even twelve hours of prison customs this seemed a remarkable and gladdening thing. Up till that moment I had incessantly wished that I should some day be able to tell the officials the entirely harmful impression conveyed by their manner to the prisoners.

It was obvious that this official manner was quite detached from the individual personality of those who assumed it. They looked and spoke in this way, not to serve their private ends, but in compliance with some strangely mistaken tradition, as a matter of conformity. When under the heel of it, one felt a conviction that no reform of prison regulations would alter the maiming influence of prison life until this tradition were altered. Now, on the contrary, I felt equally desirous of proclaiming that here was an individual with an innate gift to usefully fill the part of prison official; he had mastered the fundamental matter of treating prisoners as he would treat other human beings. I think this doctor tried some slight persuasion to obtain my release by consenting to be bound over. He quickly saw, however, that my imprisonment was not due to any hasty or unconsidered act, and he did not press the matter for long.

It was agreed that I should go back to bed for the benefit of my heart condition. After the prolonged strain I was only too glad to do this. The morning, however, was taken up with many visits of inspection. The governor made his rounds in a formal way and never relaxed his official muscles, but he seemed kindly, nevertheless, and I felt sorry for him having to play what I supposed was a disagreeable game for him. The matron wore a quite different expression from when I had seen her the evening before. She looked very tired, and I wondered whether any part of her work gave her satisfaction.

The chaplain, too, looked ill and I thought what a harrowing life his must be, always pouring out sympathy for sorrows and sufferings that he had no power to relieve. He came up to my bed with a smile and said, in a voice well-flavoured with contempt: "Well, you must have done something very wicked to find yourself in here? "I was surprised, supposed he meant it for a joke; supposed, too, that possibly from his point of view it was an entirely comic thing that we should be in prison. But it seemed odd that his imagination and sympathy should not at least have led him to inquire first what was our point of view in the matter, and he seemed not to consider it possible that our actions should have entailed self-sacrifice and the pain of bringing anxiety to those we loved. I answered: "If I had thought what I did very wicked, I should not have done it."

At ten o'clock hot milk was again brought into the ward for those who wished for it, also fruit, but, to my great relief, this was optional. The morning was taken up with cleaning the ward. The 3rd Division prisoner by a series of processes and with the aid of a long-handled polisher, first swept, then bees-waxed, then polished the wooden floor. She did it with the skill of an expert and her graceful gestures were a pleasure to watch. She never paused for a moment in her work except when the entry of some official necessitated a temporary suspension.

Then followed a polishing of metal fixtures and dusting of the walls, shelves, books, etc. To my great joy, the patients not in bed were ordered to take part in the dusting. It was a means of practising my favourite hobby of cleaning, also of keeping warm, of helping the little 3rd Division prisoner, and occasionally exchanging a whispered word with her, though this was rarely achieved. The dust was continuously stirred throughout the morning, moved from the floor, then from the wall. The grey fluff that came from the bedding and floated about the floor gathered a certain amount of dust as it was swept up and eventually burnt in the fire, but no damping or reasonable process to get rid of the dust was used, so that shelves, books, beds, were no sooner dusted than they were again covered as before.

On one or two occasions I ventured to damp my duster, but this, of course, made it very dirty, which result met with disfavour. It was no doubt felt that as the more vigorous patients had nothing much better to do, they might as well go on dusting throughout the morning. In an ordinary home the daily processes of sweeping and dusting always seem to me absurdly laborious, elaborate and inadequate; the workers at these household crafts having had so little share in the application of modern invention to their toil, and little appeal on behalf of public service and utility has been made to women of higher education and greater leisure than the workers themselves. The housecraft of prison, as one watched it day by day, pressed one's thoughts on to the subject. The collecting of dust by means of damp cloths immediately followed by a dry rubber would certainly be more effective.

At about twelve the midday food was served, it was the most solid meal in the twenty-four hours. It consisted every day of fried fish, potatoes, cabbage, bread, butter and a custard pudding or boiled rice pudding made with eggs. I, being a vegetarian, did not eat fish. After some days I had the courage to ask for a rice pudding made without eggs and was allowed this. The food was good and well cooked, but the absolute monotony of the bill of fare was a great trial to some of the prisoners, more especially the bed patients.

In the afternoon, those who were allowed out exercised for an hour walking round and round a yard with high walls to it. We were exercised at a different time from ordinary prisoners. We were not allowed to talk to each other and had to walk single file one behind the other at a given distance apart. As there were never more than four or five of us from the hospital a certain amount of laxness was allowed. We could go our own pace, the faster walkers from time to time overtaking the slower and now and then one was allowed to stop and lean up against the wall. The weather was cold, we had frost and snow, during most of my time in Holloway, and being used to furs, gloves and muffs, I felt the cold very much especially in my hands.

The only extra garment for out of doors was an unlined cloth cape with hood attached. This was warmer than it looked. I used to do arm exercises as I walked to stir my blood. The discomfort of the shoes prevented any joy in walking, there was no yield in the soles and the hard leather pressed the feet in a way to make every footstep a consideration. I have sensitive feet and may have suffered more in this respect than others, but to judge from appearance the tread and gait of all prisoners is laborious and artificial, affecting the hang of the whole body, on account of the shoes.

I did not go out for the first two or three days. In the afternoon the sense of fatigue overcame one. Unless the patients were ill enough to undress and get into bed, they were not allowed to lie on it, we, however, sometimes sat on a chair close to the bed, leaned our heads upon the pillow and slept.

Some read books, others did needlework, others tended the bed patients.

I am a little deaf, and found it a tiring business after no sleep at night to hold intercourse by means of whispers, the only form of conversation allowed, but nevertheless this was far the most interesting occupation available. People are inclined to be communicative, although total strangers to each other, when cut off from their homes and friends and all sharing the same fate. I heard life stories in Holloway hospital that would fill many novels. I wondered, as I have always done, how it is that people can trouble to read books when romance, adventure, comedy, tragedy and pathos are to hand at all times in more living form and with far greater variety of event and character.

At about five the supper was brought in, the food being the same as at breakfast. I sometimes kept back a potato from the midday meal to eat cold with the bread and butter. As soon as this was cleared away we were let out in turns to the bathroom, where a hot foot bath was provided, and privacy. This was a most welcome luxury. Two mornings after we had been in, a screen was put round the washing table so that the morning ablutions became more effective. From this time forward I experienced nothing to complain of in the washing line.

These first days of prison, although immensely interesting, were, nevertheless, longer in point of time than anything I remember in life, not excluding early childhood. The novelty of every detail and the fact that observation was sharpened to a pitch only known at moments of great emotion, no doubt partly accounted for this.

I knew that my eldest sister had intended to come and visit me as soon as she could get a permit; I supposed she would have no difficulty. The first and second day went by and she did not come. I became a prey to a morbid depression of spirits. Being completely cut off from previous existence, one rapidly fell into the belief that all friends and belongings had discarded and forgotten one. This state of mind was one of the most melancholy experiences of prison. It seems childish and absurdly unreasonable when remembered after release. It nevertheless was bitterly real at the time, and a few hours within prison walls were sufficient to develop the illusion. As with so many other prisoner sensations, it is akin to child life, engendered from complete helplessness, subjection to others, ignorance and uninformedness as to what is happening outside the cramped horizon of the life to which one is subject. The sense of continuous expectancy and comfort for present distressful monotony in the belief that undreamed of good might happen at any moment is also very similar to the mental outlook of children.

The next day, February 26, Mrs. Pethick Lawrence was summoned out of the ward. She came back radiant, having had a visit from her husband. Her happiness and the news she brought back of the outer world shed joy upon us all, but, nevertheless, I had the feeling all the more strongly that my own people had forgotten me, since they, I argued, could have obtained the same privileges as Mr. Lawrence. The ordinary prisoner is usually allowed a visitor only after the first month of the sentence has expired.

The members of the Freedom League were in great excitement, expecting that their leader would be coming to prison that day and very likely be sent to hospital. She had been arrested at the head of a deputation when the other members of the Freedom League had been imprisoned, but her case had been remanded. In the afternoon the prayer card at the head of one of the spare beds was altered to one of Roman Catholic prayers. This was taken to indicate beyond doubt the coming of Mrs. Despard. I read the Roman Catholic card and thought it compared favourably, in point of suitability to prisoners, with the selection made by the Church of England. The hymns, biblical passages and prayers were more tender and personal and less concerned with misdoing. They were rather childish, but, as I have pointed out, prisoners resemble children.

In the evening, when the curfew hour of our bedtime was already past, a stranger prisoner, a very remarkable looking woman with white hair, a fine face, and stately carriage came into the ward, and was immediately recognised by her followers as their deservedly beloved leader. She came up to greet Mrs. Lawrence, and they were about to shake hands with cordiality when the wardress interfered, angrily forbidding them to touch one another.

When the poison basket came round that night, I noticed with admiration and envy Mrs. Despard's dignified but effectively determined refusal of the proffered tonic. She discarded the hospital whisper and said out loud to the drug dispenser:

I have never taken medicine in my life and I am not going to begin now; I will explain to the doctor tomorrow.

She was a most vigorous lady. I have never heard of a prisoner before or since who slept soundly through the first night of sentence. She walked round the exercise yard, too, at a pace beyond my powers. I was fortunate in achieving one very interesting conversation with her, when she told me of how the women's workrooms instituted under the recent Local Government Board's Central Unemployment Fund had been closed down, on the ground that they were not self-supporting, although they were worked at less loss and at far less cost per head than some of the workshops for unemployed male workers. £28,000 was said to have been spent on one farm colony for men which had produced only £1,000 return.

Yet there was no complaint, no talk of closing down because of its unremunerative character. £750 had been allotted for widows' and single women's workrooms. These, too, were worked at a loss as there was not sufficient sale for the clothes they made, and because of this loss, small in total and far smaller in proportion than in the men's work, the room was closed. To our great surprise Mrs. Despard was released "on medical grounds," after serving only a week of her sentence, although she was in robust health. The weekly paper *The Christian Commonwealth* had taken up her case and the House of Commons was circularised by the editor, Mr. Dawson. This is supposed to have moved the Home Office to clemency.

One of the patients who slept in a separate cell, but came to the ward for meals, had a particularly attractive face and personality. She was exceptionally gentle and courteous in her manner, but her outward calm nevertheless suggested a reserve of inward force; her eyes had a way of lighting up suddenly with sympathy, pathos, or fun. I longed to have a free talk with her. Her name was Mrs. Clarke; she was one of three Suffragettes, the others being Miss Irene Dallas and Miss Douglas Smith, who had been arrested on a deputation to Downing Street on January 24. I had sent in my name for the larger deputation to the House of Commons. I had been invited to go instead on this smaller one to Downing Street, but I had refused.

When I saw the women afterwards who had undertaken this much more disagreeable job than mine, I felt again thoroughly ashamed of myself. I should say they were all three unusually sensitive to the odiousness of the errand which had appalled me to the point of shirking it. I did not realise until after she had left the prison that Mrs. Clarke was a sister of Mrs. Pankhurst. (Mrs. Clarke was released from Holloway the second time on December 23, and died on December 25, 1910). These three were released on the morning of February 27. We could just hear the sounds of their welcome and the band playing the *Marseillaise* outside the prison, but, of course, could see nothing through the high, grained-glass windows. One was filled with a great longing to join them. This was after only thirty-six hours of prison, I imagined what it must be to those under long sentences when a fellow prisoner is released.

On that day, Saturday, at about the time for our exercise, one of the superior officers came into the ward and, singling me out from the others, ordered me to leave my slippers, bring my shoes to put on outside and follow her. I had already learnt the order of the daily routine, and every event that was slightly exceptional filled me with hope that my turn had come for a "visitor," but I had had several disappointments in this line and so steeled myself not to expect too readily. I was taken across the yard of the main entrance and ushered through a part of the prison where I had not been before to a row of rooms looking like small offices with glass doors, giving on to a passage. On the door to which I was led was written the word "Solicitor," and almost before I had time for joyous conjectures as to who my "visitor" could be, the door was opened and my sister, Betty Balfour, was facing me.

It was like seeing the sun after a long time of darkness. I only then realised to what an extent the gloom of prison surroundings and anxiety about my home people had taken hold of my mind. The sight of my sister did not dispel them, but seemed to take me from within their grip to an independent position outside of them, the physical trials of my fellow Suffragettes in our ward, the anti-happiness get up of the prison building, clothing, food, equipment, and the general vitality-destroying framework of the prison system and its officials, seemed suddenly to be a thing apart from me instead of one with my very self.

We were told to seat ourselves on opposite sides of a small table and not to touch each other nor pass anything from one to the other. The door was left open and the wardress sat just outside so as to hear, and if necessary control our communications. She was a benignant, kindly woman whom I had not seen before; she reminded me of Madeleine de Rohan, of the Theatre Français, in *Le Monde où l'on s'ennui*. She was dignified, gentle, sympathetic. I was nevertheless afraid of her, or rather of the office which she filled, and wished her miles away. I never saw her again, either during my month in Holloway or on the many occasions when I have since revisited it on behalf of other prisoners.

I have tried several times to write down my impressions of this "visit" from my sister. I have to own myself beaten. The joy of it seems so exaggerated, I cannot trust myself to convey it for publication. All prison sensations are exaggerated from the point of view of those out of prison, that is their essential characteristic. Still more exaggerated must a genuine description of them seem to a prison official who is used to witness without sharing them. For men and women who have experienced them, it is never again possible to discredit their intensity or to be contemptuous towards those who try to give expression to them. My own recollections of prison are isolated from other parts of my life by a kind of halo of reverence. Awe comes over me whenever they are in my mind; this awe and reverence are twice as powerful in connection with those moments when joy had her turn, and these rare occasions of gladness outweigh from their importance the much more numerous experiences of gloom, anxiety, anger and physical suffering.

After twenty minutes of eager and joyful ecstasy of communication, during which I drank in the sight and sound of my sister's loved personality, the wardress told us that our time was up and I was taken away. My sister and I were allowed to kiss each other before parting. When I got back to hospital I had three very distinct sensations. That of having experienced a good thing which was over; distress at not being able to impart my joy to my companions nor discuss it with them, since none of them knew my sister; indignation when I realised that no ordinary prisoner, who needed the help of joy so much more than I did, and no Suffragette prisoner without influential friends, would be able to have a similar experience until after the first month of imprisonment. In the practical sense more especially, for the settlement of business and family affairs, it is on first being imprisoned that letters and interviews are needed by prisoners.

The glow of my own happiness, however, triumphed over all else until bed time, when with a perversity born, I suppose, of the accumulated fatigue of recent days and nights, the one flaw in my sister's visit came uppermost in my thoughts and possessed my brain with an unconquerable tyranny. Some days before the deputation, she had been in correspondence with a leading Conservative M.P., one whose lifelong belief in Woman Suffrage had become a little rusty. The questions he put to my sister proved that he had not kept pace with recent events in the movement and was unaware of the tremendous demand made by women themselves for the vote as evidenced by the resolutions, petitions, and unreceived deputations of organised societies of working and professional women, quite apart from the unions that had sprung up everywhere expressly in support of the Suffrage.

I had sent her a collection of printed evidence to this effect for the benefit of her correspondent and I inquired of her eagerly that afternoon as to the result. She told me that she had unfortunately lost the papers. I was annoyed and wasted several minutes of our precious time together in reproof. The memory of my anger came back to me now in exaggerated dimensions. Why had I allowed myself to be reproachful to her? She had been so dear to me, so prompt and efficient in her efforts to come and see me, so comforting in her wealth of sympathy, and I had rewarded her with reproaches! As I went back over the scene, my heart was wrung with longing to send her some little message of good-will and my inability to do so appeared to me then as nothing short of a tragedy. For the fiftieth time in those first hours of imprisonment I seemed to be and to feel like a child, at the mercy of fluctuating emotions extreme in their intensity.

I longed to be alone, but that night the ward patients kept unusually wide awake and I had to restrain myself over and over again. As the night wore on, the avenue of beds became less troubled, a sense of privacy grew in proportion and at last I gave way to my grief and sobbed. I covered my face in the bedclothes, but in spite of this precaution the wardress heard me and before long she came and stood by my side. I expected a scolding. She very seldom took any notice of the patients till morning, I knew it was her business to reprove me, but on looking up at her face I saw that the customary mask-like expression had vanished. She was kind, she inquired tenderly why I was crying, sat down on my bed and held my hands, told me that my sister would not remember my reproaches but would be unhappy if she knew of my present distress. She did not laugh at me, she showed as much sympathy as a friend. It was a great surprise.

She stayed talking to me in whispers for a considerable time, though looking continually towards the door as if in fear of being detected in a kindness, for through the night as through the day, she was liable to unseen inspection through the locked gate and open door, or through the spy-hole of the door when closed. I was most deeply grateful to her, it was a delightful discovery that underneath her rigid exterior she was an unspoiled human being. I longed to return her kindness and ventured to propose that I should rub her chest to ease her hacking cough. At first she would not hear of it, but at last, after I had fetched some ointment from the bed-head of one of the patients who had a cough, she consented and allowed me to open her dress. She seemed much afraid and told me she would probably be dismissed if we were seen.

My attempts to allay her distress eased my own mind of its childish trouble, for which reason she had probably allowed me to help her. I would gladly have talked to her all night about prisoners, the working conditions of wardresses, her own life, but this, of course, was forbidden. She soon went back to her table, her face resumed its former expression and I never again held any intercourse with her. If the horrors of prison existence are enshrined in an atmosphere of nightmare, the rare happy moments have the glamour of a good dream. This kind act of the night-wardress remains as one of the sunlit flower patches of my time in Holloway.

The next morning after the superior officer had been her rounds taking temperatures, she beckoned me to her. "What have you been complaining about?" she asked sharply.

"I haven't been complaining," I answered.

"Yes, you have—you complained of something to a visitor."

I then remembered that, when reassuring my sister as to my health and to prove to her the genuineness of my statements as to prison conditions being in no way harmful to me, I had mentioned two things which proved rather trying, *viz*., that my underclothes and stockings were too short to cover my knees, and the fact that one small towel had to do service for all purposes during a week. I reported this to the wardress, but explained that I had mentioned these not in complaint but to prove to my sister that my discomforts were insignificant.

"Well," she retorted, "next time you have anything to complain of come to me with it—if not I shall get into trouble."

This seemed the very reverse of prison regulations, for usually the trouble was caused by anything out of the ordinary being granted to a prisoner. From that time forward I was supplied with two towels, one of them renewed every week, and two rolls of flannel bandages were brought to me to cover my knees. I supposed that the ordinary cells, to which I expected soon to be transferred, would be much colder than the hospital, so I held the flannel bandages in reserve.

After I came out of prison I heard that my family were troubled, knowing how dependent I was upon warm underclothes, especially at night. My eldest brother had interviewed the head of the Prison Commissioners Department, Sir Evelyn Ruggles-Brise, who had said that I should at once be supplied with bed-socks. Bed-socks, of course, do not grow in prisons. They were represented, I suppose, by my flannel bandages, but the official statement had the desired result of quieting my family's anxiety.

CHAPTER 7: SOME TYPES OF PRISONERS

There was no chapel for us on Sunday and it seemed an unusually long day. My thoughts yearned towards my home people, and I rehearsed the joy of my sister's visit over and over again. The excitement of seeing her had now given way to a wholesome and relaxed fatigue and I looked forward to another night with a sure expectation of sleep. In the evening at about six o'clock, our bed time, a new patient was brought into the ward. She was carried in by 3rd Division prisoners, helped by a head officer, sitting upright in an ordinary armchair with carrying poles attached to the arms. She looked extremely ill and ashy pale. She was evidently in great pain, though she did not groan or call out. There was nothing in the way she was treated to suggest a surgical case, and I concluded that she had been brought in for some fever or acute internal complaint; from the look on her face I thought it not unlikely that she might die in the night. She was a stranger to me and after the first few minutes my instinct was to turn away and not look at her, remembering the distressing sense of publicity which I myself had felt so acutely on first coming to hospital. The news quickly spread in the ward that she was a member of the Freedom League, by name Mrs. Meredith Macdonald.

She had several friends in the ward, but they scarcely recognised her when she was first brought in. They told me that she had fallen down that morning in the exercise yard, which was slippery from frost, and had injured her leg at the hip joint. I soon got to know her myself and talked much with her. No nurse was in attendance on her during the night, only the ordinary night officer (wardress). The anguish of acute suffering in this newcomer and her harrowingly unassisted condition, drove all thoughts of my own people from my mind and all question of sleep from my eyes. The accident had taken place at about 9.30 a.m. She had slipped over a small gutter and fallen with great suddenness to the ground. She lay for several minutes stunned in the snow. The wardress in charge ordered her to "go into the middle," where those who cannot walk fast drag round in a smaller circle, but she did not attempt to move. Some of her fellow prisoners came to her assistance, they were immediately ordered away by the officers. She looked across the yard to the wardress of her own corridor who then came to help her.

"I have hurt my thigh," she said; "I think I had better go in."

The wardress answered, "Very well."

As soon as she began to walk she felt pain in the hip bone and put her hand on the wardress's shoulder for support. It was a very short distance to her block (D X) of the building and on reaching it she was handed over to another wardress who suggested she should sit down and rest before going up to her cell. She was about to do this when her right leg collapsed completely under her and she would have fallen, but that a wardress held her up and put her into a chair. She was then told to go upstairs "before you get any stiffer."

The leg was useless, but by help of the double banisters she hopped up two flights to her cell, an older wardress from the upper corridor lending her assistance. She had no control over her foot and said to the elder wardress that there must be something wrong. The wardress answered, "I am afraid you have injured the muscles and that is a very painful thing," and offered to put her to bed. She could not face the additional pain of being undressed. About half an hour later a doctor and the hospital superintendent visited her, and she was subjected to extreme pain by a reckless testing. She herself suspected a fracture and suggested having recourse to X-rays as the only means of satisfactorily testing this. She pleaded the special need in her case of, if possible, retaining her walking power on account of her young children. The doctor sent her a draught to ease the pain, but this was quite ineffective. She lay in her cell all day unable to keep still for long on account of the pressure of the injured part on the mattress, and yet every move was exquisitely painful.

In the evening the doctor came again and renewed his agonising overhauling. She was then removed to hospital, the chair in which they carried her, having no foot rest, the injured leg came in frequent contact with the porters, causing her the intensest pain. It is not surprising that she looked more dead than alive on reaching the ward. The injury and the rough methods of investigation combined produced a feverish and most painful condition in the patient. The case was taken over by another doctor (Dr. Sullivan) who at least handled the injury much less brutally, but no attempt was made to treat it surgically. A slight wound in the lower part of the leg was occasionally dressed and bandaged by the hospital wardress, who visited us twice a day when temperatures were taken and drugs distributed.

There was no other nursing whatever. The doctor's examinations consisted only of measurements to compare the length of the injured leg with the healthy one. Nothing was done, in recognition of fracture, to reset the bones or keep the limb in one position, no weight was applied to stretch the shorter injured leg; there seemed to be no aim in the doctor's recommendations beyond that of helping to restore a bruised bone by as nearly a natural use of it as the patient could be urged to make. A circular air-cushion was supplied and extra pillows; also a night table by the side of the patient's bed, and a bed pan was kept in the ward which could be used for bed-patients with the voluntary assistance either of the wardress in charge or of the fellow-prisoners.

Mrs. Macdonald was kept in bed for the first few days, but the extremely painful pressure from lying on the injured bone with the legs in flat position caused her incessant restlessness, and before long she begged leave to get up and sit in an armchair. This was allowed and soon she was urged to move about, walk and use the leg as much as possible. In spite of the most heroic efforts, the last recommendation was impossible. She moved about leaning on a chair by way of crutch and getting up or sitting down with the help of her fellow-prisoners.

The complete loss of control over the injured leg pointed, in my estimation, to much more serious harm than mere bruising. I felt the greatest indignation from that first evening of her entrance among us at the way this prisoner was treated. Her suggestion about the X-rays was ignored, her request to the governor, and eventually her petition to the Home Secretary, that she might be visited by her own doctor was refused. When the doctors talked with her about her case they seemed to pay no attention to her own views, but rather accentuated the official prison manner of ignoring individuals as though she had been a child or an irresponsible person. Yet there was no trace of exaggeration or a tendency to work up grievances over her own case.

Through all her acute and continuous physical suffering she showed keen powers of observation and a sense of humour that constantly relieved the nightmare of horror with which I watched her pain. Her heroism under physical suffering surpassed anything I have ever come across or imagined possible. During the nights I was with her in the ward, about four or five, I slept very little myself and whenever I looked at her she was awake. I did not once see her asleep by day or night while I was with her in prison. It is only since seeing her in free life that I have been able to compare her face under normal conditions and realised the intensity of distress which must have caused the continually strained expression she had in Holloway, varied at times by contortions due to acute pain. Yet she spoke little of her sufferings, seldom complained of anything, never once was irritable under her trials or indignant at the treatment of them, never once groaned or cried. She was uniformly patient, gentle, self-contained, considerate of others.

I still was unable to get any sleep at night, but when a few days had gone by I ventured to make up my bed so that I faced the wall instead of the ward. This gave a greater sense of privacy and sheltered my eyes from the blinding light of the naked gas jet. I very much missed a habit I have of doing various physical exercises before going to bed. About halfway through the night I made amends for this by going to the little ante-room near the sink and lavatory, the door of which communicating with the ward was left unlocked at night. Here, taking it corner ways, there was just room for me to stretch my arms full length.

I consider it was thanks to this midnight practice that I was able to keep my digestion in better order than is usual among prisoners.

Hospital patients are not allowed to go to the daily service in chapel, but occasionally we were taken down to a morning service, in the nature of family prayers, which was held in the ward below ours. This was given over mostly to feeble-minded patients, several of whom were in bed. My place was always the same, close to the bed of a woman whose face will haunt me, I think, as long as I live. I never saw her move, she lay quite flat, her head alone appearing above the bed clothes. She took no part in the service and seemed to be unconscious of it. She was young, her skin was remarkably smooth and devoid of expressive lines, but yellow as if she had jaundice. Her appearance illustrated to me the meaning of despair more clearly than I have seen it hitherto in any living being. She was entirely passive and unresentful, but if hope had tried to enter into her mind it would find no lodging there. It seemed to me that neither life nor death had anything to offer her, nor was there anything she possessed of which they could rob her. While I stood or sat through the service my back was turned on her, but when I knelt down I was facing her. One could not feel pity for her—there was a rigid dignity and detachedness about her as of someone living in an atmosphere different from our own. All my thoughts and prayers were bent towards her, but I never had the sensation of in any way communicating with her.

I noticed regretfully that there were no hymns, hardly any passages from the Bible were read, the prayers selected were of a dolorous order, and the greater part of the time was taken up by an address from the chaplain. He spoke to us of the temptation in the wilderness, how that Christ was tempted in the same way that we are, but that He was good and we were bad. He instanced how wrong it would be if, when we were hungry, we yielded to the temptation of stealing bread. At this remark an old woman stood up. She was tall and gaunt, her face seamed with life, her hands gnarled and worn with work. One saw that whatever her crimes might have been she had evidently toiled incessantly. At this moment her face wore an expression of strained intensity as though some irresistible tide of inward emotion had forced her to act. The tears streamed down her furrowed cheeks as she said in a pleading, reverent voice, "Oh, sir, don't be so hard on us."

The wardresses immediately came up to her, took her by the shoulders and hustled her out of the ward; we never saw her again. The chaplain did not answer nor even look at her, and continued his address as if nothing had happened. A feeling of passionate indignation took hold of me, succeeded by the feeling of helplessness and irresponsibility which stifles vitality and above all every good impulse in prison. Sympathy for the ejected prisoner, disagreement with the man who officially represented the teaching of Christianity, neither of these thoughts could find vent in words or actions; they become stored up in a brooding, malignant attitude of resentment towards the whole prison system, its infamous aim, its profound unreason, and the cruelly devitalising distortion of its results.

When we were back in our ward the chaplain came to visit us. This time, he knew who I was. I asked him about the prison library which was under his charge. I wished to send some books when I was free, amongst others George Moore's story of *Esther Waters*. I thought that novel ought to be in every woman's prison because of the heroic and triumphant struggle depicted in it of the mother of an illegitimate child. I asked the chaplain if he knew it and would allow me to send it. He answered that he did not know the book, and added, "But your ladyship is such a good judge of literature, I should leave the choice of books entirely to you." Whenever officials visited the ward we were supposed each to stand at the foot of the bed allotted to us. Complete silence was the rule. This remark of the chaplain's was, therefore, overheard by many of my fellow-prisoners. From that moment I was nicknamed "your ladyship."

As soon as the official round was over several of us came together and, as was inevitable, compared the attitude of the chaplain towards the prisoner who had appealed to him during his address and towards myself. It was on this occasion I first noticed that the dress-jacket I wore was different from those of my companions; mine was evidently quite new and without the broad arrow markings. A fellow-prisoner. Miss Povey, member of the Freedom League, to whom I had brought a glass of water during the first night, came to my rescue. She was now sufficiently recovered to be out of bed during part of the day. She had a great sense of humour and immediately responded to my need.

We seized a brief moment when the wardress was standing in the doorway, we took shelter behind the open door and swopped each other's serge shirts. She was small made and for once this portion of the clothing had been more or less well adapted to our respective sizes. The sleeves of my shirt were half a length longer than she required, and though she put a large tuck in them they retained their superfluity of size. The sleeves of her shirt did not reach my wrists and as the solitary button at the neck did not secure the closing of the jacket down the front, I had continually to be pulling it together again in the course of the day. It was marked in many places With the broad arrow, but had been so well worn, as the lining of the neck and cuffs attested, that the white paint of the markings had almost chipped off in several places. From this time onward it became a sort of game to watch for the privileges that were accorded to me. Prisoners who had been in before explained that until I came there were never knives and forks supplied as we now enjoyed, the fare, too, had been made more luxurious.

After three or four days I had practically recovered from the effects of the treatment meted out to the deputation, and, but for the want of sleep and its results, had regained my normal health. I was very anxious to leave the hospital, partly because I wanted to share the lot of the bulk of my Suffragette companions and to ensure that they should benefit by whatever unusual privileges were accorded to me. Secondly, I wished to know from my own experience the routine life of ordinary prisoners and to see more of them, which I supposed would be possible away from the ward. Finally, my appetite for solitude grew from hour to hour. I feared that continued lack of sleep (I am a slave to sleep) might tell on me in a way to seriously handicap my health and cause my friends and belongings anxiety after my release, which could easily be avoided.

Consequently, every morning when the governor and doctor came on their round I asked leave to go to "the other side," as the ordinary cell buildings were called. My monotonous request was as monotonously refused from day to day. The governor replied that I must first obtain consent from the doctors, the doctors insisted that my heart was in a condition to make the routine of floor-washing, plank bed, etc., injurious to me. One of the doctors did not trouble to continue feeling my pulse, he simply dismissed my request to be moved with the statement, "As for you, you are suffering from serious heart disease, you can't be let out of hospital."

To harden myself for the cell routine I shared more and more in the cleaning processes of the ward. Besides the emptying of basins and dusting the walls as high as my arms could reach, the big table had to be moved for floor polishing, and I helped the little 3rd Division ward-cleaner with this. She was very small and worked unremittingly all day. She used to flush very much over the floor-polishing, although she was most dexterous with the heavy, long-handled polisher, and did all her duties with admirable labour-saving skill and sequence. I wondered how much her heart condition was considered. I felt a great interest in her. Her face, expression, and manners were those of an essentially good woman, she was intelligent, had a sense of humour, was loyal to both the officials and her fellow-prisoners; she seemed in every way above the average of mortals. I wondered what offence against the law could have brought her to prison, she had several bars on her sleeve, implying a long sentence.

I found she had committed one of the most grievous crimes which it is possible to commit, the most unnatural, and opposed to all that lies at the root well-being of a race or nation. She had killed her own child. Yet when I came to know the facts, it seemed to me that her actions were fully accounted for, and even had her child-killing been more deliberate than it actually was, it was impossible to condemn this action in a human being who had been squeezed by such opposing forces. Her story was told me in snatches partly by the other prisoners, partly by one of the wardresses, and partly by herself as I used to kneel by her side to put floor refuse into the fire at the rare moments when the enormous padlock of the fender door had been released. Her story was this.

She was a servant, and had been seduced by her master. She, of course, was dismissed from his service. When the child was born, he had at first contributed to its support, but after a while had ceased to do so and disappeared, leaving no address. She had taken the greatest pride in bringing up her child, a boy, to whom she was devoted. Her cell was one of those just outside the general ward. It was sometimes used for the reception of visitors to hospital patients who were too ill to go across the way. When this happened she always asked the prisoners eagerly on their return, "Did you see the photo of my boy?" Having been in prison many months she was allowed to receive and keep this photograph.

To return to her story, as time went on the struggle to maintain herself and her child was considerable. She made a friend, a man of her own class, who knew her history, respected her for her good motherhood and promised to marry her as soon as a sufficiently good job came his way. Before long the job was said to have been offered him, marriage was in sight, and they plighted their troth with the seal which knows no undoing. The work failed, marriage prospects paled, her friend deserted her and she found herself faced with the prospect which she now understood only too well, of disabled health, unemployment, disgrace, and a second child to maintain unaided. She kept on at her employment—in a laundry—until the very hour of her premature confinement. Then worn out in body and spirit, and quite alone at the moment of her trouble, she had in her distraction and misery strangled her baby. She went on with her work at the laundry.

It was the father of her child who gave her up to the police; according to one rendering, he did so because she was so ill he thought it the only way to secure for her "a rest." She had an uncle, a citizen of London, a publican, who used his influence on her behalf at her trial so that she was condemned on the charge of "concealment of birth," not of child-murder. Prisoners are allowed visitors once a month, but no one had been to see her for several months. I determined I should be one of her visitors as soon as I was again free, so that we might hold a sustained conversation of a kind impossible to fellow-prisoners.

I often tell the story of this girl as an example of the neglect of women's interests and the consequent need for the recognition of their citizenship so that legislation and administrators of the law should be responsible to both sexes. My listeners have sometimes commented:

But what difference could the vote make? and how could legislation alter these admittedly tragic situations?

At this very time (March, 1909) the women of Norway who had recently been enfranchised, but had not yet exercised the vote, were drafting a bill for the protection of illegitimate children. I think there could not be a better example of how a fundamental change could be made in both the educative and protective side of legislation as between men and women, pre-eminently just and without any reactionary vindictiveness on the part of women. The essence of this law is simply recognition of the fact that every child has two parents and that the burden and responsibility of producing children should, therefore, be shared by both in so far as law can secure equality. According to this Norwegian law, *the mother is given the right during 'pregnancy to inform the local authorities of the name of the father. The man whose name is given may deny responsibility within fourteen days. If he does not, he is registered as the father; if he denies it the burden of proof rests with the mother. The father can be compelled to support the mother for three months before* (in England the law gives her no claim upon the father until after the birth of the child), *and, in certain instances, for nine months after confinement, and he is bound to support the child until it is sixteen years old.*

A man at the time of intimacy is comparatively willing to undertake his share of these situations; after the lapse of many months he is more inclined to try and shirk them. In the case of denial on the part of the man, how much easier it would be for the woman to prove her case when the friendship had been recent and witnesses could be brought forward in support of corroborating evidence. Ten or twelve months later such witnesses have often dispersed or their memories grown hazy. Owing to the undefended, economically unsupported position of these mothers, certain results inevitably follow—loss of respectable situations and consequent necessity for the women to have recourse to more precarious, more laborious, and worse paid employment, with their lowered social status pressing heavily upon them in every direction.

These conditions, reacting on the exceptional physical state of the mother, claim their inevitable toll from the lifeblood of the child. It is not surprising that the deaths of illegitimate children are nearly double those of children born in wedlock; for 1911, the statistics, the latest issued, show deaths of infants under one year in England and Wales, in wedlock 249.37 per thousand births, illegitimate 489.99. With the mother's maintenance secured, something tangible is being done to save the health as well as the life of future generations. *The woman can draw the amount of her claim through the local authorities who recover it from the father.* This is an immense safeguard. Constantly under the legal conditions here, when the mother's claim has been proved, admitted by the father and paid by him for a few weeks, he moves away before long, leaving no address and the woman, even if she knows of his whereabouts, cannot enforce her claim without irksome and difficult legal procedure.

It is far easier for the public authority to pursue him, but even if this proves in some cases impossible, it is better for the State to lose its money than the life or health of its citizens. The State always pays in the end. *The child has the right to hear the father's name and, in the event of his intestacy, has the same rights of succession as his legitimate children.* Just imagine how this clause would alter the outlook of parents when educating their sons, more especially in those spheres of society where such unions on the part of men are almost invariably with women of a lower class than their own, and it is these unions which produce tragic and evil results far more socially and racially injurious than illegitimate unions among men and women of the same class. (This bill, I believe, was passed in Norway, with some alterations).

Another of the hospital patients, a member of our deputation, Miss

Leslie Lawless, was gravely ill with her lungs. She seemed in a high fever and we were very anxious about her. The prison clothes hang loosely upon one, and, though this is healthy in principle, they seem draughty and cold after modern garments, such as close-fitting under-vests, etc. She had caught a severe chill waiting about for more than an hour in the draughty passages after the reception bath. She had been very ill and suffered much in her cell before being brought, only after the third day, to hospital. Mrs. Duval, a member of the Freedom League, was another really suffering patient. She had come up to London to see the results of the Freedom League deputation. She was walking about the street when the deputation had already been arrested. She was not taking part in any form of disturbance or demonstration. She was arrested on the ground that she was "known to be one of them."

Two gentlemen, total strangers, who witnessed her arrest, volun-teered to come into court and speak on her behalf. She was never-theless found guilty and sentenced to six weeks' imprisonment. She had twice been in prison before; she had not intended to risk arrest as she was in a very delicate state of health, having suffered consider-ably from her previous imprisonments. She was now in hospital with acute neuritis and a most irritating rash. She had many children at home and was anxious about them, not having been able to make ad-equate arrangements for them owing to her sudden and unexpected imprisonment. When I looked into her suffering face and heard from our whispered conversation that this was her third imprisonment I felt overcome. I envied her courage, but felt myself quite incapable of following her example.

Flowers were provided by the prison authorities, both in our ward and the one below; sometimes, too, our friends sent them to us. We were not allowed to know from whom they came, and they could not be destined for any particular prisoner, but flowers are expert ambassadors, and their messages of good-will from our friends were generally understood. They had to be taken out of the ward at night and returned to the ward in the morning; they had to be refreshed, the water changed and dead leaves picked off. I usurped this office. I feel ashamed, on looking back, to remember with what selfish greed I took it over, never giving the others a choice or chance in the matter. The joy of handling the flowers seemed like food and rest rolled into one. All the patients rejoiced in them.

When a new lot were sent in they were handed round for each

prisoner to see them and smell them at close quarters. Their appearance in prison used to remind me of Filippino Lippi's Florentine picture of the Virgin appearing through the sky with a trail of coloured angels behind her to St. Bernard in his ascetic and joyless surroundings. They brought moments of rapture which revitalised one's spirit and counteracted many of the stunning effects of prison existence. Some people whom I told of this have resented the fact that prisoners should be given the joy of flowers, but unless it be recognised as part of the punitive system to impose physical illness, I think the prison hospital authorities are to be congratulated on their wisdom in this respect; the flowers did more than the drug-basket to heal our complaints.

One of the reasons I took on as many housemaiding jobs as I could was that it enabled me to be let out of the ward for the emptying of slops, and this afforded a good opportunity for seeing and occasionally communicating with ordinary prisoners. They seemed to come and go pretty quickly from our floor of the hospital, and I seldom saw any of them more than twice or three times. The prisoner's dress has a wonderfully disguising and unifying power, and it was a never-ending interest to try quickly to diagnose the type of prisoner, so as to make the most of any possible communication by whispers. Washing up was done in the bathroom cell and the door left open.

Sometimes the handling of plates would prove that such work was unaccustomed and uncongenial, others were skilled but sullen and grudging in their service, some again would be keen and willing and showed the pathetic eagerness of a newcomer to inquire as to rules, to be friendly with her fellow-prisoners, to court the approval or advice of the wardresses. But such liveliness was not the fashion and was always repressed. One could watch the light and spirit of these human beings wane, as a lamp wanes for want of oil. Sometimes many days would go by without opportunity for the smallest communication with ordinary prisoners, then again there would be occasions of unexpected good luck.

Once when emptying a basin at the sink a little woman, newcomer, who was dusting the top of the walls and fittings with a long-handled broom, came close up behind me. In prison one seems to develop eyes at the back of one's head and that kind of cunning which is engendered in human beings and animals who are much restricted I realised that no official eye for the moment was upon us. The splashing of the tap covered the sound of our low voices; without looking round, without changing expression or gesture so as not to arouse suspicion, the following conversation took place.

Self: "The dust collects quickly here, doesn't it?"

Prisoner: "Yes, how long have you got?"
(The invariable first question for all prisoners.)

Self: "A month."

Prisoner: "I'm on remand for a week."

Self: "What is it for?"

Prisoner: "Attempted suicide."

Self: "Poor you. Why did you do that?"

Prisoner: "Well, I had a pot of trouble and I thought it was the quickest way out."

Self: "I remember feeling like that too, once, but I don't now."

Prisoner: "And nor do I now, life's sweet while it lasts, isn't it?" This with a beaming smile.

We had meanwhile exchanged furtive glances at each other. She had a round, rose-like face, with a look of abundant health and kindliness. Apparently, the "pot of trouble" had been of no long duration.

Self: "It seems odd to send people here for suicide?"

Prisoner (eagerly): "Yes, it does indeed. It seems a shame." Then, with some hesitation, "What are you in for?"

Self: "Suffragette."

She looked at me wonderingly, as if she supposed this to be the technical term for some form of vice unknown to her, though her sympathy and respect were not withdrawn. We were, however, interrupted at this point and I was summoned to return with my much scrubbed basin to the ward. I never saw the little rose-like face again.

Beside the sink there was a tiny sash window about the level of my head. When this was open I could catch sight of the yard where remand prisoners exercised. I was surprised to see that many of them wore prison dress. This meant either that they had been made to change their clothes, or that remand and convicted prisoners were exercising together. Seeing a great number of prisoners in a group was a most depressing sight. They were packed quite close, touching each other as they went round the narrow asphalt path in single file. They nearly all of them looked ill. Their faces wore an expression of extreme dejection; the lifeless, listless way they walked, enhanced the look of entire detachment of one from the other; in spite of being so closely herded, each seemed in a world of her own individual sorrow. Anxiety, suffering, bitterness, and a harrowing tale of want or degradation was told by the clothes of those not in prison dress.

The procession was more heartrending than anything my imagination could have conceived; it took away my breath to look at them. Why are they there? What has driven these poor wrecks into this harbour? What is being done for them here to give them courage, self-reliance, hope, belief in better possibilities for themselves and their children, opportunity to mend their own lives, better conditions of work, fairer payment, and above all a more honourable recognition of their services as women, of their needs, and of their rights; the vitality to fight for their own welfare against unjust handicaps, prejudiced ignorance of their wants and tyrannous repression of their attempts to cry out for wider labour markets?

We of the remand hospital No. 2 most often exercised in this same yard in the afternoon. We were only about six in number, sometimes only two or three, but, since seeing the procession of the morning, their personalities seemed to haunt the yard. I thought of them as beads of a necklace, detached, helpless and useless, and wondered how long it would be before they were threaded together by means of the women's movement into a great organised band, self-expressive yet co-ordinated, and ruled by the bond of mutual service. The test of a chain's strength is in its weakest link. Where is our chain weakest? Not in the wretched victims who daily paced this yard, not in the debtor, the drunkard, the thief, the hooligan, the prostitute, the child murderer. These miseries were mostly the direct outcome of harmful and unjust laws.

Amongst the few that remain of spontaneously criminal type, their number is insignificant, their influence negligible; they act as cautions rather than instigators, although they call for all the remedial forces which the State or individuals can devote to them. They themselves are diseased exceptions, but they belong to groups of women, home workers, wage earners, skilled craftswomen, who have kept alight the old traditions of serviceableness, utility, and the powers of women. They have already made many efforts to unite and to preserve their nobility of independence. They, moreover, are quick to respond and eager to serve the modern women's movement. No, the weakest link in the chain of womanhood is the woman of the leisured class. Isolated and detached, she has but little sense of kinship with other women.

For her there is no bond of labour, no ties of mutual service; her whole life is spent in the preservation of appearances, and she seems hardly ever to probe down to the bone of realities.

Child-having remains her glory, the one bit of full-livedness in an otherwise most arid desert. This is the one basis on which she feels herself united to other women, and the wrongs and sufferings of child bearers stand out as the exception on which you can sometimes get her to move on behalf of other women. Until these women can be educated as to the lives of the bulk of women, brought up against the laws with regard to them that now disgrace the statute book, made to feel the horror of custom which still undermines their own existence, and to burst through the gilded bars which hold their own lives in bondage, they act upon the social organism in a way that is almost wholly harmful. Only when their eyes have been opened will their "influence" and "example" bear out a reasonable meaning of those words and their position of privilege make them worthy to lead.

As I had watched the prisoners I saw before me a counter-procession of women of this leisured class, herded as I have so often seen them at ballrooms and parties, enduring the labours, the penalties, of futile, superficial, sordidly useless lives, quarrelling in their marriage market, revelling in their petty triumphs, concerned continually with money, yielding all opinion to social exigencies, grovelling to those they consider above them, despising and crushing those they think beneath them, pretending to be lovers of art and intellect, but concerned at heart only with the appearance of being so. Subservient to a superficial morality, tested not by the question, "What has been done?" but "What is the general opinion about what has been done?"

And immediately the procession of Holloway yard seemed human, dignified, almost enviable by the side of that other. It is these leisured women the women's movement has hitherto cast aside. They are the dross, the dead fruit. All others have responded in some way, however feeble their power of service, when they have heard the call; but these have not. As I thought of them my pity moved from the procession in Holloway to these other women. Success is impossible for a social system that takes no heed to its outcasts, the pathological victims of national existence are the symptoms which can lead us to diagnose its fundamental flaws. Whether or not the women alive today in the ruling class can be cured is of comparatively little importance, but clearly the causes which have brought them forth must be altered at the root. The conditions which go to produce a ruling caste are shifting their ground throughout the world.

Such things are moulded by involuntary forces; they cannot, except in the immediate future, be foreshadowed or decreed. But it is now obvious that, whatever this basis, women must have a fair and honourable share in it. Rulers of the best are not reared by bond-women. The bi-sexual powers must be released at all costs in those sections of the community which, whether by intellect, by birth, or by wealth, have the guiding reins of national life in their hands. The question of what that basis shall be is an altogether separate matter. Who can turn the force of our women's movement in that direction, who can be a missionary to preach war in their peace-bedeadened country? The answer that came to me in Holloway, and ever since it has seemed to me the only answer, was this—the example of working class organisations, and above all, of those few splendid women who have given their lives to lead this movement. Where doctrine, precept and example all fail to penetrate, the spirit of sacrifice, which wakes an echo in all human hearts, will find a way.

Chapter 8: "A Track to the Water's Edge"

On March 2, as a result of my pleading to be dismissed from the hospital, I was put to sleep in a separate cell along the passage of our ward. This cell had a floor of unpolished wooden boards, contained a fixed iron bedstead, movable washing stand furnished with tin utensils, a wooden chair, a square plank fixed to the wall near the door as a table, and a corner shelf under the window to hold Bible, prayer and hymn book, prayer card, list of rules, salt cellar, toilet paper, slate and slate pencil. A small basket to contain my clothes was kept under the bed. A bell near the door communicated with the outer passage. The cell was lit by a thickly barred window of small panes of glass, having in the centre a box-like apparatus, with a lid, opened by a rope pulley to let in the air without enabling one to see out, as in church windows. There was a grating ventilator below the window.

In the wall of the cell giving on to the passage was a glazed aperture, through which the cell was lighted at night from a gas-jet, as in the "reception" cell. Besides the heavily metalled door, these hospital cells had iron gates, so that the door could be left open when patients had to be watched. At eight o'clock the night wardress went her rounds, lifting the spy hole and shouting through the door "All right?" to which the prisoners have to answer "Yes." If they are asleep, the question is repeated until they wake and answer it. The gas was then lowered to a light by which it would have been difficult to read, but not extinguished.

It was explained to me afterwards, when I pleaded for darkness, that I was an "observation" case on account of my "serious heart disease." The luxury of privacy after five nights and days of unrelieved publicity seemed very great, and as soon as this last "inspection" was over my imagination conjured up into my presence every friend I have ever had, including my dog who died twenty years ago. I held intercourse with them, "dreamed true," and had a happy time. I then rolled round and gave myself up to perfect sleep.

After, as it seemed, a very short night, I woke with a start and a feeling of great horror. I supposed I had had a bad dream, but quickly realised that the nightmare was on the waking side of my existence. I sat up in bed. There was a sound of footsteps which I could not at first locate or interpret. They came nearer, clear foot-falls and a shuffling sound in between, as if some of the feet were reluctant and were being dragged along. Then a voice in great distress, half shriek, half groan, that came in broken snatches. The sounds came rapidly nearer and grew more definite. The massive walls of the building seemed to become thin and the doors flimsy with the penetrating noise. I expected that any moment these night-wanderers might enter my cell, I supposed it was a case of delirium tremens or madness.

The footsteps stopped. A violent scuffle was apparently taking place. Then followed a jangle of keys, the banging of a gate, more turning of keys, and I realised that a frenzied woman had been shut into the cell below mine. She immediately seized hold of the gate and shook it so that it rattled on its hinges, suggesting almost more than human strength. The wolf-like barking sounds of her voice turned into a human yell as she screamed out, "Nurse! Nurse! Let me out." It seemed a most reasonable remark.

The words broke the spell of horror and woke instead my intensest sympathy. She was expressing the one desire that is constantly uppermost in prisoners' minds, the walls echoed it as a thought most familiar to them. The gate shivered unceasingly under her onslaught as she hurled herself against it, and her words came at intervals, "Nurse! Nurse! Open the gate." The sounds suggested in turn madness, fury, despair. I strained to interpret and understand, but there was no clue. I yearned to console her. Presently footsteps came outside my door, a rattling of keys and locks, my door was burst open and a wardress I had not seen before put her head in, saying, "I thought you might be startled."

Her face was inflexible and revealed nothing. I threw out questions, "Was it a maternity case?" "Was she ill?" "Why was she so wild?" but the door was slammed to without any answer being given. However, even this attention was a relief and unfroze my blood a little. I wondered if the other prisoners, if the poor distracted woman herself in the cell below, had been offered as much consolation.

I was kept in bed that morning until after the rounds of inspection. The governor was very civil. He urged me to give the required assurance and bind myself over "to be of good behaviour," that I might leave the prison. He asked if I had "considered" my mother. I have no doubt he thought it his duty to talk in this way, and probably he was trying to be kind as well. At the time, however, his insinuation seemed more like a blow in the face. The words rushed to my lips: "If you knew my Mother, if you had seen her only once, you would know that it was impossible to risk causing her anxiety without immensely considering it," but I restrained myself and merely said: "I am not the only woman here who has a mother." I remembered that when Mrs. Pankhurst had been imprisoned she had been punished for exchanging a few words with her daughter. The governor then brought out a stethoscope to examine my heart. This was surprising, as I had not realised that he was a doctor. He urged tonics, but did not insist. Eventually I consented to take maltine and a banana after the mid-day meal, as they were distressed that I was so thin.

The shrieks and cries from the cell below had grown less towards morning, but they were renewed at intervals throughout the day. When I went into the general ward the horror of the night was still hanging over my companions. A wardress told one of us that the woman had killed her child and been put into the condemned cell after being sentenced to be hanged. After my release it was officially stated that the woman who had been sentenced to death for baby-murder had been perfectly quiet and that the "condemned cell" was in a part of the prison far removed from the remand hospital.

The shrieks we had heard were those of a mad woman, under remand for larceny, who had since been removed to a workhouse infirmary. The distressful cries went on intermittently for several days, after which they lapsed into groans like those of the dying. My longing to communicate with her became at moments almost unendurable. I hoped she would die; she seemed too far gone in distress for any other remedy. One morning before it was light I thought I heard the throaty sound of the death rattle from her cell. After that she was removed, whether dead or alive I could never find out until after my release.

I went into the general ward for the greater part of the day. I made my bed and dusted my cell, but was not allowed to wash the floor or clean the tin utensils because of my "heart disease." The quieter nights enabled me to eat more food, and I think I gained in weight and became generally restored to quite normal health. It was obvious that no ordinary prisoner nor Suffragette prisoner would, in my state of health, have been put in hospital, and that I was being kept there either to give me a soft time or for some other impenetrable reason. I told the Senior Medical Officer that unless I were allowed to the "other side" I should feel obliged to protest by means which he would probably regret when it was too late. He looked very much alarmed, but my threat produced no practical result.

I then asked leave to petition the Home Secretary, a right allowed to all prisoners. Blue official paper, ink and a pen were brought to my cell, only one sheet of paper being allowed, but it was a large one. I forget the wording of my letter. I stated that I had been rather severely knocked about by the police while on a peaceable deputation to the House of Commons to petition that, when the accepted conditions for which voting rights are granted have been fulfilled the vote should follow, in the case of women as of men, a claim which he, the Home Secretary himself, and a majority of the Cabinet and House of Commons had recognised as just.

That I therefore was grateful for the privilege of being placed in hospital during the first few days, where the careful and kindly treatment of the officials and excellent food had quickly restored me to my normal health. I told how I had asked permission to join my companions in the cells, but hitherto had asked in vain. I explained that the cell routine of floor scrubbing, tin polishing, etc., would be no exceptional exertion in my case, since I was an amateur scrubber, having patronised that craft in much the same spirit in which other unemployed women took up water-colour drawing or hand-embroidery.

I found that my fellow prisoners were kept in the cells when much more seriously ill than I was, and I was driven reluctantly to the conclusion that the preferential treatment meted out to me was for no better reason than that I had influential friends whose criticism, if my health should suffer in prison, was feared by the authorities. I resented such favouritism on the part of officials, both as a Liberal in politics, as a believer in the teachings of Christ, and as a woman, and if the special treatment of my case continued I should feel bound on my release to make it known from every platform of our campaign throughout the country.

I found there was a tradition amongst prisoners that petitions to the Home Secretary were always in vain. As I put forward a moderate and reasonable request, consistent with the prison regulations, I hoped it would serve as an instance for proving this tradition to be false. This letter, perhaps, gave a slightly coloured version of the hospital regime, but I knew that, in spite of their aims to the contrary, officials are human, and that if I could express some sort of praise that was fairly justified, my letter would be more likely to reach the higher dignitaries and be attended to by them. Perhaps, I thought, the combination of a very reasonable request with an allowance of judicious flattery might even result in the request being granted.

The following day I noticed a peculiar and welcome expression on the faces of various officials as of a smile hidden behind the mask, plainly indicating that my letter had been read in Holloway, however much the valentine might be destined for waste paper basket furniture at the Home Office. I piled on my good behaviour and ate as much food as I could, to conciliate the prison authorities. On the third day following I received a written answer, a formal statement that my petition had been received, but that the Home Secretary did not see his way to granting it. This led to further altercations with the governor and doctor. They insisted that the cell regime would be too severe for me. I replied that unless they allowed me to experience it for myself I should probably carry away an exaggerated version of the hardships imposed on my companions. They pleaded that my exceptional physique and heart disease required "rest."

I answered that prison was not a "rest cure "and that in the case of my fellow prisoners, more especially of Miss Lawless and Mrs. Meredith Macdonald, no such reverend attention had been paid to their physical needs. Every day I put forward the request and argued the point, always in vain. I felt that the time had come to carry out my threat. My mind brooded on what form it should take, but for various reasons it had to be deferred. I had contracted the cold which was rampant in the ward. The prisoner's handkerchief, a duster hanging from the waist of the skirt which did service for a week, was an inevitable conveyer of infection.

This forbidding form of handkerchief became doubly a trial with a cold in the head. I used when at exercise to hold it out as I walked, in the style of a bull-fighting matador, in order to dry it and shake it out, and I used toilet paper in its stead whenever opportunity offered, but no efforts could counteract the disgusting overuse and exposure of the duster. I determined not to press my request to go to the cells while there was any rational excuse for keeping me in hospital. When my cold was wearing off I had the misfortune to meet with an accident and cut myself with some broken crockery. This necessitated bandaging, and again I put off my threat. The days went by with unvarying monotony. Although I had known for several weeks of my decision to go on the deputation and had full time to prepare for a likely imprisonment, I was continually remembering some concern of my home life, the wheels of which would be getting clogged in my absence.

At first these thoughts were very worrying and kept my mind continually on the fret at my inability to communicate with the outside world, but the realisation of one's helplessness gradually subdued these desires. One day, however, I heard from a more experienced "gaolbird" that permission to write a letter was sometimes granted if "on business." I promptly determined to try for this privilege, since it had been granted to other Suffragists. I chose a matter connected with the village in which I lived, so that the fact of my being "all right," as the cell inspectors put it, might be conveyed to my mother. I asked leave to write to the rector's wife about a flower show committee of which I was secretary.

Leave was granted. I was asked to confine myself exclusively to the "business" for which permission had been given; the luxury of writing it was nevertheless very great. Later on I was allowed to write a second letter to a friend on the Stock Exchange who manages my money affairs. I wanted some money for a prisoner friend who was to be released before me. Cheque books were, of course, not available in prison, and although a letter to my banker would probably have been sufficient, I thought a personal friend would be more likely to let the news of my continued "all right"-ness filter through to my mother, although I was not allowed to send a definite message. There seemed, too, something attractive in addressing a letter direct from Holloway to the Stock Exchange, as I did not know my friend's private address.

This letter, of course, required an answer which I was allowed to receive and keep. The rule for prisoners is that letters addressed to them by a spontaneous correspondence from outside are forbidden, but if permission is granted to a prisoner to write a letter which requires an answer, that answer can be received and kept. This answer was about the money I had asked for, duly enclosed, and contained also a casual reference to a remote relative. "I suppose you have heard that X. has been down with influenza." Evidently the writer assumed that I had been carrying on my correspondence as usual. I ungratefully wished that if I was to be allowed news of the outside world it might have been an item connected with my more immediate belongings. But the letter gave me a pleasure difficult to describe, bringing, as it did, a ventilating whiff of ordinary human, free existence into prison life. I clung to every particle of it, envelope and all, and generally carried it about in my clothes for fear it should be destroyed while I was out of my cell; no love-letter was ever more watchfully guarded by a girl of sixteen. It, of course, had been opened and read before it was delivered to me.

I pleaded that as the cell prisoners were allowed a change of vegetables, cabbage, onions, haricot beans, succeeding each other in turn at the midday meal, the hospital patients might be allowed the same, anyhow the bed patients, to whom the daily cabbage became extremely distasteful through monotony. The medical officer who took the inspection rounds that morning was not favourable to petitions of this kind.

He answered gruffly, "If you were given the variety, depend upon it you'd be petitioning before long to be put back on one kind only," and the daily cabbage continued. But one gets used to snubs in prison and before long I tried again. For three days in succession we had been given salt butter of a rather rancid kind, instead of fresh butter as had been supplied before. I kept a small sample of it in a saucer and showed it to the Senior Medical Officer when he came round. This man, according to my experience, was uniformly obliging, just as if he had been an ordinary man and not a prison official. He did not scoff, but took the saucer in his hands and marched out of the ward with it, saying: "I think I had better see to this myself." We were not given salt butter again. Emboldened by this success when next he came I put the vegetable question before him. He said nothing, but from that time forward we were given a change every day.

One day there was a stir in the atmosphere owing to an unusual event, the fortnightly visit of the Visiting Magistrates was due. This was an opportunity for prisoners to air their grievances. Experience had taught us that, at any rate as regards Suffragettes, prison officials and Visiting Magistrates were one and the same authority, indeed prison officials. Prison Commissioners, Home Office, police, and police magistrates, all played to the same tune as conducted by the attitude of the government, and we knew that there was no tribunal of an independent character to which we could make appeal. Nevertheless, as a matter of principle, we left no stone unturned to get injustice redressed by constitutional means. Among the hospital patients there were several cases of glaring injustice. The false charge before mentioned on which Mrs. Duval (Freedom League) had been arrested and sentenced to six weeks' imprisonment. Mrs. Pethick Lawrence's sentence of two months when other second offenders in the same deputation were given only four weeks and some six, and when Mrs. Despard, also a prominent leader, had been sentenced to only one month (second imprisonment) and released after one week "on medical grounds," her health at the time being excellent.

Finally, the disgraceful medical diagnosis and treatment of Mrs. Macdonald after her accident in the yard. Mrs. Macdonald and Mrs. Duval were unable to leave their beds to appear before the magistrates. Mrs. Macdonald decided not to appeal on her own behalf. The magistrates were not medical men and an appeal against the doctor would have been useless and perhaps would have aroused fresh prejudice against her. She was allowed to send a written communication suggesting some excellent reforms on general lines for prison management.

That afternoon, when I was locked into my cell, at an unexpected hour a wardress ushered in a gentleman, apparently an official, whom I had not seen before. I expected him to order my dress to be opened and to begin stethoscoping my heart—that was the usual procedure when a male official appeared. Listead he stood before me and said with some dignity: "I am Sir Alfred Reynolds." The name conveyed nothing to me, so I did not answer, but merely bowed. He went on to ask if I wanted anything, to say he might be seeing Lord Lytton soon and did I want any message conveyed to him or to my home. The sense of bewilderment which prisoners feel when the unusual happens, breaking into the monotonous routine of their lives without explanation, overcame me . I did not know with what object the stranger put these questions, the wildest interpretations rushed through my mind—that the authorities were seeking some fresh excuse to release me, that my home people had heard some untrue report and were in a panic, that there was some underlying purpose connected with my fellow prisoners, to which I had no clue.

My instinct was to be on my guard, and to shield myself against intrusion. I answered coldly that I was "All right, thank you," and that I had no messages to send. That evening I was told that this gentleman was one of the Visiting Magistrates. After my release I realised that he was a neighbour in our county of Hertfordshire and knew my brother. It was very kind of him to visit me in that considerate way and I much regret that I did not respond to his friendliness at the time.

Mrs. Lawrence put her case, guarded by a wardress, standing before the seated board of Magistrates. They had nothing to say in explanation or defence of her sentence, but offered no redress.

On Friday, March 12, I had an unexpected and altogether delightful surprise. In the afternoon I was summoned out of the ward and taken across the yard. Was I being changed to the other side? A deliriously joyful thought suggested itself, could it be a visitor? I had already had my due in this respect, but several visitors were occasionally allowed to prisoners. Since privileges towards me were the order of the day it was a possibility. I was shown into the same "solicitor's" room as before; this time it was empty. I was left in charge of a wardress I had not seen before; she was very amiable. I felt quite distraught with the unusual excitement, and with the torrent of questions that ramped through my brain.

Although I had had no reason to expect another visitor, I had recently longed for one with accelerated zest because of the patient with the injured leg. I had grown daily more exasperated over the attitude of the authorities towards her case, and felt that the seeming brutality on their part was probably due to an official inability to realise all that it entailed to this suffering woman, that if only one could get the facts known outside the prison a reconsideration might bring about the granting of some of the very moderate requests she had made with regard to her release, and also by exposure of her treatment make it unlikely that physically injured prisoners should be subject to the same hardships in future. She was a woman of abnormal courage, and in spite of her crippled condition was planning to go straight home by rail to Mariow on the day of her release. She did not keep a servant; her three children who had been cared for by friends were to return with her. It seemed to me she was unfit for her ordinary life and I was most anxious that she should see a surgeon before attempting the journey by rail. I urged her, too, to make some arrangement for being nursed in her own house or to go for a while to a "home" or hospital.

For all these matters it was imperative that she should see her husband and discuss possible plans with him. She asked leave of the governor to write to him. This was refused unless she obtained a permit from the Home Secretary. It took three days to write to and obtain an answer from the Home Office. When the reply came, permission was granted to write to her husband, but no mention was made as to his visiting her. The prison authorities would not allow this without a further permit from the Home Office. There was no time to receive and act upon this before her release. When I compared such treatment of an urgently needful situation with my own, the ease with which I obtained leave direct from the prison authorities to write two letters, one of them of no particular importance, and the ease with which two of my relatives had been allowed to visit me, I felt exasperated. The action of the authorities made no pretence at inflexible, even-handed justice, and the partiality shown was all on behalf of the prisoner who needed it least.

After a few minutes, to my surprise and intense delight, my eldest brother was shown in. He gave me good news of those at home. Before long I was pouring out to him the facts and my pent-up commentary concerning Mrs. Macdonald, in spite of frequent protests from the wardress, who exclaimed from time to time that it was against the rules to make communications to outsiders about fellow prisoners or the prison authorities. This time I was careful not to reprove my loved visitor for anything, and before our all-too-short interview came to an end I was able to send a message to my sister to make good my regrets about her visit.

The variety of leniency of the different officials, and of the same officials on different days, gave a certain savour of adventure to the dreariness of prison life. Here are two instances of the brighter side. Mrs. Lawrence and I were one afternoon allowed to walk up and down the length of the ward side by side talking in low voices. She told me about the early days of the militant movement and supplemented my book-study of that miraculous fairy tale in which I was now privileged to take part. As I listened and reproached myself continually with the thought, "Women had all this to face and I was not helping them," there seemed a positive charm in the trials of imprisonment—the suffering about my home people, the grim sights and sounds of our surroundings, the rudeness of prison officers, the physical discomforts of unaccustomed clothing, thunder-stuffed pillows, etc.

Now that I passed the nights in a cell and came into the ward only for meals and part of the day, I noticed with keener insight how remarkably the atmosphere of leadership clung round Mrs. Pethick Lawrence. Her clothes and the disciplined routine were exactly the same in her case as in ours, she conformed to all the rules and seemed to adapt herself to the life as if it had been of her choice and not imposed upon her. Yet the authority, and above all, the wisdom in her personality seemed to shine out more prominently even than they did in free life when she was controlling the many departments of the office at Clement's Inn for which she was responsible, or of the public movement from a platform. Everyone came to her for advice, even the prison officers seemed instinctively to refer matters to her. It was, for once, quite intelligible why they had separated her from the bulk of the Suffragist prisoners by putting her in hospital.

It was obvious that her control over them would far outweigh the authority of prison rules and rulers should she choose to exert it. The reason given, however, was that she too was suffering from heart disease, but this medical verdict did not prevent her being sent to the cells, where the full prison labour of floor washing and tin polishing was exacted of her, as soon as our shorter sentences had expired and she was left to finish her unjustifiably longer term in solitude.

Another unexpected privilege had been carefully planned so that the joy of it was spread over several days. The Freedom League prisoners were soon to be released. We schemed a jollification to take place on the Sunday evening before their departure. The Sabbath day reflected national customs in prison as outside. The morning was characterised by clean clothing and an unusual rigidity of behaviour, but towards the latter half of the afternoon the air of solemnity wore away, some of the officers had an afternoon off, bringing back with them an indefinable sense of the outer world, and the evening hours sometimes produced an atmosphere almost of amiability. Much would depend on whether a lovable wardress, who often did duty in our ward and had shown herself invariably friendly towards us, should be "on" or "off." The patients, who had increased to nine, were all of them now out of bed during part of the day. We were to gather round the fire, and to tell yarns, stories or poems, as if we were in camp in the free world.

A sense of excitement and expectancy pervaded the ward all day. I felt as children do before a self-schemed escapade into the dominions of forbidden joys, my delight only slightly marred by the prospect of having to contribute to the recitations, a performance not at all in my line. I spent the spare moments of the day trying to remember and write down on my slate Coventry Patmore's poem *The Toys*. Parts of it had constantly floated into my mind while in Holloway from the striking resemblance between prisoners and children. I treasured more especially the actual list of toys which the child, a seven times breaker of the law, when punished and dismissed *"with hard words and unkiss'd,"* had put beside his bed:—

A box of counters and a red-vein'd stone,
A piece of glass abraded by the beach,
And six or seven shells,
A bottle with bluebells,
And two French copper coins, ranged there with careful art
To comfort his sad heart.

When evening came after the supper meal our little plot developed with unexpected smoothness. The kindly wardress was in charge, activity and "inspection" in the passage outside subsided altogether and we were left to our own devices. What chairs there were we set round the fire and the rest of the company sat on the floor. An unwonted expression of happiness beamed from the fire-lit faces of these prison-clad individuals, drawn together from many parts of the country and from widely-differing walks of life. Each one contributed her share to our spontaneous entertainment. Even the wardress, completely casting aside her official manner and addressing herself deferentially to Mrs. Lawrence, for whom she had a great admiration, told a pathetic little story with a surprising gift of narration and concentrated expression. I remember I had dreaded lest one or two of the company besides myself should not be "up" to an adequate contribution, and that our little entertainment would be marred by those uncomfortable moments of both conscious and unconscious failure such as are common to "social" gatherings, no matter where they take place.

However, everyone played up. There was great variety in the different speakers, each in turn adding a new element to the programme, each was good of its kind and there was no need for pity anywhere. My friend with the injured leg contributed a remarkable political poem of her own making, but far the most artistic items were given by Mrs. Lawrence. She told us first an Arab story which she had heard from a Dragoman sitting round a real camp fire in Egypt. It was full of the detail dear to the East, which suited the associations of superfluous time in our then experience. It was intricate and humorous, lifting our minds completely out of our present surroundings. She was pressed for "more." She then repeated Olive Schreiner's *Three Dreams in a Desert.*

I had read this allegory many years ago when it was first published. I remember that the painter Watts and my father had been enthusiastic over the poetical beauty of these *Dreams*. Their lyrical force, the imaginative woof and warp of their parables and the dignified cadence of their language had impressed me in my youth so that I read them many times for sheer emotional joy, but their meaning had evidently not penetrated to me. Olive Schreiner, more than any one other author, has rightly interpreted the woman's movement and symbolised and immortalised it by her writings. Now after even so short an experience of the movement as I had known, this *Dream* seemed scarcely an allegory. The words hit out a bare literal description of the pilgrimage of women. It fell on our ears more like an A B C railway guide to our journey than a figurative parable, though its poetic strength was all the greater for that. The woman wanderer goes forth to seek the Land of Freedom . . .

'How am I to get there?' The old man. Reason, answers, '*There is one way and one only, Down the hanks of Labour, through the water of suffering. There is no other.*' . . . 'Is there a track to show where the best fording is?' . . . '*It has to be made. . . .*' And she threw from her gladly the mantle of ancient-received opinions she wore, for it was worn full of holes. And she took the girdle from her waist that she had treasured so long, and the moths flew out of it in a cloud. And he said, '*Take the shoes of dependence off your feet.*' And she stood there naked but for one white garment that clung close to her, the garment of Truth, which she is told to keep. She is given a staff, Reason, 'a stick that curled.' '*Take this stick, hold it fast. In that day when it slips from your hand you are lost. Put it down before you, where it cannot find a bottom, do not set your foot.*' The woman having discarded all to which she had formerly clung cries out: 'For what do I go to this far land which no one has ever reached? I am alone! I am utterly alone!' But soon she hears the sound of feet, 'a thousand times ten thousand and thousands of thousands and they beat this way.' . . . '*They are the feet of those that shall follow you.*' . . . *Have you seen the locusts how they cross a stream? First one comes down to the water's edge, and it is swept away, and then another comes and then another , and at last with their bodies piled up a bridge is built and the rest pass over.*' . . . And of those that come first some are swept away, and are heard of

108

no more; their bodies do not even build the bridge? ...'*What of that? They make a track to the water's edge.*

And in the last dream she sees in that land of Freedom where Love is no longer a child but has grown to a man:

On the hills walked brave women and brave men, hand in hand. And they looked into each other's eyes, and they were not afraid.

We dispersed and went back to our hard beds, to the thought of our homes, to the depressing surroundings of fellow prisoners, to the groans and cries of agonised women—content. As I laid my head on the rattling pillow I surrendered my normal attitude towards literature, and thought "There is some point, some purpose in it after all."

Since I had left the general ward there were more opportunities for the officers to show kindness without being detected in "favouritism," and I had come to be on very good terms with several of them. Even the ward superintendent, who made a special hobby of outward severity, had relaxed on several occasions. For instance, she stood in the doorway one morning watching me make my bed. She remarked, with the same outward air of contempt that was habitual to her, but with a kindly look in her eyes; "You're not much used to that, I expect?"

I answered: "Do you think I do it so badly?"

She smiled and seemed distressed that I had interpreted her that way. Her anxiety that I should put on flesh while under her charge made her almost motherly at times. I accounted for my small appetite by explaining that I did not spend myself in prison life. "Don't know about spending yourself, but how about your sensitiveness? Doesn't that 'spend' you?" This taunt was because when she renewed the plasters on my cut, which she did very skilfully, I winced a good deal. The sticky plaster adhered closely and the process of removing it generally made me feel faint. I didn't know till she said this that she had even noticed it, but her contempt was softened by a kind smile. I had determined to begin my strike in real earnest the following week if I failed by reasonable pleadings to get sent to the cells. I was anxious that the responsibility of my bad behaviour should not fall on her, and I wished to make very clear that I had no malicious intentions towards her, or anyone else, beyond giving proof to the doctors that I should be better the "other side." She was extremely busy and her visits to me never lasted more than a few seconds.

I took the first opportunity to say unconcernedly and not looking at her, but with the hope of arousing her curiosity sufficiently for her consent: "If you should have a spare minute before Sunday, come in to me when I am in my cell, I want to ask you something."

She looked surprised, but said nothing and avoided me for the rest of the day. The following afternoon she looked in hurriedly, saying in her most official voice: "What is it you want? "I resented the scolding tone and answered without humility, as one would to a fellow-being outside, "Come near to me, I want to speak to you, but only if you can spare the time."

I was lying on my bed, a privilege I was allowed in the separate cell. She came in, pushed the door to, stood close to my bedside and said again gruffly, "What is it?"

I reached out my hand to take hers, but meeting with no response I drew it in again. I did not want to get angry with the rebuffs of her officialdom, so I kept my eyes down as I said: "I like you because you have always treated me the same as the others, yet you have never really been unkind to me. I want to ask you something now, because by Sunday either I shall have had leave to go to the other side or I shall have begun my strike in real earnest and you will be getting more and more angry with me."

She stooped down and said in a low voice of extreme tenderness as if I had been a child: "Why, I have never been angry with you yet." I looked up into her eyes. They were lit with kindliness and her whole face beamed on me with genial goodwill. It was a surprising change. The personality was the same, but the mask was off and I realised something of the sacrifice it must be to this woman continually to conceal her good nature under so forbidding a manner. I felt more than ever how wasteful and unreasonable is a system which represses the natural powers of good influence in such a woman and exacts of her, in their stead, an attitude towards the prisoners of so much less worth. Her kindness made my determination to carry out my strike at all costs a much harder job than any amount of her official hardness and reproof would have done. If it had been for any less object than a matter of principle I could not have done it.

"No," I answered, "but I haven't yet begun my strike seriously." I added: "I don't wish to discuss that now. I want you to tell me when you could come and see us after I am out. Mother will wish to thank you for being kind to me, and to hear about my wicked ways from you. You must come down to us in the country. We are on this line and quite near London."

Her face grew serious again, but remained without the official mask. She shook her head. "That's impossible," she said with decision, "it would be against the rules."

"There are no prison rules for me once I am free again, and you surely have some holidays when you can do as you like."

"No, that would be quite against the rules."

I pleaded afresh and with determination. She then tried another tack, said that she had friends of her own to visit in the little time at her disposal. I answered she must bring one of these with her and they would spend the day together with us. But she would have none of it. I said she, of course, felt obliged to rub in the rules and regulations while I was prisoner under her charge and that I respected her for that. It was obvious, however, that such rules would have nothing to do with me once I was free again, that I should write to her after my release, as an ordinary outsider, and make fresh suggestions. I had in mind several instances in which prisoners and warders had continued friendly after release. I asked her to give me her home address or, at least, to tell me her Christian name, for, as several of her sisters were also prison officers in Holloway, I did not want my letter to go to them. She, however, would not tell me any of these things. I asked why it would be against the rules.

She answered, "We are not allowed to hold communication with ex-prisoners," and vouchsafed no further explanation. I said I thought we Suffragettes might be looked upon as different from the ordinary ex-prisoners. She remained adamant. I felt fresh enmity for the system which continually admitted variation from its rules on the side of less kindness or for reasons of snobbish privilege, but which showed itself rigid and unelastic when it was a case of reasonable, unharmful good-will. But, of course, I immensely respected this woman's loyalty to the system she served and her punctilious adherence to its rules. She had, nevertheless, let go her own voice and her own smile just once upon me. They remained among the joy experiences of Holloway. I wondered if she had ever shown them to the poor woman who screamed and groaned in the cell below mine, or to the yellow-faced patient in the lower ward.

I began my strike gently; I knocked off all diet extras, such as the maltine and its accompanying banana or the pudding at the mid-day meal, and kept to the food which would be mine the other side, *viz*.:

Breakfast: Brown bread, butter, milk.

Midday: Brown bread, potatoes, one vegetable.

Supper: Brown bread, butter, milk.

Both doctors and wardresses talked of the plank bed as one of the hardships likely to be too much for me in the cells, so I took one of the two mattresses from my bed and slept with it on the floor. I clambered up on the furniture and cleaned the windows of my cell to show I could do some extra housemaiding without harm. The first night of my floor-bed I was left undisturbed. The second night, at the time of the "All right?" rounds, the hospital superintendent came in. To my surprise she was not angry, did not scold. She asked quite gently and interestedly why I was lying on the floor. "Because the doctors suggest that I would get ill or die if I laid on a wooden bed instead of an iron one, so I am just showing that I can manage it all right; I am very comfortable, thanks."

But she didn't go away. The cell, of course, was small, the fixed bedstead down the centre of it taking up most of the floor-room, so I had laid the mattress cross-ways under the bed, my head sticking out on one side, my feet on the other. The wardress suggested that if I woke suddenly in the night I might hit and hurt myself against the bed. I assured her that sleep in Holloway was not of a kind heavy enough to wake from it unconsciously. It was true I had enjoyed such a sleep one night, the first in my private cell, but the ghastly sounds of human desperation and suffering by which it had been broken had driven away sound sleep for the remainder of my imprisonment. At last she went away. The following night she again came and argued about the bed.

She said she would worry lest harm should happen while she was responsible for me and it would drive away her own rest. I respected her for at last using a sensible form of argument, but for the moment I did not relent. When she had gone, however, I managed by judicious shifting of the movable furniture to find room for the mattress along the wall with my head behind the door. I rang my bell, the night wardress appeared. Peremptory fashion, I sent her with an invitation to the superintendent to come again if she had not yet gone to bed. The wardress positively laughed at my effrontery, but evidently delivered my message, for in a few minutes my friend the superintendent returned. She tried to look severe, but a broad grin enveloped her face when she saw my new contrivance. "However much I jump about now, I can't hurt myself. Will you be able to sleep all right?" I asked. She said she would try, and left me.

My continued appeals to the authorities to treat me as they did my fellow-prisoners and not keep me in hospital now that I was in normal health, having proved unavailing, I entered upon the last phase of my strike. I had decided to write the words "Votes for Women" on my body, scratching it in my skin with a needle, beginning over the heart and ending it on my face. I proposed to show the first half of the inscription to the doctors, telling them that as I knew how much appearances were respected by officials, I thought it well to warn them that the last letter and a full stop would come upon my cheek, and be still quite fresh and visible on the day of my release. My difficulty was to find suitable tools.

My skin proved much tougher than I had expected and the small needle supplied to me for sewing purposes was quite inadequate. I procured another and stronger one for darning my stockings, but neither of them produced the required result. I thought of a hairpin but had only three left of these precious articles and could not make up my mind to spare one. I had the good luck, however, while exercising, to find one, the black enamel of which was already partially worn off. I cleaned and polished it with a stone under my cloak as I walked the round. The next morning before breakfast I set to work in real earnest and, using each of these implements in turn, I succeeded in producing a very fine **V** just over my heart. This was the work of fully twenty minutes, and in my zeal I made a deeper impression than I had intended. The scratch bled to a certain extent. I had no wish for a blood-poisoning sequel, and, fearing the contact with the coarse prison clothes, when the wardress came to fetch me for breakfast I asked her for a small piece of lint and plaster.

On a previous occasion I had been allowed these without further inquiry, when the frosty weather, cold water, and lack of gloves had produced a sore on my hand. But this time the superintendent herself appeared and refused to produce the dressing without hearing for what purpose it was required. I was anxious to proceed further with my inscription before letting the authorities know of it, fearing that it was not yet sufficient to be imposing and that all tools might be taken from me. However, thanks to our previous conversations, my friend was suspicious. She ordered me to show the scratch. She looked very much startled on seeing it and asked how it had happened. I explained. She at first did not know how to take it, but evidently did not think it a laughing matter, to my great relief, for I hoped this meant the misdeed was grave enough to suggest to the authorities that I was becoming an awkward customer in hospital.

She was restrained in manner, but looked rather angry as she solemnly applied a large piece of lint and many plasterings which, to my delight, gave the scratch a quite imposing look, as if half my chest had been hacked open. So that no blame should fall on her, I gave her all the information for which she asked and the incriminating tools were gathered together as if they had been witnesses in a detective case. After breakfast I was summoned into the presence of the governor and given a scolding, but no sentence of punishment was passed and I remained in doubt as to whether my evil deed had been sufficiently impressive. Later on I was taken down to the Senior Medical Officer. Scolding was not in his line and the official requirements of the occasion were evidently effortful to him, but his laborious sermon of reproofs was all the more punitive on that account. As he had invariably been kind to me and civil to all other prisoners, I was sorry to have to vex him. I reminded him of the warning I had previously given and how often I had patiently renewed my request in a reasonable way before having recourse to these stronger measures.

Of course he had to pretend that he saw not the remotest connection between his refusal to let me leave hospital and my "outrageous" conduct of the morning. He and the ward superintendent, who ushered me into his presence and exposed the scratched "V" for his inspection, were evidently much put out. I felt all a craftsman's satisfaction in my job. The V was very clearly and evenly printed in spite of the varying material of its background, a rib bone forming an awkward bump. As I pointed out to the doctor, it had been placed exactly over the heart, and visibly recorded the pulsation of that organ as clearly as a watch hand, so that he no longer need be put to the trouble of the stethoscope.

I also explained how useful the mark would be at the inquest, to which he had alluded, when they wanted quickly to extract the heart in proof that its "serious disease" was responsible for my demise and not the prison regimen. But he was not in a mood for chaff and became more and more distraught as to how to deal with the situation. At last he hit on a brilliant idea and said, "If you go on like this we shall have to dismiss you from the prison altogether." I could have congratulated him with both hands for this really understanding remark. It was obvious that such a sentence wouldn't at all meet with my aims, and would secure my return to good behaviour if anything could. He had effectively checkmated me, at any rate for the moment. I promptly capitulated and capped this suggestion by saying:

I think I had better be sent back to the general ward; I seem to give a lot of extra trouble in the separate cell.

The superintendent wardress exclaimed with gusto, "Yes, you do," and the doctor jumped at the suggestion. As there were now only ten days before our release I had decided to push through my efforts to get to the cells regardless of all else, but I was exceedingly anxious about the patient with the injured leg. Her release was due, with other members of the Freedom League, the next day (Wednesday, March 17). I had a feeling that I could to a certain degree watch over her welfare and was to this extent glad of the opportunity to return to the hospital. While waiting for the hospital gate to be unlocked a small gang of ordinary prisoners had for some reason or another congregated in the passage and blocked the way. My friend, the superintendent, took the opportunity to give me a severe scolding in their presence.

Now that the extent of my criminality had been duly notified and received, as it were, official recognition, her pent up indignation let fly and she gave me a regular dressing down. She did not, of course, allude to the nature of my crime; this was left to the imagination of the onlookers, but, as on all other occasions of the kind that I can recall, the sympathy of prisoners turns automatically to a fellow-prisoner, not to the officials. Intercourse by means of speech being forbidden, the language of the eyes becomes perfected. Inquiry, interest, fellow-feeling, loyalty, encouragement, sympathy of the best, all these emotions are expressed in prisoners' eyes in a way that outbids the meaning of words and the intonations of the voice. I respected this superintendent as before, because of the impartiality with which she treated me, but this example of public reproof before other prisoners was typical of the way this sort of prison discipline defeats its own ends.

Mrs. Macdonald was still suffering acutely. She had been taken out of the ward for the injury to be photographed by X-rays. She was carried up and down the stairs, as before, in a chair with no rest for the feet. She had been told that the photographs had not been distinct and left them "none the wiser," but "Depend upon it," said the doctor, "you had better keep moving about as much as you can." The prison authorities recognised that she was unfit to travel by rail. As she had no home in London and could not afford to rent rooms, they proposed sending her to a hospital. For various reasons, the thought of an ordinary public hospital was extremely repellent to her. The prison officials now discussed the matter with her and seemed to show a certain amount of interest and even kindness towards her.

My wound being the nominal ground on which I had been returned to hospital, it had to be treated with official respect. The ward superintendent told me she would come and inspect it the last thing before she went to bed herself. I looked forward to this opportunity of pacifying her displeasure with me, but when she came she was already in her most benignant mood. My chief concern was to inquire her view as to my chances of ever being sent to the other side. "They'll never send you out of hospital, nothing you can do will make any difference, so what's the use of going on trying? "In some mysterious way this despairing speech of hers put new mettle into me, and I determined I would renew my attempts. To reassure her with regard to my villainous intentions I told her that the doctor had hit on a really effective deterrent by threatening to turn me out of prison.

"That's what you deserve," she said, severely, but with something of a wink.

"So you think," I retorted.

The hospital atmosphere soon drew my thoughts away from my strike and its object. Several of the patients were less restless than when I had last been amongst them. The night wardress with the hacking cough had been changed. The sick patients had agreed to make no complaints for fear they should get her into trouble or perhaps be given a more disagreeable wardress in her place. But when our numbers had been increased by a patient who was in fairly vigorous health but for the most painful neuritis in her arm, she found the continuous disturbance of her all too precious sleep intolerable and she reported the wardress's cough to the doctor. We were then all questioned and had to admit the fact, whereupon we were given another night wardress. This one, as had been feared, was more rigid in her ways and interpreted the absurdly inhuman prison regulations literally.

For instance, one night a patient who was quite incapable of moving out of bed had been given medicine which disturbed her during the night. The wardress at first refused to wait upon her, but after reluctantly consenting to do this, she then refused to empty the slops. A fellow-prisoner volunteered to do this, but was not allowed. At last, after putting the patient to much distress, the wardress did the work. On hearing of this the next morning I was indignant and reported the matter to the ward superintendent. She answered, "The officer was quite within her rights. She is not a nurse and it is no part of her duty to wait on the patients. She was quite right, too, not to allow the other patients to do it." I expostulated as to the brutality of putting a patient who was really ill to such distress and on the unwholesomeness of having slops in the ward all night. "The only thing that can be done in such a case," she replied, "would be to ring the night bell for me." As this woman was on her feet for sixteen hours, from six in the morning to ten at night, the patients would be most reluctant to disturb her, apart from the fact that they would never dream of this being the right thing to do unless they had been specially informed of the regulation.

I found that my poor friend of the injured leg was suffering more than ever. I did my best to ease her pain by rubbing and trying to lift the cruel pressure from the disturbed bones. The wardress did not interfere with me as I had rather expected she would, but the next morning she said, "I must report you for being out of bed half the night." When the doctor came on his rounds he had, I suppose, received the "report," for he shook his head at me reprovingly but with a kind look as if he at least understood the motive of my most recent crime. I felt very despondent all day. The members of the Freedom League were released that morning, all except Mrs. Duval, who had to serve a longer sentence, and Mrs. Macdonald, as the authorities had not yet decided what was to happen to her on release.

In the afternoon the sun shone brightly and the air was full of that indefinable sense of spring. The "spring-running" of the jungle seemed to penetrate even through prison walls and into the minds of prison officials. Whether because of this or for some less good cause we were accorded exceptional benefits. Hospital patients who had not been out before were allowed to come to exercise and we were told to walk in couples, arm-in-arm, the healthier patients supporting the others. Amazing privilege! It seemed like a bit of heaven. We, of course, discarded the "silence" rule at the same time. We were exercised in a larger space, not one of the narrowly-enclosed exercise yards. The prison officials passed by—governor, matron, doctors—but they made no comment at the unusual sight, seemed, on the contrary, quite pleased as we grinned our pleasure boldly into their faces.

CHAPTER 9: FROM THE CELLS

The following morning, Thursday, March 18, I was again summoned before the governor. He looked as if he had an important announcement to make to me. "Do you still wish to leave the hospital?" he asked.

I was afraid this might mean my dismissal.

"Do you mean going to the other side?" I said.

He answered "Yes."

"Rather! "I exclaimed, and could hardly contain myself for surprise and delight.

He proceeded to explain: "The weather having changed, the medical officer gives his consent to your being moved to the cells."

I should not be allowed to scrub my floor nor do any of the routine "labour," but if my health and behaviour (!) remained good, I might be moved next day.

The weather, of course, had changed many times since we had been in Holloway, varieties of cold or mild, damp or dry succeeding each other day by day, after the familiar fashion of our national climate in February and March. But I was too well content to be sarcastic over the reasons given for the official surrender to my request. I simply said "Thank you very much indeed."

I had already announced this decision to several of the ward patients, when the superintendent came on her rounds and I rushed up to her unceremoniously with, "Have you heard my good news?" Her official mood was on and she ordered me off with a "Hush! not now." I gathered from various questions put to me by the governor that the authorities hoped I had not told of my carving-strike to the other patients. It would never do, of course, to conciliate the wishes of a striker! But I was not able to comfort them on this score, and my triumph was public as well as complete.

Later in the morning the superintendent took me before the Senior Medical Officer. With him it was a real temptation to say, "If now, why not before?" to point out how effective had been the behaviour which two days previously he had professed to find so incomprehensible, also to draw the analogy between this little prison episode and the women's fight for the vote—a reasonable demand, continuously pressed in a reasonable way and with great patience; result, blank refusal on the part of responsible powers. Militant action, by means of strike and protest; result, anger, condemnation, and the request is granted. The vote is not yet granted to women, but who now doubts that "they'll get it" before long; but I restrained myself and trusted that the lesson would sink home unassisted. The doctor pointed to a chair by the side of his desk for me to sit while he sounded me. In my excitement I forgot all prison decorum and shook him cordially by the hand. He and the ward superintendent seemed nearly as pleased as I was myself. I felt how differently the prison system would work and with what different results if the officials were more often allowed to please themselves by pleasing their prisoners.

That afternoon Mrs. Macdonald was released and sent, by arrangement with the Prison Commissioners, to a private hospital. The ward superintendent accompanied her, but on the return of this officer no word escaped her as to how the patient had stood the transit, nor as to the result of the further radiograph which had been taken the day before. As soon as I was released, I heard that her leg was broken and had been from the first. A committee was formed for her care and her redress. The Home Secretary, Mr. Gladstone, was sure that the leg had been broken before and refused to read our statement. It was not till 1910, when Mr. Winston Churchill was made Home Secretary, that he read the case and paid her £500 compensation. She was taken to another hospital and had a serious operation to her leg. Had it been treated at once, the fractured bone would have been restored to its own length, but after about eighteen days of her being in prison, when nothing was done for it, the bone had overlapped and the muscles hardened round it. This, of course, inevitably shortened the bone. The operation was successful, but she is lame for life.

The only item in the cell-life routine to which I looked forward with considerable misgiving was discarding the hospital slippers and having to wear the hard shoes continuously all day. I felt quite absurdly pleased with the reward of my efforts. At the mid-day meal I drank, or rather ate, the doctor's health in rice pudding and insisted that the wardress in charge should do the same. That day there happened to be on duty one of the outwardly least human of her kind, but my good spirits were irrepressible, and these being so rarely seen in prison, they gave me a certain air of authority, I suppose, for her severity melted and she ate the rice pudding, as ordered, with even the flicker of a smile.

The luxury of a bath was allowed once a week, my turn was due that evening. The superintendent said: "If I let you have it, will you promise me not to cut yourself about or any nonsense of that kind?"

I answered: "Is it likely now that I've achieved all that I've been struggling for?"

That evening, when she came to my bed for a last inspection, I said, "You see, they have given way after all."

"Yes," she answered; "I never thought they would, but there, you never can tell what is happening behind the scenes." I cordially agreed with this last sentiment.

119

"That is why," I answered, "one should never grow disheartened when things seem to be impossible."

The next morning, while dusting the ward, the little 3rd Division cleaner came up to me and, without looking at me after the manner of prisoners, said in a low voice, "I shall miss you." I took her to mean that my housemaiding had to a certain extent lightened her labours, and I was filled with pride; I have seldom received praise that gave me more pleasure. I redoubled my energies and turned over and dusted the beds that were unoccupied.

The superintendent passed and said, "What are you doing there?" I explained.

"Oh!" she answered, "That's good of you."

It's wonderful how luck, good or bad, never comes singly. Everything seemed to win approval that day.

In the afternoon I was sewing a new stripe on to Mrs. Duval's sleeve, a good conduct badge that had been dealt out to her, as the first month of her sentence had been served (she was in for six weeks), when a stranger wardress came into the ward and summoned me to "bring your things and come with me." This meant the other side at last! Now that the long-fought privilege was actually mine I felt self-reproachful at leaving Mrs. Pethick Lawrence, but she thought I had done right to try and join the others. No time was allowed for good-byes. As I retreated through the gate I waved the hated shoes at my companions, in token of my good wishes. I was made to change all my clothes. The wardress was reluctant to allow me to wear my nightdress, as I had done from the first in the daytime. I insisted, fearing that I might catch cold without it, and I promised the doctor to care for my health in every way if allowed out of hospital. She relented, but told me I must inform the matron about it.

I was taken over to the new building "D X," and shown to a cell on the third floor. No. 10. It was very clean, had no bars on the window and no gate, and was in every respect much brighter looking and without so much of the death's-head element as the hospital cell I had just left in the older part of the prison. It had a hot pipe and, to my surprise, was considerably warmer than the hospital cell or general ward, so that the official excuse about the change of weather seemed less to the point than ever. After depositing the sheets, towel, soap, etc., which I had brought with me, I was taken to join the others, who were sitting at associated labour on the ground floor passage.

The building had a strange appearance, as of an enormous bird cage. The cells are ranged on either side of a barrack-like hall giving on to narrow galleries with iron rails. The different storeys are reached by a small iron stairway in the centre. These and the balconies are covered over with wire netting for the prevention of suicide, a precaution in every way most characteristic of the prison system, a symbol of the suicide of its own success. The wire netting gives the building an abnormal appearance; newcomers question "Why is it there?" The explanation fills the mind with horror and revolt. A deeper investigation into prison life brings to light the fact that nothing is done to prevent or counteract the desire for suicide in prisoners, the evil is only met by artificial prevention of its consequences when the mutilation of all spontaneous wishes, human instincts and reasonable paths of self-interest have engendered the passionate longing to cease existing.

The moment of joining my companions was most exhilarating. They were sitting on chairs placed in regular rows, knitting stockings or sewing women's underclothes and men's shirts. I was put into a vacant place about six rows from the front. Patients who had returned to the cells from hospital had spread the news of my continued but vain attempts to rejoin the bulk of my fellow-prisoners, so that my appearance among them caused great surprise. Some of them were almost unrecognisably changed by the prison dress, others I was distressed to see looked extremely ill, but, as the news spread amongst them of my presence, they looked my way in turn and gave me a welcoming smile that momentarily changed prison into paradise. I quickly understood that the right we had claimed to talk with one another at associated labour had been effectively maintained, but for the sake of not getting the wardresses into trouble we talked only in low voices or whispers to our immediate neighbours.

The greatest eagerness, of course, was for news of Mrs. Lawrence. She had sent a special message of thanks to Mrs. Corbett and to Miss Carling, news having reached the hospital that these two had been particularly active in maintaining the rights and decencies that had been won by our predecessors through much hardship, also in their efforts to secure fresh reforms of the same kind. These were mostly connected with ordinary prison routine and affected the welfare of all prisoners besides ourselves. They were, amongst others—the use of an earthenware mug for drinking purposes instead of a tin; permission to empty slops more frequently; a chair with a back to it had been substituted for the stool; a better standard of food, cooking and clothing through complaint whenever these were amiss; the right to appeal direct to the governor—previously the applications to see the governor had frequently not been delivered, this being, of course, more especially the case when it was suspected that complaint would be made about any of the officers; protest whenever prisoners were unjustly punished for offences they had not committed; the right to speak to each other at associated labour.

The prisoners near me were eager to point out these two valiant women and cordially endorsed the report of their splendid persistency. They were sitting near the front, and it was several days before I achieved getting a place near enough to convey to them Mrs. Lawrence's message. They were immensely pleased. One of the reforms for which they had asked most continuously, but always in vain, was for alteration in the lavatory doors. These, which we nick-named "the cowsheds," were only about three feet in depth and left a space of one foot from the ground, there was no lock or bolt or catch of any kind and they could not be fastened.

As the lavatories occupied a position next door to the sink and in the very centre of the gallery, there was no sense of privacy whatever. Both feet and head of the occupant could be seen from the passage, and in the hurried passing to and fro of prisoners to the sink to draw water or empty slops the lavatory door was frequently flung open. The excuse given for this arrangement was that it was in the interests of cleanliness and because of the tendency amongst prisoners to commit suicide. If they were invisible or could lock themselves in, it was stated that besides foul behaviour they would seize the opportunity to kill themselves.

Obviously neither of these precautions were necessary in the case of Suffragettes, and we pleaded that when our numbers exceeded sixteen, the number of cells to which a lavatory was provided, one might be set apart for our use. With the W.S.P.U. and Freedom League together the Suffragette prisoners during my time amounted to about forty. We asked that a bolt should be put on the inside of the door, and a curtain hung from the top of the doorway. This would have been easy and inexpensive, and the wardress in charge could, at any time necessary, draw the curtain and open the bolt from outside the door.

It is difficult to see how this arrangement would be harmful even to the ordinary prisoner. The modern cells are fitted with electric light, the lamps of which have glass shades. The prisoners are locked into these cells and pass the night without inspection. If they intended suicide nothing would be easier than to break the glass and open a vein with it. The lavatories contain no such easy implements for suicide. The almost unanimous experience of our prisoners, and of many ordinary prisoners with whom I have compared note since my release, is that prison life disorganises digestion.

The unaccustomed food, the many hours of sitting still, the want of air, the inability to leave the cell except at stated times, and the great depression of spirit, are all of them certain to produce digestive disorders. Bread is the staple food of prisoners. The prison brown bread is excellent in quality and in nutritive properties to those who can digest it, but to most moderns, of whatever class or sex, it is an unaccustomed food. To some people it is too coarse and acts as an irritant, while producing the opposite effect on others. The white bread of the hospital, also excellent of its kind, though not so irritating, is also not easily digested because of the stagnant life and small quantity of vegetables or butter allowed.

The part played by the drug-basket in prison routine, and the surprise of its attendant if purgatives were not required, is proof sufficient that prison conditions in this matter are abnormal. The cells are supplied with tin chambers fitted with a lid which can be used in an emergency, but the close atmosphere of the cells makes this extremely undesirable to people trained in any sense of cleanliness. Every cell has an electric bell for summoning a wardress, but frequently no notice is taken of such a summons, and the bells are often out of order and do not work.

Many of our Suffrage prisoners have had their health permanently impaired, some have had to undergo operations, as a result of the prison life in these respects. From the writings of ordinary prisoners and from what I have heard from them direct, digestive disorders seem to be common to most prisoners. My own comparative immunity I ascribe to the following precautions: Doing physical exercises twice or three times a day, saving potatoes from the midday dinner so that I had some vegetable food at every meal; keeping my allowance of bread until it was stale; the extra milk and butter allowed to vegetarians; the freedom from drug taking made possible by these precautions; the privileges extended to me in the way of occasional permission to leave my cell out of the drill routine limitations.

After we had returned to our cells the matron came to visit me. I reported the fact that I was wearing my nightgown under my day clothes. She said I could not be allowed to do this without special permission from the medical officer. I accordingly put in "an application "to see him the next day.

I think there must be something of Asiatic origin in me, for, contrary to Western customs, I never feel that meals are a suitable time for conviviality, but, on the contrary, that eating should be in solitude. I enjoyed the change to the cell routine in this respect. It was good to have always the same drinking mug, the cleaning of which I had done myself, and I was glad to be rid of the hospital tablecloth, for this was changed only once a week, and the over-filled dishes of fish and vegetables, as well as tea and milk, left their mark upon it abundantly, so that during the last days of the week it presented anything but an appetising appearance.

In the cells, milk was poured into my own pint mug, vegetables were served in an unpolished tin which looked very dirty and sometimes smelt objectionably, but the potatoes were in their skins and I ate of the vegetables only that part which did not touch the tin. A tin plate and spoon were provided in the cells, and a curious piece of tin, oblong in shape, doubled over up one side to make a rounded surface and corrugated on the other to make an uneven saw-like edge, was handed in with the meal to serve as knife. This I used as it was put out again with the empty tins, but I soon learned that if the plate and spoon were greased with food it was very difficult to get them clean again, as they can only be washed in cold water.

The pail of water allowed to stand in the cell quickly became greasy itself, and there was no time, when let out to the tap to draw water, to wash up these things at the sink. I therefore used some of the freely supplied brown toilet paper to cover my plate and helped myself with my fingers instead of the spoon as they were much easier to wash. We were allowed a small supply of hot water at the same time that supper, consisting of hot milk and bread, was brought round. It was rather a trial that under conditions where luxuries were scarce, two should be supplied together in a way to make the full enjoyment of them both impossible. I preferred a hot wash to a hot supper and performed my ablutions first.

I had hoped that having left hospital I should be allowed to sleep in the dark, but it was a disappointment to find I was still an "observation case" because of my "heart disease." I did not sleep much and when morning came I felt strangely tired, but supposed it was due to the unusual excitement of rejoining my companions and of having at last attained to "the other side." One of the hospital patients had kindly given me elaborate instructions as to the mysterious and dexterous craft of bedrolling in the cells. As the failure to achieve this correctly was a frequent cause of reproof and as the instructions given by wardresses were often inadequate I was very grateful for this special training.

I remember that the patient, Mrs. Manson, of the Freedom League, was reading George Elliot's *Mill on the Floss*, and it was on the cover of this book that she elaborated to me the furniture of the cell, where each thing should be placed and how the bedding was to be folded, then rolled into a kind of Swiss-roll coil. In the cells the mattress is stuffed with some kind of chaff, a not uncomfortable form of bedding if not stuffed too full. But mine was a new one, it seemed filled to its utmost capacity, so that it was as hard as a pincushion to lie upon, and it was only after repeated efforts, requiring my utmost strength for about fifteen minutes, that I succeeded at last in curling it up and buttoning it together in the required fashion. I was sufficiently exhausted after doing this to necessitate a long pause before I started afresh on the folding of the sheets and blankets which had to be done with minute exactness.

Much more prolonged physical labours in hospital had never produced this effect upon me even during the first days when my heart was in an actively disturbed state. I wondered whether there was some health-maiming condition in this much-yearned-after "other side" which had really justified my retention in hospital.

I then remembered the ventilation system of the cells against which Suffragette prisoners had made such a determined stand. The governor and doctors had never once mentioned this lack of air in the cells as among their reasons for keeping me out of them, but now I became convinced that this was the cause of my faintness. Beyond a general feeling of what might be described as extreme slackness I did not notice anything peculiar until I exerted myself, but then the absolutely stagnant quality of the atmosphere seemed to overwhelm me. The window had no opening of any kind, the sixteen small panes of glass in their wooden framework were hermetically sealed. There were three ventilators in all, but on placing my hand upon them there was no feeling whatever of a current of air. The window was not fogged, so proving that the air was not yet vitiated to that degree, but whatever the scientific diagnosis of the results of this ventilation, there could be no doubt to an occupant of the cell that it was difficult to breathe in it after the eleven or twelve hours of close confinement.

★★★★★★

In the Report of the Commissioners of Prisons for the year ending March 31, 1911 (Part 1), the Surveyor of Prisons tells that: "The provision of opening panes and clear glass in cell windows has been continued . . . another two years' work (if funds are forthcoming) should complete the prisons." Two years to wait—and for want of money from the richest exchequer in the world! But they would have waited much longer if it had not been for the Suffragettes.

★★★★★★

During the morning, following on my "application," I was visited by the medical officer. I put the request, as ordered by the Matron, of wearing my nightgown in the daytime. He turned to the wardress and said, "What an extraordinary request to put before a doctor. That has nothing to do with me." I explained that the leaving off of this garment would probably affect my health injuriously, but as it was contrary to prison discipline a doctor's permit was required. He made some contemptuous remarks, but, when pressed, reluctantly gave his consent. This seems a very trifling incident as I record it here, but I vividly remember how it seemed another link in the chain of degradation which is forged afresh continuously around every prisoner. Some exceptional treatment becomes necessary, one is ordered to apply for it through some particular channel, on application the prisoner is refused, reproved or laughed at, as if this were a fresh instance of misdeed or foolishness.

In this instance I reminded the doctor that the authorities were anxious that my health should be good at my release, and that in making this request I was assisting them, otherwise I should prefer to go without a privilege which would not be extended equally to all prisoners under like conditions. I had intended bringing forward the question of ventilation, but felt that it would be useless to appeal to this particular official, who had invariably treated all my requests as unreasonable.

On looking back after my release on this man's conduct, it has occurred to me that possibly he adopted his attitude towards me from a righteous indignation at the orders for specially favourable treatment which were ordered for my case from headquarters. I have heard from other Suffragette prisoners and also from ordinary prisoners of his considerate kindness to them on several occasions. I afterwards told the Chief Medical Officer about the airlessness of these cells, I think with some effect.

We were exercised in the morning, not in the afternoon as from the hospital. It was a moment of great delight to see my companions in the yard, where I had a better view of them than at associated labour. We were exercised in sections of about sixteen at a time for an hour, in the central yard of the prison, as it seemed, a triangular yard flanked by high walls of the oldest blocks of cells and adjoining the high central tower, which enables Holloway prison to stand as a landmark for many miles distant. It can be seen from the Great Northern Railway on the line between Holloway and Finsbury Park Stations.

I never look at it without recalling the sensations that gripped my soul and checked my breath when I first set eyes on this inner yard. It seemed the quintessence of prison, the very heart of it. The length of each side of the rough, triangular formation is, I should think, about twenty-four feet. The walls facing southwest and east are very high, so that a deep shadow lies across the yard at all hours; on the right, as we entered from D X, is a low walled building used apparently, for cooking and laundry purposes and facing south. This seems to be a more modern erection, and from its low, single-storey construction is responsible for most of the sunlight allowed to enter the enclosure.

The remarkable feature of the yard, which caused the first feeling of horror that has remained a nightmare in my mind ever since, is the tier upon tier of cell shutters, they could not be called windows, in the two high walls giving on to the yard. They are designed to let in the very minimum of light or air, the shuttered layers of wood are, moreover, coated with refuse of the pigeons which fly freely about the yard, and are in every other respect a great delight to prisoners. The prison from here looks like a great hive of human creeping things impelled to their joyless labours and unwilling seclusion by some hidden force, the very reverse of natural, and which has in it no element of organic life, cohesion, or self-sufficing reason. A hive of hideous purpose from which flows back day by day into the surrounding city a stream of evil honey, blackened in the making and poisonous in result. The high central tower seemed to me a jam pot, indicative of the foul preserve that seethed within this factory for potting human souls.

Sometimes, in momentary reaction from the pent-up feelings of indignation and revolt, which were chronic with me during my imprisonments, I could have laughed out loud at the imbecility and pathos of human fallibility, that civilised (?) educated beings could continue such processes by way of ridding themselves from the dangers and active harmfulness of crime. Wardresses stood at different points of the yard. Whenever in our march round there was a tendency for the single file to draw closer together, the wardresses would say nothing, but catch hold of one of us by the arm until the spacing was again correct. This handling of prisoners instead of appealing to their ordinary intelligence was typical of the mistaken routine, as in hospital, imposed upon prison officials.

Once, to my delight, I recognised among these superintending wardresses one who had been with us, and exceptionally kind, in hospital. I hoped that she would manage somehow to give me news of Mrs. Pethick Lawrence and possibly also of my friend with the injured leg, whose fate I thought must surely have filtered through to the wardresses. For some days no opportunity occurred, although this officer smiled at me once or twice with a friendly recognition that was quite unofficial, but only at carefully chosen moments, showing that such a smile would not be allowed by higher authorities.

At last, when I purposely crowded up rather near to the prisoner ahead of me, she took the opportunity to check my progress by putting her arm in front of me in the recognised fashion, meanwhile telling me in a hasty whisper and without looking at me, just as prisoners communicate, that Mrs. Lawrence was well, but that Mrs. Macdonald had been found to have a fractured hip-joint and would have to stay in hospital a long while.

Although my cell was considerably warmer than that in the hospital, I still had not grown accustomed to the insufficiency of my underclothing, and as now there was no worse condition of things ahead of me I put into use the strip of flannel that had been given me for knee-binders. I found that either they slipped off immediately or had to be bound so tight that they impeded circulation and the free use of the limbs. As one had to be constantly kneeling down for bed making, etc., this device proved quite impracticable. Fearing lest fresh suggestion on my part would have to be passed by a series of officials and finally submitted to the judgment of a doctor who might, as in the nightgown question, satirically exclaim that this was a point not suitable to put to him, I took advantage of the light that was left on all night, and during the uninspected hours sewed the strips of flannel on to the flannel drawers; this enabled me to tuck them into the stockings knickerbocker-wise.

The chaplain kindly came to visit me and remained for quite a long talk. He is the only male prison official who visits the prisoners without an attendant, the governor and deputy governor being accompanied generally by the matron, and the medical officer by a hospital attendant or wardress. He told me that many prisoners after release wrote to him with gratitude for his kindness and help; nevertheless he seemed to me to have but little fellow-feeling for the flocks he shepherded in Holloway.

I appealed to him, in a way I had not been able to do within hearing of the other patients in the hospital, about the case of Mrs. Macdonald. I told how it seemed to me an instance of the way in which prison officials left to themselves could not possibly have shown such brutality and neglect as was actually the case, had not the tradition of the prison system exacted a lower standard of conduct than was natural. I summed up the special grievances—her being made to walk across the yard, to walk up the three flights of stairs, being left a whole day in her cell before being conveyed to hospital, the refusal of the doctors to use the X-rays for investigation in the first instance, the contempt with which they had ignored the suggestions of this unusually intelligent woman, the refusal to allow her to see a doctor from outside when she was dissatisfied with their diagnosis, in spite of the fact that she could not in any sense be regarded as a criminal, having been charged for "obstruction" only when on a perfectly peaceable deputation to the House of Commons.

The difficulties put in the way of her communication with her husband relative to her release. The cruel, needless physical suffering as well as mental worry which such treatment had entailed, perhaps resulting in maiming her for life. He had no word of sympathy to offer in connection with this case, and when I compared the treatment with that meted out to myself, when much greater consideration was shown with much less need, he took the official line that all that was done by officials must be right, and that his own wife had had a similar fall, some friends had advised X-rays, others had said they would be useless. Nothing was done, the injury turned out to be slight and her recovery had been complete. At the time he was using such arguments to me, it was already known that in Mrs. Macdonald's case the hip-joint had been fractured.

I know that it is a very serious matter to tell of these things in a published book. I shall be reminded that officials are unable to answer back or to defend themselves in public. It must, however, be remembered that prisoners are in a yet more defenceless position, and that having personally witnessed and experienced the effect on prisoners of certain kinds of official infallibility, it is a matter of conscience to speak out. But in all these instances it is the bad tradition, the wrong standard of conduct exacted, not the personal character of officials, that has to be attacked. This chaplain, given ordinary surroundings, would no doubt be according to his light a well-meaning, and according to his powers a well-doing man.

If his work were in a West End parish or in a rural district among people whom he genuinely revered, I can conceive that his sympathy and understanding would be considerable. The blame of his attitude towards prisoners should rest on those who selected him for a prison job and on the many elements responsible for a system which instils contempt for the prisoner as a fundamental tenet of the prison official. I was told by a fellow-prisoner, a Suffragette, who on admission had entered her religious beliefs under the title "atheist," that this chaplain several times discussed religious matters with her in a spirit of tolerant reverence for points of view differing from his own.

The combination of the two offices, priest and prison official, seem to be almost incompatible, anyhow while the prison system rests upon its present basis. It would be more suitable if religious and moral teachers could come into the prison solely as representatives of the ethical bodies they represent. They could then offer their spiritual guidance and consolations to the unfortunate inmates, as they would to free individuals, without in any way compromising the "system" or the officials who have to carry it out.

On Sunday we were allowed to go to Holy Communion. This impressed one very strangely. An attempt was made to treat one more freely, combined with many of the same restrictions as at other times. There were about ten or twelve women altogether, of whom about six were Suffragettes. To our great delight Mrs. Lawrence was one of them. It seemed ages since I had left her, and I was delighted to see her again. The beautiful words of the service were almost more than one could bear, and every one of them seemed to contain freedom. It seemed as if we must be holding it privately among ourselves.

"Drink ye all of this, for this is My Blood of the New Testament, which is shed for you and for many for the remission of sins: Do this as oft as ye shall drink it, in remembrance of Me."

Yet there was the wardress with her face from which neither good nor bad could be told, neither kind nor unkind, and the face of the parson which seemed of the very nature of officialdom. After the service we left the chapel by different doors, Mrs. Lawrence's batch and ours, and we did not see each other again.

The next morning when we were returning, through the many halls of the building, single file, our huge boots ringing out on the stone floor, at one door a hospital superintendent stood and said to each one as she passed: "Any application for the doctor?" When it came to my turn, I saw that it was my friend from the hospital, but no look of recognition betrayed itself in her face. She put out her arm to stop me and wheeled me round to the back. When several others had passed her she turned to me, began quickly undoing my dress and said rapidly, but with still no look of recognition: "Well, have you been all right?"

"Oh, yes," I said, "but surely you are not going to look at it here?" She made no answer, but began to inspect me even more quickly. I insisted on turning my back on the long file which seemed never to end. She asked kindly questions, and said she would come and see the other wound that afternoon. She did not come, however, but sent one of the younger superintendents. She came once in the early morning, and it was very nice to see her again; it was the last time.

On one of the latter days a girl was wrongfully accused of laughing in chapel, and confined to her cell in consequence the following day. It is possible that someone was guilty of this. The severity which some of the wardresses used at chapel seated above the prisoners, one at every two or three rows, their backs to the altar and their attention completely taken up with the prisoners, gave one a strange sensation in church; it took away all reverence of the usual land, and made one nervous and possibly inclined to laugh. But, as it happened, the girl punished for this offence was far removed from the possibility of laughing. She was one of those I had noticed with particularly long hair; it must have reached below her knees.

We had come away together once from an Albert Hall meeting in a four-wheel cab when I had been lucky in securing it, and a wet evening made me invite strangers who were anxious to get away. She was particularly deferential and modest in her ways, her manner in chapel was irreproachable, and that she was picked out for punishment was most singularly ill-judged. We volunteered punishment of the same order as hers, and neither chapel, exercise, nor concerted labour had the benefit of us during the day.

The last days were spent in burning excitement. Nothing that I can say will explain the feeling I had that I was going to be free once more. The food, the clothes, the getting up at 5.30 a.m., these were bad enough, but they were as nothing compared to the incessant brutal treatment of the official manner, as with Mrs. Macdonald more especially, but also with Mrs. Duval, Miss Lawless, and others; in the constantly being ordered about and spoken to as if one had no feelings or perceptions, there was nothing but an extreme severity of manner without the smallest variation. On the third or fourth day before our last, someone had a visitor while we were at associated labour. On her return along the line she said to me: "A speech is expected of you; they hope great things of you at the feast."

My heart gave one bound. This meant release without a doubt, but a speech! How was it such a thing was expected of me? "I'll simply tell some of the things that take place here," I thought, and I felt that this was necessary.

The morning of March 24 we were released. My excitement was great, I had not slept, and from 4.30 onwards it was impossible to keep quiet. At 5.30 we were called in the regulation way and towards 7 we were taken down to other cells. I was put into one with a stranger whom I had not seen before. She was a servant, a lady's maid, who had left her last place, or, rather, they had left her, because of her opinions. She had determined to go in for the deputation, although probably it would mean that she got no place again. (I heard afterwards that the married daughter of the lady she was last with had taken her gladly and at once).

The cell where we were was dirty and smelt horribly, but I said nothing, hoping that my companion would not notice it. She soon did, however, for the smell nearly made her faint. I was given a packet of letters—a large heap from friends and strangers all the world over. At the head of the telegrams was a two-sheet one from our baker in the country, sent off the moment I was a prisoner, addressed to "The Castle where Suffragettes are confined, Holloway," most anxious about my food, and might he send the special bread he always made for me! I read my mother's letter again and again; it was all kindness, and I could hardly wait to see her. We were arranged in a long, close file, in the same order in which we had been ushered in, and put to stand in the big gateway. I never knew what it was that kept us, but there we stood for nearly an hour. A wardress or two were watching us, and we were not allowed to move.

At last the big doors were unbolted, we were half pushed from where we stood, we were out in the open—we were free. My sister and her eldest girl and boy—had somehow gained permission to come within the outer gates. I saw them and forgot all else. There was no release-breakfast feast; we were told that we were to meet that evening at the Inns of Court Hotel and make our speeches there.

Some days had passed when I went back to the prison. I thought I should be glad to get within reach of the ordinary prisoner, I in no way dreaded it. I had more to find out about X., the 3rd Division prisoner of the hospital. But, strangely enough, when I saw the big tower of Holloway, that looked quite different from anything else, and which brought back the inevitable picture of the women that go in, are kept in durance, and let out again to a life more horribly unnatural, I felt my legs begin to shake, and by the time I was shown in to the governor, who kindly saw me, it was all I could do to walk upstairs. I could not see X.; they said that someone else had been to visit her that month. I got in touch with her case through the Prisoners' Aid Society but they said that she was being "attended to" by another lady.

I went again to Holloway the morning that X. was to be released. Her freedom was due at 8 a.m. Two women and her little boy were waiting for her, they had kept the boy from all harm during the long months of her imprisonment. They didn't know where she was going to live, or what she would do, they had heard nothing from her. Soon after eight the great doors swung open, and the prisoners for that morning were let out, but there was no X. among them. I inquired at the door, but they would give no information there. After waiting another three-quarters of an hour I put in an appeal to see the governor.

The little boy of four years old had waited more than an hour outside, I had petitioned for him and one of the women to wait inside, but in vain. I was shown up to the governor, who kindly saw me and made inquiries for me about X.'s case. She was booked to go out that morning, but was waiting for her uncle, a well-to-do man, to take her away. I said her little boy was there, might he not spend the time with her, as she would be taking him away. The answer was "No." The governor said it was a case in which the chaplain and a lady visitor had taken a special interest, that he knew very little about it. He asked me very kindly to wait in his room, but as he had nothing more to tell me I went back to the women outside.

They told me more fully about X. She seems to have been in every way a good and hard-working woman. She had killed her child, knowing that it would be impossible to keep it alive. The man, the father, lived in the same street, but now he had gone, they did not know where. They hoped that she would come back and live where she had been before, but they feared the rich uncle, a publican. X. had been to live with him and her aunt when quite a young girl, but they had insisted that she must tout the men for them, and engage in illegal intercourse as an attraction. She had run away, and would not live with them. At her trial the uncle had been called in, and he, being a citizen of London, had kindly managed that she should be tried only for concealment of birth. He had done well for her at the trial, but now they feared he would get hold of her again.

My feelings were indeed torn when I had to tell them the governor's news. They had kept the child without help from anybody, sometimes it was a very hard thing, but they had always kept it in good health. Presently a tall man came by and went into the prison. About a quarter of an hour after he came out. X. was with him. She walked head down, her face in tears. Scarcely knowing what she did, she advanced towards her little boy, stretched out both arms and gave him a passionate embrace. He had rushed towards her calling out "Mother!"

Then, sobbing as if her heart would break, she followed the man to the public-house opposite. The two women made as if they would follow her, and I slipped into her hand a letter I had written in case I did not see her. The man then rounded on the women, and driving them away with his hand, said: "Keep away, we don't want you—your money shall be paid you all right," and he fled along the pavement, taking X. by the arm. We went and had some belated breakfast at a shop. I took the address of the women and the little boy, but I unfortunately lost it when I was abroad. I had given them mine, but I have never heard of them from that day.

I went abroad with my mother, and in the meanwhile things happened apace in England. The deputations, in ever-increasing numbers, succeeded one another with imprisonments of two or three months. The officials treated all the deputations with the utmost indifference. Miss Wallace Dunlop wrote up on the walls of the House of Commons:

Women's Deputation, June 29. Bill of Rights. It is the right of all subjects to petition the king. All commitments and prosecutions for such petitioning are illegal.

This is one of the most fundamental laws of Great Britain, but the vote has rendered it unnecessary for men. For this she was given one month's imprisonment, and she it was who began the hunger strike, and was let free after four days. For several months succeeding prisoners followed Miss Dunlop's fine example, and the Home Secretary, Mr.

Herbert Gladstone, let them out after four or five days, some of them were kept five or six days. When they were let out they were released unconditionally. Towards the middle of September, Mr. Gladstone thought that he would make another move and, instead of releasing them, he had them fed by force in the prisons. The horror this created was at first small, for there were but few people who realised what it meant. I shall never forget the impression that it made on me.

CHAPTER 10: NEWCASTLE: POLICE STATION CELL

I was at Birmingham in October, 1909, and I had two meetings with Mrs. Pankhurst. Whenever this happened one felt most singularly useless beside that great woman. I was overcome by the sense of being superfluous, and oppressed at having to go through the same ordeal in the evening. After the first meeting she took me with her to a nursing home to see the girl who had been the first to be released after the hunger-strike and forcible feeding. It was a fine evening, and a beautiful red light lit up the window as we came in; against it was merely the shadow of a girl, sitting in an armchair. She did not look ill in an ordinary way, but young and fresh, only so absolutely thin and wasted, it would not have surprised us if life had gone out.

She told her story very simply, just the bare facts and nothing more. She had been fed for a month. Mrs. Pankhurst, in cross-questioning her, elicited some of the horrors. She had resisted the gag as long as possible, then, with the increasing weakness, she had not the strength to resist much. Yes, the tube was a long one, pushed down the throat, in spite of all attempts to prevent it, and into the stomach. The feeling was that the tube was absolutely choking you, and when it was withdrawn that it dragged after it the whole of your inside.

She looked absolutely ethereal as she smiled at us and said "Goodbye." For several days her face haunted me, it was startlingly like something. Then I remembered the paintings of Fra Angelico in the Chapel of St. Mark's at Florence. I bought one of the little sixpenny editions of his pictures. There it was, the thing I had seen lately, the look of spiritual strength shining through physical weakness.

I looked through the book to choose one specially like the girl at Birmingham; there were several that reminded me of her. I had looked at these pictures in my younger days, and their great beauty had given me joy, but I had felt annoyed with the man for painting beings so inhuman, women that were ethereal but so little real, a look of purity that no living creature has. Now I had longed for them, having seen the thing portrayed in life. As I looked through the book, I turned over suddenly on a picture that was quite different. There was a crowd of women, real women, doing battle with men. One hit out at a soldier—the men were soldiers—another thrust out her arm, and with her hand over his face, kept him away with all the strength she could, a third had been thrown to the ground, but, with a face of raging despair was thrusting out in every direction.

The soldiers were simply carrying out their duty, an order had gone forth and they obeyed it; in the arms of the women were little babies, they had been told to kill them, and they did as they were told. In a seat above, looking on quite calmly, was Herod. It was the Massacre of the Innocents. The picture made a deep impression upon me, yet it all seemed so small compared with the unnecessary death rates of now. I was, just then, reading some facts that dealt with the death rate of infants. I found in one of the booklets by J. Johnston, Esq., M.D., 1909, this passage:

> The first big fact which faces us upon this subject is that while the death rate for England and Wales for 1906 was 15.4, the infantile mortality—the death rate of children under twelve months—was 132. This means that one in eight of the children born in this country dies before its first birthday—a death roll of 339 per day—a massacre of the innocents greater than that of King Herod at Bethlehem. And this wholesale slaughter of young life goes on, not for one day, as did that historic butchery, but is repeated every day, every week, every month, year in and year out, until in the year 1900 the army of baby martyrs reached a grand total of 123,895. Well might the African monarch. King Khama, say, 'You English take great care of your goods, but you throw away your children.'

I left that room in Birmingham in a maze of feelings. An angel had been in my presence and I, who agreed with all she did, had left her and many others to go through with this alone. My mind was made up. I would take the very next opportunity of making my protest with a stone.

On Friday, October 8, Christabel Pankhurst and I were on our way to Newcastle. We were seated opposite to each other in the midst of a crowded third-class carriage. It was on this occasion that I realised, as I had not yet done, the wonderful character, the imperturbable good temper, the brilliant intellect of my companion. As we could not talk in this crowded train, I showed her some letters and papers on which I wanted her advice, or which I wanted her to know about. Whether they were print, typewritten, or manuscript, she had read them all in a moment, so as to discuss them with me afterwards.

When we arrived at Newcastle we found that we had accompanied Mr. Lloyd George; there was a small crowd that welcomed him and that cheered half-heartedly. We went, after depositing our things at an hotel, to join an outdoor meeting. Christabel spoke. I sold *Votes for Women* in the crowd, which, though a large one, was mostly composed of out-of-work men, who took little interest in what was said. We drove round the town in honour of Miss New, who had just come out of prison, and went to a tea in her honour in an hotel where some fifty or sixty women were assembled.

After this there was a strange meeting in the ground-floor room of a lodging-house. There were twelve women; we were all intending stone-throwers, and Christabel was there to hearten us up and to go into details about the way in which we were to do it. Mrs. Brailsford was there, whose husband was lately on the staff of the *Daily News*; he and Mr. Nevinson had resigned their posts because of the shameful way in which that paper and the Liberal Government had forsaken the women.

I had made up my mind that I was going to throw a stone—that was as sure as death, but the manner of it was going to be my own; I was equally sure of that. I was not sure of "the stone-throwers." I had vaguely felt that they would have different reasons from mine for this errand, that perhaps, though they could not be more certain than myself, they would mind it less. I had not been in the room with them five minutes before I realised that I was mistaken. I was the "hooligan," if there were one amongst them.

One I specially remember. She was pretty, with a great deal of fair hair. She had not, I thought, the look of determination, of silent, unhesitating determination, which gave an air of inflexibility to the others. She leaned forward and asked many questions: the wardresses, would they, too, be disagreeable, would they pull down her hair and tear out the tortoise-shell combs? One somehow knew by her voice that she was not ready, she asked her questions as if something of a nightmare was in her mind; they were asked quite simply, but seemed to say, "Oh! save me from this!" I asked Christabel, when alone with her at the hotel, if I might tell her there was no need for her to do it, that I thought she was not quite prepared.

"Of course," she answered, "if she does not feel up to it, let her stand aside. One cannot tell how one is going to feel, she has never done anything before."

Not long ago Mrs. Pethick Lawrence had met her, it was at a bazaar. She wore a big hat and looked as remote as it is possible to look from stone throwing. She expressed the greatest admiration for the militants.

"There is only one thing," she said, "which I cannot think worthwhile—that they should go to prison."

I was to get her out of it the next morning, the day of Lloyd George's meetings and of our militancy.

That evening there was an immense meeting at the drill hall where Christabel was to speak, but before she began a gang of about forty students howled and threw squibs, so that nothing could be heard. When she got up for a moment the applause drowned everything, but it soon was again impossible to hear her. The students broke up the seats and threw everything about. Then some ten of them charged the platform. A row of stewards hastily ranged themselves and tried to check their advance, but their arms were wrenched apart, until the husband of one of them took his turn and gave it to one of the students, whereupon the other men turned tail and ran.

At this man coming forward the police interfered, they had been appealed to in vain by some of the stewards. It was most difficult not to help them, but I had sworn to keep myself till the next day. The row made by the other students went on unabated. Meanwhile, Christabel remained perfectly good-tempered. For the first quarter of an hour she spoke up, but as it was impossible for her voice to carry above the noise she lowered her voice and spoke only to reporters. The next day her speech appeared in full in all the local press.

The next morning, October 9, we were to meet early at the same lodging-house. The morning papers were full of Mr. Lloyd George, and in biographical sketches emphasised the glory of his having been militant, and successfully militant, through several questions that he cared about in his early days. It was different in the lodging-house from the night before. All was hurry and determination. Two of the women had gone already to deliver their stony messages. The organiser, a very straightforward and reasonable woman, was sending each one to a different place. She said:

"There is a stone wants to be put through the door of the Palace Theatre in the Haymarket. It must be done at once or the gang of detectives will have become too thick."

A firm voice said: "I'll go." It was the young girl with fair hair who had asked so many questions the night before, and whom I was going to set free.

"Oh, no," said the organiser, "this job will have to be done alone—two would be detected at once."

"I'll go." It was like a force of nature that reiterated this, and there was something of adamant at the back of the voice. She picked up two or three papers to sell, and was out in the street before we any of us knew what she was doing.

I dashed after her. I couldn't believe that there was so much change in her since the night before. I moved quickly, but it was only down the street that led out of the lodging-house street that I caught her up. I said:

I had thought of getting you out of it, because you seemed too young to do the work. That was last night; today all is quite different. But let me try and say what I have in my mind. You are going to throw a stone. Think, as you lift your arm to do it, of the majority in the House of Commons who for years have said they are for Votes for Women, who over and over again for twenty years have voted for the second reading of a Woman's Bill, and were quite content that it should stop there. Think of the nearly total Cabinet for Woman Suffrage when the Liberals came in, under a Suffrage Prime Minister, but all attempts to pass a bill were treated as futile.

Think of the women who work with a sweated wage, who have not the energy to rebel, who are cloaked with poverty; the thousands who, stricken with poverty more hideous than we can think of on one side, and tempted with money on the other, sink into a life of shame, which is endured for five or six years, till death releases them. Think of Lloyd George, whose speech is always fair but who carefully prevents anything being done for women. Think of the women who have been sent to prison for their protest against these things, who have hunger-struck as a fresh protest and who now have been fed by force. Then throw your stone and make it do its work.

"Thank you," she said, "thank you."

I looked up at her, as I had not liked to do till that minute. A changed being stood before me. I had noticed that she had changed from the night before, she had changed unbelievably at this minute, and all that strength, determination, complete forgetfulness of self could give her, were with her now.

We parted. I went back to the others. The next thing I heard of her was in the other office, where we provided ourselves with stones. A little girl of about sixteen, who kept on running messages for us, came rapidly into the room. "Miss X.," she said, "has thrown her stone, broken her window, and been arrested." Then she went out.

From that moment I knew that all was well. Miss X. got through the two days in the police-court, the trial, the hunger strike, and the forcible feeding that followed for the space of fourteen days, as did the others. Her body was weakness, but her soul was strength.

No particular job was given to me. Miss Emily Davison and I were to keep together. It was still early, and first we had to make sure of our stones. We went to the other office to get them. I was doing up mine in brown paper, double thick.

"You will not be able to throw those," said the organiser, "if there is the least bit of wind, it will get inside and send them you don't know where."

That was true. I found some much thinner paper which kept closely round the stone. I took four or five. On each one I wrote a different thing, I think they were all taken from Mr. Lloyd George's recent speech. I put them into my pockets and went out. Miss Davison had been speaking from every part of the town during the last week. I recommended her to buy another hat for partial disguise. We went into a hat shop and did so. In the shop there was a fascinating little black kitten which it was hard to leave. Then we went into an eating shop, thinking it was as well to have some luncheon. The shop was overpoweringly stuffy and hot. I had not met Miss Davison before, and it was most interesting to hear her experiences.

Still, we could neither of us speak nor listen with anything but effort. We decided to go and see what it was like at the Haymarket, a large, open space, where the car with Mr. Lloyd George would probably pass. There was still more than an hour before he could come. The crowd was already considerable. Nearly every woman that I saw looked friendly; this was probably my imagination, but it did me good. The Suffragettes were greatly thought of that day.

The place, we found, was divided in two by a hoarding of about ten feet in height; there was a space, guarded by police, that could be opened to let a carriage through. We looked round at the windows of all the adjacent buildings, but they were not of an official or of a sufficiently conspicuous character for our stones. Presently a man in front of us—the crowd now was pretty thick—was twirling round one of his cards in his hands which were folded behind him. He then held it up, so that we could see there was writing on it. At last his signals grew more desperate. One of us took the card from him. On it was written his deferential greeting, that he knew what we were out for, could he help us in any way, run messages for us or anything? We answered, writing on the other side, that we thanked him cordially, but as we had no particular job, it was best for him to "wait and see."

He had a kindly face and looked the right sort, but we thought it was just as well that this was the true answer. There was a monument to the soldiers who had died in the war in the midst of the open space. Their names were written on it, and the little boys were clambering up the monument to see above the crowd. They had died for their country, that was the one fact which seemed to stand out very clearly from the monument. Yes, nobly, and in a good fight, they had died—where is the statue to the women who had given their lives to the nation?

We heard cheering in the distance, it was the arrival of Mr. Lloyd George at the theatre, he having driven by another way. My companion began to think that our chance was over until the evening. A feeling came over me that I could not wait any longer, and that somehow or other I must throw my stone. As it would anyhow be but symbolical, it seemed to me one could find an occasion as well here as elsewhere. One thing, however, I was determined upon—it must be more zealously done, more deliberate in its character than the stone throwing at ordinary windows, which had been done lately. I was determined that when they had me in court my act should inevitably be worse than that of other women. At this moment there was a hurry in the crowd, the police were making a clearing and opening the carriage entrance for a motorcar. We found ourselves on the very edge of the crowd. As the motor appeared, I whispered to Miss Davison: "Is this any good?"

"Not the least in the world," was her reply, "just one of the motors coming back."

I knew this, of course, but the instinct was too much for me. To throw a stone against the car as it ran along the side was dangerous, as there were two men in the front. I stepped out into the road, stood straight in front of the car, shouted out "How can you, who say you back the women's cause, stay on in a government which refuses them the vote, and is persecuting them for asking it," and threw a stone at the car, but very low down. I thought I had thrown it too low, so that it would not hit the car. I was going on, in the space of time which seemed infinitely long, to tell the car to turn back and get their answer from Mr. Lloyd George, then call to the people to come through the gap and hear his answer.

I had time to think out all this. Miss Davison came to my side, and I saw someone take hold of her before she could throw her stone. Then two plain-clothes detectives caught hold of me, but what was my intense surprise, without any violence whatever. They simply led me back through the crowd which surged around on every side. I had thought there were no actual friends where we stood, but I at once saw one or two ready to come and help me if I wanted it. So I was still and said not a word. My part was finished, and I saw that anything said might easily cause a tremendous disturbance at those close quarters.

Miss Davison was arrested at the same time, though she had done nothing, and we were led away together. It was a business getting through the crowd. When we had left the Haymarket the crush was very much less, and the two detectives in plain clothes who were responsible for me walked on either side without touching me. This went rather strangely with the newspaper contention that I was "very excitable." Another incident which got put into the papers was, that when we were going down a main street, two tramcars, going different ways, were about to meet. This pressed the crowd that followed us and pushed us all together. We were walking, of course, in the roadway. A little girl with a baby in a perambulator and a small boy on foot had got on to the island and were wishing to pass to the pavement, being afraid of the two trams. I realised that I was the policeman of that show. I stopped and just held out my hand to the detective on my right. We let the baby and its leaders pass, then we moved on.

We were taken to the central police station of the town. The police here were most civil, and, indeed, kind. We gave our names and addresses, and then we waited in the main room. Poor Miss Davison was very distressed at doing nothing. Her heroism had to wait for another day.

★★★★★★

Soon after this Miss Davison was forcibly fed in Manchester Prison, and, on barricading her cell, the hosepipe was played upon her from the window, a process of force that caused her infinite pain. She fainted, and it was many days before she recovered. She owed her life probably to being released from prison, and to the fact that she was a great swimmer, used to the shock of cold water and to withstanding its force. In 1913 she met her death with the most heroic courage at the Derby race. It was her opportunity of proclaiming to the whole world, perhaps heedless till then, that women claim citizenship and human rights. She stood in front of the race and was knocked down by the king's horse Anmer, rendered unconscious, and died the following Sunday, June 8. Millions of people, not only in our own but other countries, knew, from this act, that there are women who care so passionately for the vote and all it means that they are willing to die for it.

★★★★★★

Mrs. Baines came into the police court and spoke to us. I was filled with disappointment that I had not been able to do more. She told me that she was quite content, that I had thrown my stone straight, and, she believed, hit the car. She was delightfully encouraging, and made one think one had done well. Presently Mrs. Brailsford joined us, she had done exactly what she meant to do, and with a hatchet had hit one of the barricades.

I noticed in this central police station a large iron cage. It was empty, and we wondered what purpose it could serve. On one of the benches a little boy was sitting, of about seven or eight years old. He had on ragged clothes, but seemed quite happy with a cup of soup which he had been given. It seemed odd though to bring small children to such a place, with nothing but policemen, although several of these were good-natured.

After we had been here a considerable time and were joined by some of our companions, we heard that it was unlikely they would allow us bail, and we were taken off to the cells. Who could have believed that in the central police station of a place like Newcastle they could be so dirty? Mine was No. 2. It was on the left side of a broad gangway, which could be shut off by an iron gate. It was October and inclined to be dark, and when I was first put into the cell it was impossible to see what it was like or what it contained. It was rather high, the very small window opposite the doorway was either of foggy glass or grimed with dirt, it scarcely lit up anything but itself. To the right was a plank, rather wide and long, and with a kind of bolster made of wood. This was all for seat or bed.

143

When the evening light was lit above the door, where it was barred with iron on the side of the cell, I saw that the wood was filthy. There was a plenitude of fleas, but no lice. Under the window to the right was a lavatory, it was extremely dirty, the water could only be turned on from outside. There was a ledge about three feet high, which sheltered the seat. Under the window, but this I could not see till the second day, was a men's urinal, there was a gutter in the floor for this, but no water. The cleanliness of the wall can be imagined. The smell in the cell was continuously foul.

★★★★★★

I have been in police station cells in several other places—a variety in London and two in Liverpool—but never have I seen anything like this. The other cells were scrupulously clean.

★★★★★★

I was very tired, but only liked to sit, not lie, on the bed. After what seemed a very long time, a policeman summoned me, and said we were all to have food together in the wardresses' room. As I was let out I noticed seven of the others being let out too—Winifred Jones, Ellen Wines Pitman, Kathleen Brown, Kitty Marion, Dorothy Pethick and Emily Davison. Mrs. Brailsford was the only one I did not see. The four others—Violet Bryant, Ellen Pitfield, Lily Asquith and Dorothy Shallard—had all done their work the previous evening, and had been sentenced on this, Saturday, morning to two weeks' imprisonment. It was, of course, a joy to see them. It seemed so very long since that morning.

When we had passed the central police office, and were ushered into the wardresses' room, it appeared that Mrs. Brailsford was shut into the wardresses' bedroom—whether for a more honourable imprisonment, she being a woman whose public work none could call deficient in selflessness and courage, or whether because she was a "dangerous criminal," having used a hatchet in making her mark on the barricade, we did not know. I remember catching sight of her as the door was opened to let in a cup of tea. There she sat, calm and erect, and Mr. Brailsford, who had been let in to see her, in piteous trouble, having the one thought—"Will my wife be fed by force—how can they dare to do it? How will she be able to bear it?"

Most of the others I had not seen before, yet I felt exuberant delight at being with them. One only I knew well, and that was Miss Ellen Pitman. She was in the deputation of February and, after being in prison some ten days, she was brought to the hospital for neuralgic

144

pains in her leg. She was a trained nurse, we had got to know each other well, and her fine face will always be very dear to me.

We now got to know the wardresses—they were as kind to us as possible. I was so tired I could scarcely see, and after a time we retired to rest. There was a deafening noise; the cells were filled mostly with drunkards, for it was Saturday. Thundering blows on the doors, accompanied by a string of oaths, went on all through the night. The police were very kind to them, bringing them fresh water to drink, chaffing them and coaxing them. No bedding of any kind or rugs were provided by the police, but our friends outside were most wonderfully good to us, and, when they found we were not to be bailed out, they were busy collecting rugs and blankets. At about 12 they sent me in a rug and a sort of air-cushion bed, which would have been most delightful, but I tried every end in vain, I didn't know how to put air into it. I was stiff for several days from my rest on the plank, but I owed it to the friends that I did not have two nights of it. On Sunday they brought a mattress instead of the air bed, and my flannel sheets which gave me a restful night.

On Sunday I sent for the district visitor, supposing she would be a woman, but was told there was no district visitor; a police-court missionary? not one either; finally, I sent for the doctor. My complaint was that no toilet paper was provided, and no sanitary towels for the women. Prisoners are kept from Saturday afternoon until Monday. I said, were not these people the same as those who go to prison, they have these necessaries there?

I don't know about a prison, I'm sure they would never use them in Police Station cells.

Exactly the same remark was made about the prisons, but all the same these things were instituted and now used by prisoners. I begged that, at least, they might be kept in charge of the wardress.

Not long after I had seen the doctor, I was summoned out to see someone else. To my great delight it was Mrs. Pankhurst. She was all sympathy, and it was delightful seeing her.

I was had out of my cell yet another time, for my name, age, etc., to be "taken down" by a policeman in a book. I was able to look over the book as he wrote, and I saw, to my intense surprise, that the law brought three charges against me, first, of assault on Sir Walter Runciman, who was in the car; secondly, of malicious injury to the car at £4; thirdly, of disorderly behaviour in a public place. I felt very exalted to think I had done so much, and thought that three months was the least they could give me. I could not help being pleased to think that the car had contained the host of Mr. Lloyd George, not merely the chauffeur. But what pleased me most was the £4 damage.

How I could have done it was indeed a mystery, but I was glad to know that the stone had not gone on the ground, as I had feared. As I went through the central room on one of these occasions, the cage which I had seen before, to my astonishment, was inhabited— by a man, I expected to see some fierce brute, but he was small, frail and miserably degraded, without power to do anyone an injury, with marks of abnormal weakness in his face. When I saw him, the feeling came over me with a great tide, that I should throw myself at his feet and try to bear something of his burden, because if I had done my duty, and if my contemporary women and those who went before had done their duty, we should have given him another life, by securing better, more human conditions, for himself and for his mother who gave him birth. He had lived in that terrible state of things which make it hardly possible to survive. Here, at any rate, was a man intensely feeble in his body, and he was put in an iron cage as the only suitable place!

We were called out and made to stand at the doors of our cells. Presently, the plain-clothes police came to "learn our faces," and after looking at us steadfastly for some minutes, we were put back again.

The food was brought for us by our friends from outside, who provided for us deliciously, and we had our meals all together in the wardresses' room. Only Mrs. Brailsford never appeared, being shut in the inner room, but we sent her some of our food. On Sunday night, the wardress had brought us a little basin with some warm water to our cells, which was indeed a boon.

That Sunday night the police were most kind, they allowed me to sit at a table outside my cell and write. My cell was much too dark for writing. Tonight the place was more full of noise than it had been before. The wild yells, and blows on the doors, made my hand shake so that at first I could not write, but by holding the pencil, lent to me by the police, over the paper, it came sufficiently legibly at last. I wrote to my mother and my sister. I also wrote to the *Times* the following letter, from the eleven who were imprisoned, (I handed this letter to a friend on Monday morning, at the trial Miss Davison was dismissed, so her name was taken from the signatures):—

Sir,—We ask you to give us our last opportunity, before we go through the ordeal awaiting us in Newcastle Prison, of explaining to the public the action which we are now about to take.

We want to make it known that we shall carry on our protest in our prison cells. We shall put before the government by means of the hunger-strike four alternatives: To release us in a few days; to inflict violence upon our bodies; to add death to the champions of our cause by leaving us to starve; or, and this is the best and only wise alternative, to give women the vote.

We appeal to the government to yield, not to the violence of our protest, but to the reasonableness of our demand, and to grant the vote to the duly qualified women of the country. We shall then serve our full sentence quietly and obediently and without complaint. Our protest is against the action of the government in opposing Woman Suffrage, and against that alone. We have no quarrel with those who may be ordered to maltreat us.

Yours sincerely,

Lily Asquith.	Winifred Jones.
Jane E. Brailsford.	Constance Lytton.
Kathleen Brown.	Kitty Marion.
Violet Bryant.	Dorothy Pethick.
Ellen Pitfield.	Ellen W. Pitman.
	Dorothy Shallard.

Central Police Station,
Newcastle,
October 10, 1909.

I wrote on the wall of my cell my name and the words which rung in my head over and over again, from the Book of Joshua:

Only be thou strong and very courageous.

I received a letter in the police cell, saying that I had thrown my stone not far from a family residence of relatives of ours—did I not feel it hence a double disgrace? In answer to this I had thought some time. Who were those for whom we fought? I seemed to hear them in my cell, the defenceless ones who had no one to speak for their hungry need. The sweated workers, the mothers widowed with little children, the women on the streets, and I saw that their backs were bent, their eyes grown sorrowful, their hearts dead without hope. And they were not a few, but thousands upon thousands. Side by side I considered what they could do, what they had done, where women had the vote. The wife has half her husband's wages, by law, and when he does not give it, she can have the amount paid direct to her. She is given money for her children by the State when her husband dies. When she is not married, if she has a child she is paid for it, not by the father direct, but through the public authority, and she has not to apply to the father for her money. I thought of all these helpless women, of the Parliament that had given its theoretic consent for over twenty years, but refused to pass a Bill, and I thought what are my relations? I do not know, but if anything, they are for us, and if they are still asleep, in the fog of the "don't know and don't care," am I bound to consider their dreaming? I wrote on the wall:—

To defend the oppressed,
To fight for the defenceless,
Not counting the cost.

Chapter 11: Newcastle Prison: My Second Imprisonment

The next morning, Monday, October 11, we got up early, with a sense of excitement that we were to be "tried." We were allowed to wash in a basin arrangement all together. The water was cold, but clean and fresh. The roll towel was horrible, I have never seen anything so dirty—blood had freely been wiped upon it. Nothing could surpass the kindness and civility of the wardresses. One, who thought only of the hunger-strike, cried as we left. We were then led off to the cells upstairs, which were rather cleaner and much lighter. A man came to mend something outside my window; it was open and I could see out by two or three square inches. He looked in at me with great curiosity, but-without ill-will. I had the policeman's pencil still, and wrote on a paper to hand up to him that he should not be afraid of the Suffragettes, but help them to get the vote. I was still thinking about it when the police began to rattle the keys, so I refrained, although it was some time before they came to fetch me.

They led us forth to the other side of the building where the court was. We waited in a passage underneath it, and were led up in turns to the prisoner's box. The others, who had done nothing but break glass, were sentenced to the 3rd Division and hard labour for fourteen days, and some a month, without any option. Mrs. Brailsford and I were both given the alternative of being bound in money sureties for a year. In reality, this offered us no alternative, but in the estimation of the magistrate, I, who had done deliberately most harm, was given the option of going free, while the others, who were many of them younger than I was, first offenders and all had done much less damage than I had, were prisoners beyond their recall.

When it was my turn, I was prepared for the three charges I had seen on the paper the day before. First came the charge of assault on Sir Walter Runciman. I said that I did not know it was Sir Walter Runciman in the car, and that I threw the stone low down, so that it should not hit the chauffeur or anyone. They did not take up this charge. Then came the charge of damage, at which I was well pleased. But the man facing the magistrate, the clerk, who conducts most of the affairs in several courts I have been into, would not let this charge come on. He said that I had evidently not intended the damage to the car, and that part of the case was dismissed. I tried to tell him that I had no concern for the motorcar, and, though I didn't know how a stone so small could have done so much harm, I was not in the least concerned over the £4 worth of damage, but he would not let me speak and passed on to the third charge, "disorderly behaviour in a public place."

I put in, with a loud voice, "My disorderly behaviour of throwing a stone with violence in a public place was deliberate and intentional."

After this, they could not but go on with it, since the whole court had heard what I had said. They apparently treated me as a lunatic, and began to ask if it was through not knowing what I was doing that I had thrown a stone?

"If I had not known what I was about to do, I should not have held a stone in my hand," I answered.

I had made up my mind, at one time of the trial, that I would deny the tales that had circulated about the Suffragettes and Mr. Lloyd George's children. It had been said that we tried to kidnap them, that we had wished for their illness, and all kinds of invented evil. Who are the Suffragettes that they should make war on children? If the child of Mr. Lloyd George were ill or in any way suffering, we were sorry, we were sympathetic, as with every other child, and we were sad for him as the loving father of that child. I tried to speak, when I first was called on, and repeatedly afterwards, but I was always stopped and could get no innings. Finally, the magistrates convicted me of "disorderly behaviour with intent to disturb the peace," and bound me over, myself in the sum of £50 and two sureties of £25 each, to be enforced for twelve months; in default, one month's imprisonment in the 2nd Division. I, of course, had no option of finding sureties for twelve months, and was sentenced to the month's imprisonment. My companion, Miss Davison, was dismissed, as she had literally done nothing.

Mrs. Brailsford, who had struck at the barricade with an axe, was also given the option of being bound over, which she, of course, refused, with the alternative of a month's imprisonment in the 2nd Division. She had not, as I had, committed any offence before. She was a splendid woman who had gone out to help with the Macedonian relief fund in 1903. She had fed the hungry and nursed the sick and wounded until she contracted typhus fever. The whole "trial" was unworthy of the name—it was a device whereby Mrs. Brailsford and I should be separated from the others and treated with more respect, I having been the only one to do a glaring act and an, apparently, harmful or greatly risky one. The others, without exception, were treated to the 3rd Division.

We were put again into a van, but had only a short way to drive. We were shown into a passage of the prison where the governor came and spoke to us. He was very civil, and begged us not to go on the hunger-strike. Then the matron came, a charming and very refined woman, who walked with a stick, being lame. Miss Davison had headed our little band of twelve; when she was dismissed, Miss Dorothy Pethick, Mrs. Pethick Lawrence's youngest sister, was our head and spoke for us. Her face had all the beauty that freshness, youth and grace could give it, and with it all for her age—she was twenty-seven—there was a wonderful strength about it. She spoke civilly to the governor, but in a very determined way. He could not do enough for us. "Don't break your windows—please don't break your windows."

> We will not break them if they can open. You must understand that we have come here, not to please ourselves; we have pleaded for windows to open in the cells through two years in vain. Now we break the glass to make more sure. It is for the poor things who are shut up in these little cells for weeks and months at a time. Whether they know it or not, their bodies know it—it is all that is bad for them to sleep and live in a room supposed to be ventilated, without a window, and to be given a book telling them elaborately how a window may be kept open in all weathers by placing a board in front of it on a slant, will not make things any better. And what is more, if you feed us by force, we shall break every window we can lay hands on.

"Very well," said the governor, "choose your own cells; come round and see."

Then, with the governor and matron, we went round. Several cells were shown to us. We were left in some that were small but new—the windows did not open. Finally, Mrs. Brailsford and I were taken to different cells on the ground floor where we were separated completely from the others. We were allowed to have our doors open all the time, and some iron gates only shut us in. Compared with Holloway, their good manners made a great difference, but the kindness about the cells was mostly put on; at least, they had not windows that opened, so they could do little. Mrs. Brailsford and I had cells next door to each other, we spoke together frequently all day. The wardresses were dear northern women, affectionate in their ways. The matron we found to be even more charming than she looked. She took Mrs. Brailsford and me for exercise, and we talked to her nearly the whole time. She was quite a Suffragette and understood our rebellion.

There was no attempt to put us into prison clothes; we had small packages of things with us. My underclothes were not all that one could wish after two days and nights in the police-station cells. They were amongst other things covered with fleas, and I had at my trial, and on various occasions, become exceedingly hot, which, now that the hunger-strike had begun, was exchanged for extreme cold. The prospect of a month in them as they were was extremely undesirable. I wrote to the Home Secretary, as I was told this was the only means, but I knew that anything I asked for from him might as well be let alone.

The first day, Tuesday, was fairly fine. At exercise in the morning we looked around and we noticed some broken glass windows. We shouted "Votes for Women, Hurrah! Hurrah!" but were not sure of any response. They had put our companions, of two days before us, into the punishment cells. We were scarcely back in our cells before there were hasty footsteps; they slammed our doors shut, we could only dimly hear the steps as they passed our cells and then above. Soon after we heard shrieks, always coming from the same direction. It seemed as if the others were being fed by force. During about half an hour the sounds were terrible.

Then the doctors, two of them, came to us. They had on white jackets, as if they had just come from an operation, as indeed they had. I said to them, "You have been feeding our friends by force?"

One of them answered, "Well, yes, we were bound to have a food trial with one or two of them."

They felt my pulse, first one, then the other; they felt it over again, then they went out. Mrs. Brailsford and I discussed the feeding of our friends, which had sounded most awful; we did not know what to do. We had, of course, not touched any food since our breakfast in the police-station cells. We ourselves had met with nothing but kindness.

The knotting in my stomach from lack of food was fairly painful by the second night. Whenever I fell asleep I woke with my knees curled under my chin. I had also a great aching in my back, probably through fatigue and the plank bed in the police-station. The night wardress was very kind to me. I asked once if she couldn't come in and rub my back just a little. "Why, my dear, the gate's locked and I have nae got the key."

Mrs. Brailsford said she felt well in every way, save that she could do nothing but think of the other prisoners who were being fed by force. When we walked round the exercise yard on Wednesday morning it was snowing hard. It made me think of Robert Buchanan's poem, *"The Ballade of Judas Iscariot."*

> *'Twas the wedding guests cried out within,*
> *And their eyes were fierce and bright—*
> *'Scourge the soul of Judas Iscariot*
> *Away into the night!'*

> *The Bridegroom stood in the open door,*
> *And he waved hands still and slow,*
> *And the third time that he waved his hands*
> *The air was thick with snow.*

> *And of every flake of falling snow*
> *Before it touched the ground,*
> *There came a dove, and a thousand doves*
> *Made sweet doves' sound.*

> *'Twas the body of Judas Iscariot*
> *Floated away full fleet,*
> *And the wings of the dove that bore it off*
> *Were like its winding-sheet.*

> *'Twas the Bridegroom stood at the open door*
> *And beckon'd, smiling sweet;*
> *'Twas the soul of Judas Iscariot*
> *Stole in, and fell at his feet.*

As I looked upon that dreary scene I saw the prison walls, the cell windows, looking more like tiny shutters, the infinitesimal small windows of the punishment cells in the ground below where we were. The matron stood on a ledge above us. She was considerate and kind in all her ways. We were either alone and quite unguarded or else she was with us. One evening, when a wardress was letting me back into my cell, I heard the most melancholy sound of a woman calling out to herself again and again, in a tone of uttermost misery.

As always, I thought, in a prison, no one answered her, no one said anything. Presently there came the matron's consoling voice. Very gently I heard it on the floor above ours, it sounded almost like a mother's voice: "Oh! there is that poor woman again. Can't you some of you go and comfort her?" And someone did, for all was quiet after that. I watched at my gate all day, and was pleased to notice that the prisoners who worked outside the cells moved happily, ran about with a springing step and seemed like ordinary servants about their work. How different this was from Holloway!

The first morning the chaplain came to visit me. He was a pleasant-looking man, with a fine beard. He laughed as he told me he was the father of fifteen children; he said this as he left. I longed to tell him I hoped that he had had at least two wives to bring them into the world!

The second morning, Wednesday, October 13, when the doctors came, I stood in the corner of my cell with my arms crossed and my fingers caught in my nostrils and my mouth. It was the best position I knew of for them not to be able to feed me by nose or mouth without having first a considerable struggle. They came, and after I saw that they had no tube I came out from my corner and let them both look at my heart. They thumped, each of them in turn, and felt my pulse as well. Then they appeared to be agreed and went out.

I said to them, "You seemed to be puzzled by my heart; I can tell you about it if you like." But they had made up their minds about something, and did not want any help from me. Later in the day they came in again with another man in their company. I was again in the corner, my hands in my mouth and nose, but they brought no feeding things. At first I thought the third man was another prison official; but soon, from the way they talked to him, I gathered that he was an outside doctor, apparently from London. He was very civil. He tapped my heart repeatedly and then brought out a tube, which at first I thought was a feeding tube, but it was only another way of testing the heart. He was about a quarter of an hour or twenty minutes over the whole thing, then they went out.

As I had no answer from the Home Office, though I had written on the Monday of my arrival in the prison, I thought I would begin to wash some of my things, as the doctors would not come back unless to feed me, and that would be nearer six o'clock. I washed my brush and a few other things in the large pail of my cell, then asked if I might empty it, and as I did this, I held the things some seconds under the tap. It was only cold water, of course, but I was glad of even that. I then put them on the chair to dry as best they might, and lay down on my plank bed, for the pain in my back was terrible, when a wardress came in and announced that I was released, because of the state of my heart! Though this was fairly evident from the visit of the outside doctor, I had not realised it.

I gathered my things together and went out. I called to Mrs. Brailsford; she was released too. We were put to wait in the governor's room; he was not there. We wondered if we were the only two to be released, and if so, why not the others? How about the heart of Nurse Pitman, who was close on sixty, or of Miss Brown, who had only just been released from a recent hunger-strike! Mrs. Brailsford had seen a doctor before she came on this expedition to Newcastle, and he had declared her absolutely sound in every way, so we did not know why she was released, except for the fact that she was, through her husband, closely connected with Liberal journalism and herself had the noblest reputation for public service in Macedonia.

I had heart disease, though only slightly; it had been marked in me since the Deputation on which I had been to the House of Commons, at the beginning of this year. But I was not in so bad a condition as either Nurse Pitman or Miss Brown. After a time the news came that we were the only two released! Poor Mrs. Brailsford was so overcome at this news that she was unable to drink the glass of hot milk that was given to us before we were let out. The governor came back to his room. He had always told us how keen he was for the vote, and he seemed very glad for us that we were to be released. The cab was ready and we drove away, I think at about 3.30 in the afternoon. It seemed appalling to go and to leave the others in prison, to the hunger-strike and to forcible feeding.

Nurse Pitman and Miss Brown were released the next day. It was not possible to understand for what reason they should have been kept twenty-four hours longer on hunger-strike than Mrs. Brailsford and myself; the only reason that we could see was that our names were known, theirs were not!

The only thing which made an impression on me, not told in the above, was that once the wardress led me out to one of the lavatories. Just in front of it a woman had been sick, and I was taken away to another. It showed the great loneliness of prison life. There, in rows thickly set all around me, were the cells, in each a prisoner. One had been taken out immediately before I had, but she was put back and all the cells were locked before I came. The mystery was intense, the silence, the loneliness as great as they could be.

My sister, Betty Balfour, came from Scotland to see if she could do anything to help me when she heard that I was in prison. She was convinced that I should not be forcibly fed because of the state of my heart, but that I should be let out after a day or two of hunger-strike. It was delightful to be with her, and the next day we travelled south together to my home.

In December I went to speak at Glasgow, and Dr. Marion Gilchrist listened to my heart. This was her verdict:

> I have examined Lady Constance Lytton's heart and find she has a chronic valvular lesion, but it is acting well in spite of the fact that she has just undergone great exertion.

She said it was easily understood why I had been let out of Newcastle Prison.

CHAPTER 12: JANE WARTON

Under a government which imprisons any unjustly, the true place for a just man (or woman) is also a prison.

I was sent to Liverpool and Manchester to join in working an Anti-Government campaign during a General Election in January, 1910. Just before I went, there came the news of the barbarous ill-treatment of Miss Selina Martin and Miss Leslie Hall, while on remand in Walton Gaol. They had been refused bail, and, while awaiting their trial, their friends were not allowed to communicate with them. This is contrary to law and precedent for prisoners on remand. As a protest they had started a hunger-strike. They were fed by force, in answer to which they broke the windows of their cells. They were put in irons for days and nights together, and one of them was frog-marched in the most brutal fashion to and from the room where the forcible feeding was performed. These facts they made known to their friends at the police court on the day of their trial.

I heard, too, of another prisoner in Liverpool, Miss Bertha Brewster, who had been re-arrested after her release from prison, and charged with breaking the windows of her prison cell, which she had done as a protest against being fed by force. She had been punished for this offence while in prison. She did not respond to the summons, and when arrested on a warrant, three and a half months later, she was sentenced to six weeks' hard labour for this offence.

I felt a great wish to be in Liverpool, if possible, to get public opinion in that town to protest against such treatment of women political prisoners. If I failed in this, I determined myself to share the fate of these women.

When I was in Manchester, Mary Gawthorpe was ill with the internal complaint which has since obliged her to give up work. She saw me in her room one day. We had been distressed beyond words to hear of the sufferings of Selina Martin and Leslie Hall. Mary Gawthorpe said, with tears in her eyes, as she threw her arms round me:

Oh, and these are women quite unknown—nobody knows or cares about them except their own friends. They go to prison again and again to be treated like this, until it kills them!

That was enough. My mind was made up. The altogether shameless way I had been preferred against the others at Newcastle, except Mrs. Brailsford who shared with me the special treatment, made me determine to try whether they would recognise my need for exceptional favours without my name.

Our meetings were always crowded and enthusiastic, especially in Manchester. This was my first experience of meetings in a really poverty-stricken district. I never shall forget one in the Salford Division of Manchester. A small room was packed as close as it would hold of the poorest working women. How eagerly and intelligently they listened, and what a wonderful light came into their eyes as the hope dawned in their minds:

Can it be that Parliament would really begin to think of *us* and attend to *our* interests?

All their questions were to the point and practical. How different was the atmosphere from that of the typical drawing-room meeting, where many women came together with the remark: "I am all for '*propertied* women having the vote," but their fear is lest the electorate should be flooded with working women voters. I have never yet been asked by a working-class woman whether our bill, to give votes to women for the same reason as men have it, would not give undue power to propertied women. That is a man's question, though often taken over by women of the leisured or professional class who identify themselves with the objections of theoretic politicians.

To the working-class women the matter presents itself easily and naturally, as it actually is—a woman's question, not a class question. To have their right to labour unrestricted, their protection controlled by themselves, their economic position independent and on the straight-forward footing of being judged by its value and by that alone; their property, earnings, and their persons to be defended by law, and their right over their children to be acknowledged by law. In fact, their freedom as human beings, their full recognition as equal members of the community with men—that is how the Votes-for-Women ques-tion appeals to them. They see it neither as a party question nor as a class question.

Suddenly I had my opportunity. The Press and the people in each different constituency were entirely engrossed with the elections. Up till now, protest meetings were being held by our Union every week outside Walton Gaol, Liverpool. These were not held during the elec-tions, but I told the Liverpool organiser, Miss Flatman, and the general organiser, Mrs. Jennie Baines, that if they would have one more of these protest meetings on Friday, January 14, it was my intention to go in disguise, call upon the crowd to follow me to the governor's house, and insist upon the release of the Suffrage prisoners who had been tortured by forcible feeding. It was not our wont to do any militancy or to hold any protest meetings during election time, that being a time, as it were, when no government is in, but it seemed to me that this was the opportunity to make the governor of the prison respon-sible. It was a case of nothing less than cruelty and did not specially concern, unless they chose to back it up, the government.

I joined the W.S.P.U. again, filling up the membership card as Miss Jane Warton. The choice of a name had been easy. When I came out of Holloway Prison, a distant relative, by name Mr. F. Warburton, wrote me an appreciative letter, thanking me for having been a prisoner in this cause. I determined that if it were necessary to go to prison under another name, I should take the name of Warburton. When I went to Newcastle, my family raised no objection. Now nobody was to know of my disguise, but Warburton was too distinguished a name; that would at once attract attention. I must leave out the "bur "and make it "Warton." "Jane" was the name of Joan of Arc (for Jeanne is more often translated into "Jane" than "Joan") and would bring me comfort in distress. A family sympathetic to our cause, who lived in the suburb near Walton Gaol, were informed that a keen member, Miss Warton, would call at their house in the afternoon before the protest meeting, to investigate the outside of the gaol and the governor's house by daylight, and that she was ready to be arrested if she could not obtain the release of the prisoners.

I spent the previous day and night in Manchester where no one knew of my intentions. In the afternoon, at a drawing-room meeting, I was introduced, after I had spoken, to a woman who was a factory inspector. She had very often to attend in the police courts. She said to me:

> I think it is impossible to attend these cases, and hear the other cases while you wait, and not be a convert to votes for women if you were not one before. The other day a man and two women were had up before the magistrate. They had been found in the street, the man and one woman had been cohabiting together, the other woman mounted guard. The case was quite clear, and the facts were not denied, the man had bribed the women. The man was let free, the two women were sent to prison. If women had the vote such things could not be; in those countries where women have the vote they get altered in less than a year.

In the evening we went to a meeting in a large hall. It was full of working men and working women; it looked as if there were not room to move, so crowded were the seats and gangways. They were tremendously enthusiastic, many of them shook me by the hand, and the thought of them remained for a long time in my heart.

The next morning I took leave of my two kind hostesses. Their last injunction to me was, the agitation of my impending task having affected my appetite, "You should eat more; mind you eat more."

I accomplished my disguise in Manchester, going to a different shop for every part of it, for safety's sake. I had noticed several times while I was in prison that prisoners of unprepossessing appearance obtained least favour, so I was determined to put ugliness to the test. I had my hair cut short and parted, in early Victorian fashion, in smooth bands down the side of my face. This, combined with the resentful bristles of my newly-cut back hair, produced a curious effect. I wished to bleach my hair as well, but the hairdresser refused point-blank to do this, and the stuff that I bought for the purpose at a chemist's proved quite ineffective. A tweed hat, a long green cloth coat, which I purchased for 8s. 6d., a woollen scarf and woollen gloves, a white silk neck-kerchief, a pair of *pince-nez* spectacles, a purse, a net-bag to contain some of my papers, and my costume was complete. I had removed my own initials from my underclothing, and bought the ready-made initials "J. W." to sew on in their stead, but to my regret I had not time to achieve this finishing touch.

All this sounds simple enough, but I suppose it was due to my preoccupation of mind that I have never known a day's shopping fraught with such complications and difficulties. At the frowzy little hairdresser's shop, the only one that seemed to me inconspicuous enough for so important a part of my disguise, the attendant was busy, and I had to return in an hour's time. I told him that I was going a journey and wanted the hair short, since that would be less trouble. He cut it off. Then I wanted what remained to be worn in a parting, with the hair falling straight on either side. This part of the process was most absurd, for that way of wearing my hair was obviously disfiguring to me. "Ah! now that looks very becoming," said the hairdresser, and with that I left the shop in haste.

The eye-glasses I had first bought made me feel giddy from the quality of the lens. I had to take them back and have the glasses changed to the weakest possible. At the first place, in spite of all my protests, the shopman insisted on elaborately testing my sight, afterwards requiring me to wait for half an hour or so while he fitted up the glasses. So I went to another shop, and in self-defence invented the story that the glasses were for stage purposes, for a friend of mine who had very good sight, and that if she was not to trip up in her part the glasses must be as nearly plain as possible. This time I was more successful with the lens, but the grip of the folders was still galling to the very large bridge of my nose.

When I had finished this errand I was startled to see walking along the street one of my kind hostesses, whom I had parted from early that morning, professedly to return to Liverpool without delay. I took refuge down a side-street until she had passed by. Then I had strayed into the more opulent quarters of Manchester, in my search for another spectacle shop. All the shops were of a high-class order, and Jane Warton could find nothing to her requirements. On inquiry for a "cheap" draper, three different people recommended me to a certain shop named "Lewis."

Jane Warton

A sale was on there and Jane found that it was the very place for her. So many Miss Wartons were of the same mind that the street was blocked with customers for some distance down; but I was obliged to wait, for no other shop was of the same description. The hat was a special difficulty; every article of millinery was of the fashionable order, warranted to cover half the body as well as the head. This did not suit Jane. Finally she succeeded in getting the right one of stitched cloth, with a plait of cloth round the crown. Before leaving Manchester I realised that my ugly disguise was a success. I was an object of the greatest derision to street-boys, and shop-girls could hardly keep their countenances while serving me.

I had done my shopping at last, and hurried off to the station. I took out my box, put in it my own hat and jacket, put on the label "Miss Jane Warton, Cloak Room," and left it there. In the refreshment room, where I went to take a last hurried meal, a delightful big, brown dog, a mongrel, came and talked to me. He was with a party of two men and a woman, who sat at a corner of the room. The dog came up to me at once; he put his head on my lap and was most dear.

After this I got into the train. I finished a letter to my mother, telling her of yesterday's meetings and that I might not write to her for some little time because of being so busy with the elections.

Arrived at Liverpool, and not knowing my way to Walton, I took a cab and drove out for nearly an hour before reaching my destination. I was already racing hard with daylight and, thanks to a damp fog, it was already quite dark when I arrived there.

The house to which I had been directed was in a new quarter and nowhere to be found. We drove up and down the roads and inquired at shops and post offices. Presently I spotted the familiar sight of a woman stooping to chalk on the pavement some announcement—it was our protest meeting. I felt happy again, it was like seeing a friend. She turned out to be one of the daughters of the very house I was seeking. There were three daughters who lived with their mother. The daughters were zealots and welcomed Jane without a sign of criticism. I saw the mother gasp a little when I entered her drawing-room, but she was nevertheless most courteous and kind.

I was escorted to the gaol and took my bearings. To anyone who has been in prison, few things, I think, are more exasperating than the unrevealing face of the outer walls. On this occasion I felt an overmastering longing to inquire after the prisoners who had stirred me to my coming deed. What was the degree of their suffering and exhaustion?

161

What should I be able to do for their release? If by some miracle I obtained it, would it be too late to help them? I thought more especially of Miss Selina Martin. I had seen her in Birmingham a fortnight after her release from the weeks that she had been fed in the prison there. She was in the nursing home, together with Mrs. Leigh, that splendid fighter for the women's cause and most heroic woman. Their look of illness haunted me still.

The idea that Selina Martin was again, perhaps at that very moment, undergoing the same cruel treatment exasperated me. I felt so feeble, had so little faith in the utility of what I was about to do, yet I was athirst to do it, and the strength of my wish that it should be effective made me feel, at moments, capable of anything. But to all this the prison walls had nothing to say. They revealed nothing. They looked angry with all the world, angry above all because of an uneasy conscience.

I returned to the house of my friends, selected from their garden small, flat stones in case of need, which I wrapped in paper, and snatched a hasty meal. My kind hostess had heard that I was a vegetarian, and had provided a most appetising dish of stewed white pears. My mouth was parched with the weary work of the day and the thought of what lay before me, but I had no time except to taste the pears; the memory of them during the hunger-strike filled my dreams.

Again we set out for the prison. All through the day I had been dogged by the nightmare thought that I should be too late for the meeting, or for some other reason should be prevented from achieving my purpose. As we neared the place, a crowd of between two and three hundred men and women were following the carriage in which were our speakers. It had been agreed that I should mix with the crowd, not join with the speakers, but at the end of the meeting should have my say from below. I passed the carriage to report myself to the organisers. Many of our members were standing around, but I think most of them did not recognise me, except from my voice later on.

Miss Flatman, Miss Patricia Woodlock and Mrs. Baines made stirring speeches, but the crowd had mostly gathered out of curiosity and were not many of them likely to listen to my coming appeal. I was afraid lest they should disperse before I had my chance, so I rudely interrupted Mrs. Baines and spoke from the outer rim of the crowd, on the side of the governor's house.

I reminded the audience of how the men of Dundee, when forcible feeding of Suffrage prisoners was threatened in that town, had assembled to the number of two thousand and protested against it. How thereupon the hunger-strikers had been released and no forcible feeding to our women had been inflicted in Scotland. Could not Englishmen have done the same? Let the men of Liverpool be the first to wipe out the stain that had been tolerated up till now. We were outside the gaol where these and other barbarities were actually going on. The Home Secretary had denied responsibility and asserted that it rested with the prison officials. Let us put this to the test and call upon the governor of the prison to release these women. No violence was needed, but let us go to his house, insist upon his replying to our request and refuse to be dispersed until he had released these women.

If there are no men in Liverpool who will stand up for these prisoners, let the women do their part—I call on you all to follow me to the governor's house.

With this I turned towards the house, a separate building surrounded by a little garden. To my surprise, the crowd began to follow me. Again I shouted out to them—

No violence, remember, but call for the governor and refuse to be dispersed till you have secured the release of the prisoners.

A policeman began leisurely to follow me; there were only two or three of them about. I took to running and urged on the crowd. The police then took hold of me. As for once it was my object above all else to get arrested and imprisoned, I began discharging my stones, not throwing them, but simply dropping them over the hedge into the governor's garden. One of them just touched the shoulder of a man who had rushed up on seeing me arrested. I apologised to him. Two policemen then held me fast by the arms and marched me off to the police station. The crowd followed excitedly, and our members gathered round me, appealing for my release and saying that I had done nothing.

It had been agreed with the organisers that I should be the only one arrested. As I have said, militant tactics were in abeyance because of the elections, the less disturbance was made, therefore, the better; as it was, I feared lest my action, being out of the straight course, should be displeasing to the leaders. I said to the other members:

I am all right, don't bother about me, but take the crowd back to the governor's house.

I did not wish to be recognised.

As they marched me off at a great pace, the police, who were very civil and considerate, questioned me: "What was you a-doin'? You weren't in the carriage with the others, were you? What was that you was sayin'?"

They knew they would have to make up a charge against me, and wisely thought the best plan was to ask me direct for information! I told them that I made towards the governor's house, appealed to the crowd to follow, and refused to desist when called upon by the police. I feared that this might not be enough to achieve a conviction. I was thinking, "Was there nothing else?" when the man appeared whose shoulder had been touched by my stone; he carried the missile in his hand, still wrapped in the purple hand-bill announcing this very meeting, no doubt a most evil-looking document in the eyes of the authorities. I knew then that I was safe.

Presently, two others who had been arrested were brought in. It was a most unlooked-for consolation to have their company through the night, though I hoped, of course, that they would be let off and not share the rest of the ordeal with me. Two of the members, on hearing my voice, determined that I should not be alone, so they returned, and one of them poked a flag through a window in the governor's house, breaking the glass; the other mounted guard while she did this. They were both arrested. One was Miss Elsie Howey, a valiant as well as most dear one of our members; the other was a lo-cal member, who gave the name of Mrs. Nugent. I had twice stayed with her and her husband when at Liverpool. She was not only most charming, but also of attractive appearance, which awoke a great deal of curiosity in the police as to her identity, and luckily drew off all possible suspicions from me.

We all played up to the situation; Elsie Howey and I treated her with deference, as a person of great importance; we nicknamed her "the Princess."

The police were exceptionally friendly to us, although they were punctilious as to the regulations. For instance, Miss Howey and I were suffering from bad colds and had eucalyptus inhalers in our pockets. We were not allowed to keep these; they were removed with other things, such as a purse, stylo pen, brooches, watch, etc. We were all three allowed to be together and away from other prisoners, locked into a cell of the usual police-station description—that is, unfurnished but for the bare plank, serving as seat or bed, along the wall, and about one and a-half feet from the ground, terminating in a lavatory accommodation under a high-barred window, but now lighted by an electric light in the wall above the door. This cell was scrupulously clean and blankets were supplied to us. Our friends sent us some sandwiches and fruit, and the police themselves provided us with an evening newspaper.

We had been arrested at about 8 o'clock; the police station was some distance from Walton, so it was getting on for 9 o'clock when we were at last shut up after the charges were reported and entered, and we had been stripped by a wardress of our small belongings.

The quick walk from the scene of our arrest, hurried along between two policemen, had been a warming process, after which the cold in the cell seemed intense. The bench being wider than most in police-station cells, Mrs. Nugent lay down at one end, while Elsie Howey and I lay side by side under the same blanket and warmed each other. Mrs. Nugent and Elsie kept up an animated conversation. Elsie told anecdotes of her former imprisonments and those of the fellow-prisoners. I was short of breath and fearfully tired, so I rolled round and kept quite quiet.

At about 12 o'clock the husband of Mrs. Nugent had heard of her arrest, and came off to the police station to see her. He came to the door of our cell and was greatly distressed. It was ever so nice to see him. His visit had caused a great deal of concern amongst the police, who recognised him as one of the magistrates. He put himself out to do what he could, and we offered him the comforting news that we were almost sure that his wife would get off, as she had done nothing at all. With that, as his wife was kept standing at the little window so long as he was there, he felt obliged to leave us.

Towards about 3 a.m. we were taken out of the cell and ranged along a seat by the wall of a large room; at the other end was a desk with a policeman sitting at it. We went up in turn to give our names, ages, etc., that is, about seven or eight other prisoners, all females, and our three selves. It was the turn of Jane Warton. She walked across to the policeman, one shoulder hitched slightly above the other, her hair sticking out straight behind and worn in slick bandeaus on either side of her face, her hat trailing in a melancholy way on her head. The large, grey woollen gloves were drawn up over the too short sleeves of her coat; on the collar of it were worn portraits of Mrs. Pankhurst, Mrs. Lawrence and Christabel, in small china brooches; her hat had a bit of tape with "Votes for Women" written on it, interlaced with the cloth plait that went round it, and eye-glasses were fixed on her nose.

Her standing out in the room was the signal for a convulsed titter from the other prisoners. "It's a shame to laugh at one of your fellow-prisoners," said the policeman behind the desk, and the tittering was hushed. It was all I could do not to laugh, and I thought to myself "Is the *Punch* version of a Suffragette overdone?" As I got back to my companions they too were laughing, but I thought it wonderfully kind of the policeman to have spoken on my behalf.

When this process was finished, we three Suffragettes were taken to the policemen's room, where there was a good fire, to wait for our Black Maria. The other prisoners had disappeared. The police sat round and spoke quite pleasantly; there were two or three of them at times. We discussed the chances of women getting the vote, they seemed quite in favour. Elsie Howey and Mrs. Nugent did most of the talking. I warmed myself and saw the police looking at me from time to time, wondering why I did not talk too.

At about 3.30 a.m. or 4 o'clock, Black Maria came and we were put in. This was different from the prison vans I had hitherto seen; it was not broken up into separate cell-like compartments, but was in the form of a double omnibus, one side for men and the other for women, divided by a thin wooden partition, each side having two seats facing each other and extending the length of the carriage. There were no windows; the light filtered in only through the grated ventilators. When we got into this Black Maria there was no one but us three, but we were told to sit near the door, so Mrs. Nugent sat first, then Elsie Howey, and then myself. The jolting of the van is excessive and suggests a complete absence of springs, the noise of its passage through the streets is terrific, to the point of excluding all other sounds—a noise of thundering wheels, of jolts and jars and bumps. I have not yet made out the reason why 3.30 a.m. was selected, none was given at the time to the prisoners.

Our destination was the Bridewell Police Station, but we called on our way at the other police stations in the town, picking up whatever unfortunates they had netted during the night. We called at four different stations, if I remember right. The drive in all took about an hour, and seemed a very long one.

We had not gone far before the rumbling and jolting ceased, the door was thrown open with a sound of keys and great rattling, a shaft of light fell along the 'bus, and lit up momentarily ourselves and those who were thrown in to add to our number. These were the only moments when the occupants had a chance of seeing each other. The door then hastily closed again, darkness, jolting and noise reasserted their grim influence. Drunken voices, the smell of the gin palace, an occasional query and reply shouted through the thin wall to the men on the other side, that was all. Knee to knee, and breath to breath we sat, companions of this world of darkness, fellow-sisters of the order of the outcasts. Before we had finished, we had taken up six women in all.

At the first stop, two Irish girls were let in; some men were put into the other side. The girls were only sufficiently drunk to make them intensely cheerful; they laughed and talked gaily at first and shouted lustily to their companions on the other side. But the effect of the pitch darkness was depressing, and after a time their communications ceased. They sat opposite to us near the door, and whenever there was a gleam of light I watched them, for they gave me immense pleasure. They were quite young, with beautiful arms, which one could see as their sleeves were rolled up; they had shawls on, and their faces were fresh and strong, and pretty, too, had it not been for the effect of the drink; they were as far removed as possible from the degraded town type, in every way they were healthy specimens, fresh from an Irish fishing village.

They spoke to us several times, and there was a delightful feeling that disguise or no disguise did not matter with them, but it was difficult to hear what they said in the fearful noise of the Black Maria, and we felt that our answers were mostly lost on them. They put the question in a friendly way: "What did you get taken up for?" "We're Suffragettes," was the all-sufficient reply. This was very interesting, and they had to try to tell the men on the other side, with many a laugh, as a tremendous bit of news.

At another stop, a little woman got in with fair hair, a fluttering white boa, and in a white dress. She was dead drunk, but whereas the others smelt of cheap drink, her breath was of good brandy. She laughed, and now and then gave vent to a half sentence or two that rolled in and out of her sleep.

At the next stop, two were shot in who seemed really deformed with poverty, their complexions yellow, their hands gnarled and worn, their faces of utmost sadness. They said something to each other as they got in—something to give comfort, but their sentences were full of oaths of a senseless kind, and their speech, too, was broken with drink.

Finally, it was another type altogether who was let in. A woman who looked any age, her face of utmost melancholy had yet the appearance of having drunk heavily; she had all the hang of an "habitual," her clothes were the dregs of clothes and tumbling off her. When the door was opened for her to be put in, she murmured a few broken words to the effect that her salvation didn't lie in prison.

The Irish girls and the little woman with the white boa were young, the others looked old and worn out.

I think I shall never forget the self-reproach that stung through my whole being when I had thought my intervention necessary between one prisoner and another. On passing some unusual light in the street, which momentarily lit up our van, not enough to see our faces but only to distinguish the outlines of forms, I noticed that the prisoner opposite to Elsie Howey, my neighbour, was leaning forward and bent towards her. The momentary flash of light was too short-lived to judge whether this was a rapid movement perhaps, as I thought, of assault or drunken affection, or whether it was that the position of physical weariness could find no rest from leaning back on the walls of the jolting van.

I was unable to see Elsie, but I imagined that she too might be scared by the attention of the prisoner opposite. As the darkness closed in upon us, I thrust my hand into hers; it was welcomed, but quite unnecessary. Before the end of our drive two things were clear—the prisoners might be evil-minded towards all the rest of the world, they might be blind drunk or raging with misery at their own plight, but the one thing impossible to them would have been to hurt a fellow-prisoner.

Every one of those pathetic human wrecks, deformed by drink, so that one could not tell if they were guilty of crime besides, overtaken at a moment when their self-respect was lowest, and captured by a punitive system which would do its utmost to dissolve what remained of it, as they were thrust into the black cavity of the van, made a vigorous appeal to their own courage and met with instant response from their unknown companions. It might be only some drunken joke, it was almost invariably accompanied by a laugh, but for each one it had a call on their inmost strength, and it made its appeal to those in the van. Issuing from different spheres of existence, each one representing lives the most remote from one another, scarcely any two alike in a single respect as to detail, their one point of similarity being poverty and that they had given way to drink, the instinct of our first contact, doubtless to each one of us, was repulsion, mistrust, fear of one another.

But it lasted for less than the flash of a moment, less than the inhaling of one breath. Our differences were there, but for the time unimportant, whereas the all-embracing fact was our similarity of fate. No need for social laws to bind that company, no rules of the club were necessary, the code of instinct, expediency and honour were all one and spontaneous to us. "We are all of one blood," may be a great tie, but "We are all of one fate" is, while it lasts, a better; the bond of the outcast needs no seal.

We arrived for the fifth time in a courtyard, with a deal of jolting and din; it was the Bridewell Police Station, and we all got out. The little woman in the white dress and fur boa tumbled from the van into the arms of a policeman—she assured us that she loved him on finding herself thus closely against him; he remained stalwart as a piece of wood.

We Suffragettes were put into a cell by ourselves, it was perfectly clean. We had not been there very long before the door was opened with a clang and another woman was thrust in. She was reassuring to look at, smartly dressed with fashionably-shaped brown furs draped round her neck. She had come from Ireland that night and was terribly cold. We gave her the blankets that had been given to us; nothing, however, did much good. She had come over with another woman, who on landing had been taken as "wanted by the police."

This woman had been arrested, too, as "her friend," but she said she was quite sure of getting off, as she had only known the other woman quite a short time, and had no idea that she was in any way "suspected." The concern of this woman to get free was natural enough, but she seemed to care not at all for the other one, for whom my heart welled over with sympathy. I thought of her with a more or less deceitful face, but I loved her because she was "wanted by the police," and this woman who was with us I wanted to get off, of course, but that was all; I could not feel any sympathy towards her.

We waited in this cell until it was dawning light. It was not a place for sleep, and the cold was terrible. As it was getting towards morning, we were taken out of the cell and led off to wash our hands and faces in another part of the prison. It was fearfully dark in one part, with only a light occasionally here and there, so that one could not see where one was going. On a bench, some ten or twelve little boys were sitting.

It was the first time I thought of children as prisoners. At Newcastle, it was true, I had seen one little boy in the police court, but he was enjoying himself over a cup of soup in the central room with the police, and he was much too small to be convicted, whatever his offences; possibly, if his parents were hopeless, he would have been sent to a reformatory school. That, of course, was bad enough; one knew that for half of the money that would have to be expended there was many a woman in the country who would have cared for him with motherly tenderness. But with these boys, who looked about nine years to fifteen or sixteen years old, it was another matter. The place where they sat, though public, for it was a gangway, was terrible, it was just where the passages seemed to go underground; they were extremely dark, on one side they abutted into a regular network of cells, with small communicating alleys in between. There the boys sat and gazed at the grown-up criminals who appeared from time to time; they looked at us with the greatest curiosity. It was horrible to see them in a place so profoundly ill-suited to children.

The Liverpool organiser, Miss Flatman, and Miss Maude Joachim came to us with the daylight of Saturday, January 15. It was a most unexpected joy to see them—not alone, for that was not allowed, but in one of the many passages near a window with a policeman standing by. I was able to write a little scrap of a letter to Mrs. Pethick Lawrence in the name of "Jane Warton." This made me very happy. I believe we were offered breakfast, or should have been able to get it had we asked for it, but, in any case, those surroundings were so wretched that we almost as soon went without, and I was eager to begin the hunger-strike.

As the time of the assembling of the court, 10 o'clock, drew near we waited in different parts of a large and rambling building. At last we were conveyed, through what seemed an underground court, to the foot of a staircase that led right up into the prisoner's dock.

I was the first of the Suffragettes to be taken up. Mr. Shepherd Little was the magistrate; he seemed to be thoroughly out of temper. They took only two or three minutes convicting me. When the policeman had done his work of charging me with urging the crowd to follow me to the governor's house, with refusing to desist when called upon by the police, and with throwing a "missile" (small stone wrapped in paper), I put in, "I had three stones upon me which I let fall in the governor's garden. A man in the crowd ran past me just as I was letting go the third—it fell on his shoulder; I apologised to him."

On the strength of its being my first imprisonment, I was sentenced to a fortnight. 3rd Division, with option of a fine. Just when I had left the court I was called back. The magistrate thought I ought to have a longer sentence, thanks to my having thrown stones, but the clerk thought not, and in the little altercation he got the best of it.

The women of last night were waiting on the stairs. "How long have you got?" they all said to me. "Ah! well, buck up," they added on hearing of fourteen days. Miss Elsie Howey, with the admission of her former imprisonments, got six weeks, and Mrs. Nugent was, to our great joy, released. The policeman downstairs told me that hard labour always accompanied the 3rd Division sentences, unless stated to the contrary.

CHAPTER 13: WALTON GAOL, LIVERPOOL:
MY THIRD IMPRISONMENT

Elsie Howey and I waited together at the Bridewell Police Station for the greater part of that day (Saturday, January 15). Towards evening they took us away in a partition van, alone, to Walton Green Gaol, we arrived at about 7 o'clock at night. The other prisoners must have journeyed here when we did, though by a different van, for we were all together again when we were to give our names, vocation, etc., to the prison warders. We stood up by a wall, all in a row, and waited our turn. The prisoner with the white boa and the apparently white gown, I was able to see closely and by a high light. The boa was in imitation fur and extremely dirty, the white dress was of some thin cotton, nearly transparent; it was open on her chest and she seemed to have hardly any clothes underneath. I did not like to think what she must have suffered this wintry day, in and out of the icy cold police station cells.

The effect of the drink was wearing off, and she waved her head about as though she had a very bad headache; all her cheerfulness had gone. Poor little thing, I felt extremely sorry for her, she had been given plenty of the best brandy and she had done what was wanted of her; the next day she found herself in prison. When her imprisonment was over, in all probability, to go the same road of drunkenness and prostitution would seem the only one open to her.

There were several other prisoners besides those we had seen before. Some were so familiar with the place that they reeled off their age, religion, birthplace, calling, without waiting to be asked, and then walked through into a large hall in which were the waiting cubicles. Suddenly I felt awed, a feeling of supremest pity almost took my breath away. Passing in front of me into the larger hall was a woman

171

of great beauty, her features were intensely refined, and in every part of her there seemed to be some great determination, not in respect of the prison she was in now, that was only part of it, but with regard to her life of shame that went before; the whole face and figure were virtuous and good.

The other woman who had come over from Ireland was not there, but this was the one, I felt quite sure, who was "wanted by the police." I had not heard her tell anything to the officer, I had not seen her till that moment, and I never saw her again, but I shall never forget her face which will rest always on my memory, beautiful, commanding, and of an absorbing sadness.

It was our turn at last. We gave the required details, and then Elsie Howey said that we should refuse all food and all the prison rules.

> We are sorry if it will give trouble; we shall give as little as possible; but our fast is against the government, and we shall fight them with our lives, not hurting anyone else.

The wardress gave no answer, but with a wave of her hand showed us towards the cubicles. Before we went in there we were separated; we had to part, and I never saw Elsie again till long after I came out. A wardress came and showed me to a room with two other officers, the place where I was to undress. I said that I did not bow to the imprisonment and so would not undress myself, whereupon a wardress began to pull my things off, but I showed them this was not from disagreeableness but only through the prison strike.

On taking out of my pocket a clean handkerchief I noticed that it had the initials "G. L." still upon it, and when next there came a reel of cotton with the name "Lytton" written quite distinctly round the top, I felt overwhelmed with horror. Scarcely knowing what I was about, I seized them both in my hand and put them on the fire which burnt in a stove near where I was standing. The next moment I thought I had done wrong and that the attention of the officers would inevitably be called to my action, but they seemed not to have noticed and never said anything, so I thanked my stars that I was safe. The look of Jane Warton was still comic in the extreme, the two wardresses laughed as they undressed her. Her glasses were the subject of excessive care and she was allowed to keep them with her. I would most gladly have given them up, for they hurt the bridge of my nose which was far too wide for them, but it was good, of course, to help the disguise for some while longer.

I had my bath, and was put into a 3rd Division dress of coarse, brown serge, and my cap and apron were tied on. I was put before a large basket of worn boots, not in pairs, and told to pick out two for myself. I chose the largest I saw, but they were not nearly big enough, and it was only after a tremendous effort that I got my feet into them. I was then taken to the large hall and put into a cubicle. These were like cupboards, without ceiling, giving on to the hall for light and air, so that they had not the stuffiness of the cells.

By this time I was dropping with fatigue, the seat seemed there for me to sleep on, and being alone was immensely restful. But the sounds of the other prisoners made it too painful for rest; one of them sobbed all the time, and soon I saw we were here only to be inspected. The door opened and a wardress put in a pair of sheets for me to take to the cell. Then the matron came, a capable-looking woman, but severe. She spoke to me of the hunger-strike, and of how very wrong it was. I said that of course without an object it was very wrong, but the government had been petitioned in every other way, we thought they would not like hunger-strikes for ever, that now there were still comparatively few, but later there would, if necessary, be many more; that feeding by force was horrible, besides it did not meet the difficulty of keeping the women in prison.

When one saw what the wrongs of women were to redress, it seemed a little thing that some women should die for the sake of the others. She did not stay to prolong the discussion. The next to come was a young doctor accompanied by a female officer. He called me out, and the ordinary questions were put to me. I said that I was free from any infectious disease, but that I could not answer any other questions. He seemed to have expected me to say this, and told the officer to put it down in the book she carried with her. I had decided, as on the occasion of my previous hunger-strike, to refuse to answer medical questions, but not to resist medical inspection. However, to my great relief, it was not attempted. This was the same at Newcastle, so seemed to me nothing extraordinary.

At last the longed-for moment had arrived, and I was taken off to my cell. To my joy there was a window which opened a little bit; at night it was lit by a gas jet that was set in the depth of the wall behind the door, the passage side, and covered in by a thick glass. I was ever so tired—I laid down and slept.

The next day was Sunday (January 16), but they did not ask us to go to chapel. For several days I did not wear my cap and apron in my cell, but did not in other ways continue my protest against the clothes. The cold seemed to me intense, and I wore the skirt of my dress fastened round my neck for warmth. The governor, accompanied by the matron, came to see me, but he was in a temper about our having broken his windows, so I said nothing. He was in a fury at the way I had fastened my skirt. I answered that it was for warmth and that I would gladly put on more clothes and warmer ones if he gave them to me. Later on the Senior Medical Officer came in. He was a short, fat, little man, with a long waxed moustache. I should have said he disliked being unkind; he liked to chaff over things; but as I looked at him I thought I would rather be forcibly fed by anyone in the world than by him, the coarse doctors at Newcastle and the cross little doctor I had seen the night before. I said I had not asked to see him, but he made no examination and asked no questions.

I lay in my bed most of the day, for they did not disturb me, and I tried to keep warm, as I felt the cold fearfully. They brought me all my meals the same as usual, porridge in the morning at 7, meat and potatoes mid-day at 12, porridge at 4.30. When they were hot I fed on the smell of them, which seemed quite delicious; I said "I don't want any, thank you," to each meal, as they brought it in. I had made up my mind that this time I would not drink any water, and would only rinse out my mouth morning and evening without swallowing any.

I wrote on the walls of my cell with my slate pencil and soap mixed with the dirt of the floor for ink, "Votes for Women," and the saying from Thoreau's *Duty of Civil Disobedience*—

Under a government which imprisons any unjustly, the true place for a just man (or woman) is also a prison.

On the wall opposite my bed I wrote the text from Joshua:

Only be thou strong and very courageous.

That night I dreamt of fruits, melons, peaches and nectarines, and of a moonlit balcony that was hung with sweetest smelling flowers, honeysuckle and jessamine, apple blossom and sweet scented verbena; there was only the sound of night birds throbbing over the hills that ranged themselves below the balcony. On it there slept my sister-in-law, and on the balustrade, but making no noise, was a figure awake and alert, which was my brother. My dream was of a land which was seen by my father in his poem of *King Poppy*, where the princess and the shepherd boy are the types etherealised. I woke suddenly. I could sleep a little in detached moments, but this dream had made the prison cell beautiful to me; it had a way out.

The strain was great of having to put on my shoes, which were too small, every time I was taken out of my cell to empty slops or to see the governor. The matron was shocked that I did not put the right heel in at all and every day I was given another pair, but they were all alike in being too small for my right foot.

The next day, Monday (January 17), the wardress took my bed and bedding away because I would not make it up, but lay on it in the daytime. I told her if she wished she must roll me off, but that I did not intend voluntarily to give it up. She was quite amiable, but rolled me towards the wall and took the bed and bedding from underneath me. There was a little table in my cell which was not fastened to the wall. I turned it upside down and was able to sit in it with my body resting against one of the legs. It was very uncomfortable, but I felt too ill to sit up in the chair, and the concrete floor was much too cold without the bed.

Every now and then I got up and walked backwards and forwards in the cell to get a little warmth into me. The chaplain came in for a moment. He was a tall, good-looking man, of the burly, healthy sort. It seemed to me, from his talk, that he would be very well suited to be a cricket match or football parson, if there were such a thing, but he was totally unsuited to be the chaplain of a prison, or anyhow of a woman's prison. He thought it wise to speak to me as a "Suffragette."

Look here, it's no good your thinking that there's anything to be done with the women here—the men sometimes are not such bad fellows, and there are many who write to me after they've left here, but the women, they're all as bad as bad can be, there's absolutely no good in them.

I did not answer, but I felt inclined to say "Then goodbye to you, since you say you can do no good with the women here." Presently an officer came and led me out. The manner of nearly all the officers was severe; one or two were friends but most of them treated me like dirt. I was shown along the gangway of the ward, which seemed to me very large, much larger than the D X at Holloway, and went in various directions like a star. I was shown into the governor's room, which lay at the end of the gangway. It was warm, there were hot pipes against which I was made to stand with my back to the wall, and for a moment, as I put my feet to rest on the pipes, I could think of nothing else but the delight of their heat.

The governor was very cross. I had decided not to do the needle-work which constituted the hard labour, for this he gave me three days on bread and water. He would not let me speak to him at all and I was led out, but, before I had got to my cell, I was called back into his presence. "I hear you are refusing to take your food, so it's three days in a special cell." I was taken out and down a staircase till we reached the ground floor. I think my cell was two stories above, but I am not sure; then down again and into a short passage that looked as if it was underground, with a window at the top seemingly only just level with the ground.

The door of a cell was opened, I was put inside and the door locked. It was larger than the cell upstairs, and the jug, basin, etc., were all made of black *gutta-percha*, not of tin, placed on the floor. This would have been bad for the ordinary prisoner, as it was quite impossible to tell whether the eating things were clean or not and, in any case, it smelt fairly strong of *gutta-percha*; but as the rule for me was neither to eat nor drink, I was able to put up with it well. The bed was wider than an ordinary plank bed and nailed to the ground, so that I was able to lie on it without being disturbed.

Best of all was the fact that it was nearer to the heating apparatus and so seemed quite warm when I was led in. I did not notice at first that the window did not open, but when I had been there six or seven hours it became wonderfully airless. I only left my cell for minutes at a time, when I was allowed to draw water, and the air of the corridor then seemed fresh as mountain air by comparison. I had an idea that Elsie Howey or some of the others would have been put into a punishment cell too. I called, but in vain, my voice had grown weak and my tongue and throat felt thick as a carpet, probably from not drinking anything. I tried signalling with raps on the wall, "*No surrender—no surrender*," Mrs. Leigh's favourite motto, but I was never sure of corresponding raps, though sometimes I thought I heard them. I could not sleep for more than about an hour at a time, my legs drew up into a cramped position whenever I went off and the choking thickness in my mouth woke me.

Tuesday, January 18, I was visited again by the Senior Medical Officer, who asked me how long I had been without food. I said I had eaten a buttered scone and a banana sent in by friends to the police station on Friday at about midnight. He said, "Oh, then, this is the fourth day; that is too long, I shall have to feed you, I must feed you at once," but he went out and nothing happened till about 6 o'clock in the evening, when he returned with, I think, five wardresses and the feeding apparatus. He urged me to take food voluntarily.

I told him that was absolutely out of the question, that when our legislators ceased to resist enfranchising women then I should cease to resist taking food in prison. He did not examine my heart nor feel my pulse; he did not ask to do so, nor did I say anything which could possibly induce him to think I would refuse to be examined. I offered no resistance to being placed in position, but lay down voluntarily on the plank bed. Two of the wardresses took hold of my arms, one held my head and one my feet. One wardress helped to pour the food. The doctor leant on my knees as he stooped over my chest to get at my mouth. I shut my mouth and clenched my teeth. I had looked forward to this moment with so much anxiety lest my identity should be discovered beforehand, that I felt positively glad when the time had come. The sense of being overpowered by more force than I could possibly resist was complete, but I resisted nothing except with my mouth.

The doctor offered me the choice of a wooden or steel gag; he explained elaborately, as he did on most subsequent occasions, that the steel gag would hurt and the wooden one not, and he urged me not to force him to use the steel gag. But I did not speak nor open my mouth, so that after playing about for a moment or two with the wooden one he finally had recourse to the steel. He seemed annoyed at my resistance and he broke into a temper as he plied my teeth with the steel implement. He found that on either side at the back I had false teeth mounted on a bridge which did not take out.

The superintending wardress asked if I had any false teeth, if so, that they must be taken out; I made no answer and the process went on. He dug his instrument down on to the sham tooth, it pressed fearfully on the gum. He said if I resisted so much with my teeth, he would have to feed me through the nose. The pain of it was intense and at last I must have given way for he got the gag between my teeth, when he proceeded to turn it much more than necessary until my jaws were fastened wide apart, far more than they could go naturally. Then he put down my throat a tube which seemed to me much too wide and was something like four feet in length.

The irritation of the tube was excessive. I choked the moment it touched my throat until it had got down. Then the food was poured in quickly; it made me sick a few seconds after it was down and the

177

action of the sickness made my body and legs double up, but the wardresses instantly pressed back my head and the doctor leant on my knees. The horror of it was more than I can describe. I was sick over the doctor and wardresses, and it seemed a long time before they took the tube out. As the doctor left he gave me a slap on the cheek, not violently, but, as it were, to express his contemptuous disapproval, and he seemed to take for granted that my distress was assumed.

At first it seemed such an utterly contemptible thing to have done that I could only laugh in my mind. Then suddenly I saw Jane Warton lying before me, and it seemed as if I were outside of her. She was the most despised, ignorant and helpless prisoner that I had seen. When she had served her time and was out of the prison, no one would believe anything she said, and the doctor when he had fed her by force and tortured her body, struck her on the cheek to show how he despised her! That was Jane Warton, and I had come to help her.

When the doctor had gone out of the cell, I lay quite helpless. The wardresses were kind and knelt round to comfort me, but there was nothing to be done, I could not move, and remained there in what, under different conditions, would have been an intolerable mess. I had been sick over my hair, which, though short, hung on either side of my face, all over the wall near my bed, and my clothes seemed saturated with it, but the wardresses told me they could not get me a change that night as it was too late, the office was shut. I lay quite motionless, it seemed paradise to be without the suffocating tube, without the liquid food going in and out of my body and without the gag between my teeth.

Presently the wardresses all left me, they had orders to go, which were carried out with the usual promptness. Before long I heard the sounds of the forced feeding in the next cell to mine. It was almost more than I could bear, it was Elsie Howey, I was sure. When the ghastly process was over and all quiet, I tapped on the wall and called out at the top of my voice, which wasn't much just then, "No surrender," and there came the answer past any doubt in Elsie's voice, "No surrender." After this I fell back and lay as I fell. It was not very long before the wardress came and announced that I was to go back upstairs as, because of the feeding, my time in the punishment cell was over. I was taken into the same cell which I had before; the long hours till morning were a nightmare of agonised dread for a repetition of the process.

The next day, Wednesday, January 19, they brought me clean

clothes. When the wardresses were away at breakfast I determined to break the thick glass of my gas jet to show what I thought of the forcible feeding, it seemed the last time that I should have the strength required. I took one of my shoes, which always lay at my side except when I moved from my cell, let it get a good swing by holding it at the back of my shoulder and then hurled it against the glass with all the strength that I had. The glass broke in pieces with a great smashing sound.

The two wardresses, who were in charge of the whole ward while the others were away, came into my cell together; I was already back in my bed. They were young, new to the work, and looked rather frightened. I told them I had done it with a shoe, and why. "But that is enough," I said, "I am not going to do any more now." This reassured them and they both laughed. They took away the shoes as "dangerous," and brought me slippers instead, and, to my intense relief, I never saw them again.

As the morning wore on, one after the other of the officials proclaimed that I had done a shameful thing. On being changed to the cell next door, one of the head wardresses—I never made out exactly who she was—was in a great temper. I had told her, as I did every one of the officials, why I had broken my gas jet.

"Broken it, yes, I should just think you had, indeed. And all that writing scribbled over your cell; can't keep the place decent."

"I'm so sorry," I said; "I assure you there was nothing indecent in what I wrote on the wall."

"No, not indecent, but" she hesitated and, as the words would not come to her assistance, the remark remained unfinished.

I had not been long in the other cell before the doctor and four or five wardresses appeared. He was apparently angry because I had broken the jet glass; he seized one of the tin vessels and began waving it about. "I suppose you want to smash me with one of these?" he exclaimed.

I said to him, so that all the wardresses with him could hear, "Unless you consider it part of your duty, would you please not strike me when you have finished your odious job" (or I may have said "slap me," I do not remember). He did not answer, but, after a little pause, he signed to me to lie down on the bed. Again the choice of the wooden or steel implement, again the force, which after a time I could not withstand, in the same place as yesterday where the gum was sore and aching. Then the feeling of the suffocating tube thrust down and the gate of life seemed shut. The tube was pressed down much too far, it seemed to me, causing me at times great pain in my side.

The sickness was worse than the time before. As the tube was removed I was unavoidably sick over the doctor. He flew away from me and out of the cell, exclaiming angrily, "If you do that again next time I shall feed you twice." I had removed my serge jacket and taken several precautions for my bed, but I am afraid one or two of the officers and the floor and wall were drenched. I shut my eyes and lay back quite helpless for a while. They presently brought in fresh clothes, and a woman, another prisoner, came and washed the floor. It seemed terrible that another prisoner should do this, it was altogether a revolting business. Two wardresses came and overlooked her work, one of them said, in a voice of displeased authority: "Look at her! Just look at her! The way she's doing it!" The woman washed on and took no notice; her face was intensely sad.

I roused myself and said, "Well, at any rate, she's doing what I should be doing myself and I am very grateful to her." The wardresses looked surprised at me, but they said nothing.

The governor came in for a moment to see me. To my surprise his anger had cooled a little. He had before spoken to me in a rage and, if I asked questions which implied a complaint, had told me they were not proper questions for me to ask, or that I must not argue or raise discussions. After failing to get a definite answer as to under whose authority the forcible feeding was done, I said it surely could not be right for him to allow such a thing in the prison over which he had jurisdiction, unless he had seen it and at least fully realised what it entailed. With apparently some reluctance, he admitted that he had witnessed it.

I asked:

And after that you sanction and approve of such a thing being done to prisoners who have committed *only nominal crimes with no criminal object and in defence of a claim which they have no recognised constitutional means to enforce?*

The last italicised part of this remark remained unheard, for the governor interrupted me with "That is not a fitting question for you to ask." Later, I was had up before him in his room and was severely reprimanded for breaking the glass of the gas-box and "inspection" glass, and for defacing the walls of my cell, but I was dismissed with a caution for glass breaking, and my punishment was reserved for the

Visiting Magistrates.

When it was evening the light was lit and the doctor and wardresses came again to feed me. I asked if I could not sit up in a chair and the doctor said "Yes." I told him that I was a small eater, that the capacity of my body was very limited and if only he would give less quantities the result might be better. I also begged that he would not press the tube so far down into my body. He treated the request with contempt, saying that anyhow my stomach must be longer than his, since I was taller than he was. This third time, though I was continually sick, the doctor pressed the tube down firmly into my body and continued to pour food in.

At last this produced a sort of shivering fit and my teeth chattered when the gag was removed; I suppose that every vestige of colour must have left my face, for the doctor seemed surprised and alarmed. He removed the tube and told the wardresses to lay me on the floor-bed and lower my head. He then came and lay over my chest and seemed very sorry for what he had done. I told him I should not faint, that I was not liable to this or any form of collapse; I did not mention the slight chronic debility of heart from which I suffered. He called in the junior medical officer, who happened to be passing at the time, to test my heart.

The junior doctor, who was in a jovial mood, stooped down and listened to my heart through the stethoscope for barely the space of a second—he could not have heard two beats—and exclaimed, "Oh, ripping, splendid heart! You can go on with her"; with that he left the cell. But the senior doctor seemed not to be reassured and he was kind to me for the first time. He tried to feed me with a spoon, but I was still able to clench my teeth and no food got down. He then pleaded with me, saying in a beseeching voice, "I do beg of you—I appeal to you, not as a prison doctor but as a man—to give over. You are a delicate woman, you are not fit for this sort of thing."

I answered, "Is anybody fit for it? And I beg of you—I appeal to you, not as a prisoner but as a woman—to give over and refuse to continue this inhuman treatment."

After I had lain quiet for some time I managed to clean the cell myself. I took out two pails to the sink, but had only strength to carry them a few yards. As I was journeying like this, getting on very slowly, a wardress told me to take only one at a time; her sympathy was moved to this extent, but no further. I took one pail back to my cell, went on with the other, and then came back for the first. When I had finished this business of washing up—which I was glad to do my-self, even if it took half the day, that it might not be given to another prisoner, and also for the better cleaning of the hideous mess—I fell on my bed and lay there till evening; they now left me both bed and bedding, which was a tremendous blessing.

I lay facing the window, which was high up, and very little light seemed to come from it. As the sun went down I saw the shadow of the wooden mouldings fall across the glass,—three crosses, and they were the shape of the three familiar crosses at the scene of Calvary, one in the centre and one on either side. It looked different from any of the pictures I had seen. The cross of Christ, the cross of the repentant thief, and the cross of the sinner who had not repented—that cross looked blacker than the others, and behind it was an immense crowd. The light from the other two crosses seemed to shine on this one, and the Christ was crucified that He might undo all the harm that was done. I saw amongst the crowd the poor little doctor and the gover-nor, and all that helped to torture these women in prison, but they were nothing compared to the men in the Cabinet who wielded their force over them. There were the upholders of vice and the men who support the thousand injustices to women, some knowingly and some unconscious of the harm and cruelty entailed. Then the room grew dark and I fell asleep.

When the doctor came again with his apparatus he had Bovril and brandy, and the tube was left for only one second in my body. The next morning, Thursday, January 20, I told him that the brandy, which at first had the effect of warming me, left me freezing cold after about two hours, and I thought it was no use. As for the Bovril, I had the strongest objection to it of a vegetarian kind, and I begged him not to give it to me again; he said he would not. It was only when I was sick that I knew what were the ingredients put down my body. That morning it was again milk and plasmon that was given me, and I was horribly sick. The doctor said to me, "You are absolutely not fit for this kind of thing. How could your union send a woman like you to do a thing of this kind? It is like sending a wisp of wind to fight against a—"

I did not hear the end of the sentence, but I think he said "a rock." I was not able to answer, but the next time he came I said to him:

Our union does not send anyone; service of this kind is abso-lutely voluntary. In my case not one of the leaders even knew of my action. I did it entirely off my own bat and only told the local organisers.

From the third feeding, when the junior doctor had felt my heart on Wednesday evening, the senior doctor had been much kinder to me; in fact I noticed a change in the way I was treated generally, so much so that I concluded my identity had been discovered or was at least suspected. I left off wearing my hair in a parting, as it was almost impossible to keep it away when I was sick. I brushed it back and did it up in a towel every time when I was fed. I left off wearing my glasses, which were too uncomfortable to be tolerated now that the necessity for them had worn off and they were forcibly feeding me quite happily. I then decided to take the utmost advantage of any privilege, in order to bring the officials to act reasonably, to check their recklessness as much as possible, and to bring them to strain the regulations so far as might be—not, as heretofore, in the direction of brutality, but in the direction of hygiene, if not of humanity.

I pleaded afresh with the doctor to try the experiment of giving me less quantity of food, of putting less of the tube into the body, of using less glycerine, which greatly irritated my throat the moment the tube touched it, or to use oil instead of glycerine. He listened to what I said, and though except as to the glycerine—he wiped the tube almost free of it, and called my attention to the fact—there was not much difference in what he did, yet his manner of doing it was different.

When I was at the sink on Thursday morning, two or three other prisoners were there, and they hastily whispered to me, "It is your friend next to you, No. 21." The kindness which beamed from all their faces did my heart good, but I could never hear or see Elsie Howey next door, and eventually I imagined that they must have mistaken me for her when I threw back my hair after the third feeding.

That day I thought I would clean my window, through which I had seen such a wonderful vision the evening before. Though the day was generally spent in loneliness, I knew that I might be visited at any hour, so I put off till about 3.30, when the ward was generally quiet for a time. All the furniture in the cell was movable, so I placed the table in front of the window and the chair on the top, then I climbed up. Through the small part of the window that opened I looked down, and in a beautiful red glow of the sinking sun I saw a sight that filled my very soul with joy. In the gloaming light—it was an exercise ground that I looked down upon—I saw walking round, all alone, a woman in her prisoner's dress, and in her arms she carried another little prisoner, a baby done up in a blanket. I was too high up to hear her, but I could see distinctly that she cooed and laughed to her little companion, and perhaps she sang to it too. I never saw maternal love more naturally displayed. The words of the chaplain came back to my mind—

The women, they're all as bad as bad can be, there's absolutely no good in them.

No good in them! and yet amongst them there was this little woman who, at least, loved her child and played with it as only a mother-heart can!

I got down and put the table and chair in their place; I felt amazed, having seen a sight as beautiful as the most beautiful picture in the world.

The wardress who came most often to my cell was kind to me. I said to her, "Oh! if you only knew what a nightmare it is, the feeding. I have never been any good at bearing pain, and each time it comes I feel as if I simply couldn't endure it."

"Oh! well," she answered, "it gets better, you'll see." She said this in a comforting voice, but the *vistas* of experience it gave of other prisoners who had gone through the process made it anything but a comfort to me. Most of them had been let out half dead before the end of their time, and I had but very little faith in the assurance that it would "get better." I asked her after the other Suffrage prisoners, but she could tell me nothing of them.

This wardress came back to my cell rather late one day and said to me hurriedly: "I am going away to the other side of the prison. Will you write to me when you get out?"

I told her that I was afraid my letters might get her into trouble, for I felt sure it would not be allowed. She said she was quite sure it would be all right, if I sent it to her name, Miss ——. I said, "Very well, then, I will."

I was filled with terror in the morning when the gas-jet was put out and in the evening when it was lighted again; within about half an hour of these changes in the light came the doctor and wardresses, the gag and all the fiendish consequences. I walked up and down my cell in a fever of fear, stopping now and then and looking up at the window, from which all good things had seemed to come. I said, "Oh,

God, help me! Oh, God, help me!"

After, I think, the sixth meal, I complained to the doctor that the processes of digestion were absolutely stagnant. I suggested to him that he should leave out one meal, with a view to allowing the natural forces of the body to readjust themselves, unhampered by the kind of paralysing cramp and arresting of the natural functions which resulted from fear. I also suggested that instead of brandy—he had given me another meal of Bovril and brandy—fruit juice or the water in which a pear or apple had been stewed should be added to my food. He did not answer me, but turned to the head assistant, whom he had already assured me was a fully-trained nurse, and in a half-insolent, half-contemptuous tone of voice, said: "Do you understand her? I don't. Does she mean that she is constipated? If so, you see about it."

Very likely I had spoken unintelligibly. I seldom had interviewed a doctor on my own behalf, and am not versed in their technical language. Whenever I spoke to this doctor it was either immediately before or after the feeding, so that my nerves were unstrung. Moreover, prisoners are made to feel in the presence of nearly every prison official that they are the scum of the earth, suspected of deceit, prejudged and found wanting; this has a paralysing effect on a prisoner's powers of expression. The chief assistant was the woman who took me daily to the weighing machine. She was kind and refined in her ways. I explained to her what I wanted, I reminded her several times about this; once I spoke again to the doctor of it, but I was never given either a drug, or, so far as I know, the fruit juice in my food.

I asked the doctor if a smaller tube could not be used for the feeding. He answered, "If I fed you through the nose it would be with a smaller tube."

I suggested that the smaller tube should be used through the mouth, if he thought that process the easiest. He said, "Well, that might be," but the tube was never changed to a smaller one.

As to my suggestion about omitting a meal, he also seemed to think it plausible, but he promised nothing, and fed me in the evening, saying that I had again lost weight, so that he could not leave me without food. Of course, this quite ignored my argument that until I began to keep down the food I could not profit by it or gain in weight.

My limbs, hands and feet, were stiff with cold at all times. I was allowed flannel underclothes and an extra blanket. In spite of continued reproof from the wardresses I kept on my nightdress in the daytime, the only under-garment with long sleeves, and I passed the night in

185

all my day-clothes. At last I was able to do this without comment from the authorities. They also, as a great favour, allowed me yet another blanket when I asked for it after some days; I then had three. I was allowed to keep the cape, usually only for out-door use, in my cell. But it was like trying to warm a stone by clothing it. Hot water was allowed in a pail once a day after the evening feeding.

Most of my friends had been fed by the doctor standing at the back of the patient, whereas this doctor adjusted the tube and fed me from the front, a process which he carried out by sitting across my knees. By this time I could not feel my legs and arms, except just by the joints where I felt the pain of the cold. At night I used to get up and walk from time to time to prevent them from becoming useless. But on Thursday night, my sixth in prison, I fell really asleep and when I awoke I had an unexpected feeling of ease and freedom from pain or fear. I was unconscious of my nearly rigid limbs, the beat of my heart was scarcely perceptible; I supposed I had only a little while to live.

The prospect of release was inexpressibly welcome. Presently I heard, as distinctly as if the wall of my cell had a mouth and had spoken, the words which Mrs. Leigh has made glorious in connection with our cause: "No surrender." They beat upon my brain with a new meaning; not only to a repressive government, not only to heedless laws and their attendant punishments, but to the temptations of our inabilities, no surrender. What was I about, to abdicate my job in this ease-loving way? I rubbed the painful life back into my feet, hands and limbs, and forced myself to walk up and down my cell. Pictures succeeded each other rapidly in my mind of our fellow-prisoners in the "Black Maria," of all undefended women, of children's blighted lives, of down-trodden men and women, undeveloped or ill! of body or mind, whose fate women, through their abject surrender of the woman's part in the world's jurisdiction, must to a certain extent have laid at their door.

How misplaced, unrighteous and unwomanly did non-resistance appear to me then. With every throb of my returning pulses I seemed to feel the rhythm of the world's soul calling to us women to un-cramp our powers from the thraldom of long disuse. My whole being responded and I yearned to hand on the message as I myself had in spirit received it—

Women, you are wanted. Women, as women, because you are women, come out in all your womanliness, and whether or not victory is for your day, at least each one of you make sure that the one course impossible to you is surrender of your share in the struggle.

To you, dear, faithful Suffragettes at heart, whatever the handcuffs of circumstance which may limit your powers of visible service, I pass on this message.

I had been told that the Visiting Magistrates were due to come to the prison on Friday (January 21), and that my offences would be judged by them. On Wednesday morning I asked if I could be allowed to go to chapel, as on Thursday, probably, I should move with difficulty and after that I would not have a chance, as they would have me put in irons for breaking the glass of my gas-jet—they had put my friends in irons for less than that. The wardress seemed to think this improbable, but she gave her consent to my going to chapel.

That morning at 10 o'clock, I was taken downstairs and put in a long row of waiting prisoners, we were close enough to be touching each other, all perfectly silent. They changed me about, putting me in a different place each time, for no apparent reason. We had waited about a quarter of an hour, when the order came to move along, and we went through several buildings to the chapel. The men, who were much the most numerous, were seated below, the women in a gallery above with a screen of wood jutting out, so that nothing could be seen by one of the other. I was shunted several times from my place, and at last was put in a row by myself.

I looked in vain for any of my companions, they were not there. The service was short and with several hymns, in which, as in Holloway, the prisoners joined heartily. Then the chaplain got up into the pulpit and preached a sermon with a great deal of energy. He told of a wreck, evidently a quite recent one, in which the lifeboat men had behaved splendidly. Many were saved, and they gave thanks to God and to the lifeboat men. Then he went on to describe how we were born, helpless and ignorant, in the world. As we thought of it, we must give thanks to God. I listened with interest, but nothing further was said. There was apparently no mother to thank, who through nine months had tended the little one in her body, and through pain, sometimes excruciating, brought it to birth. These were entirely forgotten. Was it because the women were "as bad as bad can be"?

The next day, Thursday, January 20, I asked if I could go out. The longing for more air than I could get in the cell was intense, though

187

the window of this one opened just enough to let in some air. I found that I could walk all right, although it seemed as if my legs were painful things attached to my body. The wardress told me I might go that afternoon. As I was taken out of my cell that morning to be weighed, I passed a little girl prisoner. She was not more than a child. For aught I knew she may have been taken straight from the life of the streets the night before, but she had at that moment the face of an angel, and she looked down on me from the steps that she was cleaning above with a smile which you can never see out of prison. Her whole face seemed lit up with it and it touched my very soul. I never saw her again, but I felt that all my resentment and anger were gone. In a way my physical courage was no greater than before, but at least I should go on; I knew that I should last out.

In the afternoon the wardress came to let me go out. I saw none of my companions on the way, and I was put in an exercise yard quite alone. A pain in my side had by this time grown acutely. I rested against the wall, but nothing did it any good. The sight of the grey, frosty sky and the feel of air were a delight, but I could not bear the cold nor hold myself up, and after a little while I asked to come in.

The next day, Friday, January 21, as I was being fed—the wardresses had given up holding me—the pain of the tube in my body was more than I could bear; I seized hold of it and pulled it up. The wardresses reproved me for interfering, but they did not put the tube in again; the doctor said nothing. I was overwhelmed with the horror of the process, and for the first time I was convulsed with sobs. The doctor was kind to me. I said that I only cried from having no strength to resist, but that I meant to live out my sentence if I could.

This was the day the Visiting Magistrates were due. Later in the morning they came to my cell with the governor, who said, "Have you any complaint? If only about the forcible feeding, you will have the opportunity later on in my room; don't talk of that now."

I answered, "I have complaints to make not only about being fed by force, but as to the manner in which it was done."

He said, "Your opportunity for that also will come later on."

I think it was now, in the presence of the Visiting Magistrates, that I said to the governor:

"I shall be saying several things when I am out of prison, and it seems to me more fair and square to tell you of them now while I am still in your hands, and you can refute them if you like."

He allowed me to proceed, so I went on:

188

"About the governor, I shall say that while he was shocked at the great wickedness of breaking glass as a protest against forcible feeding, he sanctioned and approved of the violence and brutality of the forcible feeding itself."

He almost smiled, and replied hastily that he had never said anything of the kind. I began to ask which part of my statement he denied—his condemnation of glass-breaking or approval of the forced feeding, but he stopped me and would not allow any further remarks on that point.

Soon afterwards, when summoned before the magistrates in the governor's room, I was allowed, in replying to the charge of glass-breaking, to which I pleaded guilty, to make my protest against the forcible feeding. I said I had been unable to ascertain on whose authority it was done; if by the order of an individual it seemed to me cruel and abominable, but if by order of the departmental authority, and in the name of law, I thought it much worse; then it was sheer barbarism, for under cover of such an order, kindly and well-meaning subordinates were made to assist, for the sake of duty, in the performance of many things which they would never tolerate under different circumstances. As a protest, I owned a feeble one, against this barbarism I had actually been guilty of defacing the walls of my cell with inscriptions and of breaking a valuable piece of glass.

The latter part of my remarks, I think, were scarcely heard, for the magistrates had begun to interrupt me. My breath gave out; I looked round at the magistrates, at the governor, at the matron. They had ordinary faces, neither kind nor unkind; they were displeased with what I said, they looked angry—that was all. Then I asked if I might now lodge my complaint against various points as to the manner in which I had been forcibly fed.

The governor replied, "No, not now. You will have another opportunity for that later on." After a lengthy and severe reprimand for my prison offences and condemnatory remarks on the subject of the behaviour of Suffragettes outside, the magistrates waived the matter of the wall inscriptions as having been already dealt with by the governor, and with regard to the broken glass they deferred judgment *sine die*.

When back in my cell, the governor presently visited me. I said I had understood I was to have an opportunity of seeing the magistrates again to lodge my further complaint against the manner of feeding. The governor said, "You will not see the magistrates again; but now is your time, I have come on purpose to hear your complaints." I had the impression, probably not uncommon to all prisoners, that the higher the authority the less likelihood would there be of an appeal to them taking effect.

Certainly there had been nothing in the manner and remarks of the Visiting Magistrates to alter this impression. I was therefore well pleased to make my complaint to the governor alone. It is no part of the prison protest to plead for merciful or even rational treatment, and though I had deliberately decided upon a different course, I was haunted by the fear of breaking our policy and proving disloyal to my comrades then in prison. The matron was present, as always when the governor visits prisoners in their cells, and he allowed me to remain on my bed. For the first time he listened to all I had to say without attempting to interrupt me, or to curtail or change the drift of my remarks.

I reported to him having been forcibly fed without my heart having been tested or the doctor even feeling my pulse? I said I mentioned this in no spirit of personal complaint, for, though suffering from slight chronic heart disease, my heart happened to have great resisting and recuperative power; but I didn't suppose it was possible to diagnose this fact merely from looking at me, and that on general medical grounds, as a matter of principle, I thought the heart ought most carefully to be tested before any prisoner who had been on hunger-strike was forcibly fed, since both these processes were theoretically believed to tax the heart.

I said:

There is another thing which I think I had better mention. After the first time of feeding me, the doctor seemed very irritated and, before leaving, he slapped me on the cheek; he did not hurt me, but seemed to wish to show his contempt; about this, too, I do not wish to complain as of an insult to me personally. He no doubt was irritated by his repulsive job, but this is hardly the right mood for an official, and what he could do to one woman he might possibly do to another. I think such things should not be done. I asked him the next morning, unless he thought it part of his duty, not to do such a thing again, and he never has.

I made further complaints about too much food at a time being poured in through the tube, and about the one occasion when the tube was left in for some considerable time and the feeding repeated again and again, in spite of my continuous vomiting. I did not, however, complain of these things in any detail to the governor, since they seemed to be matters chiefly suitable for the medical officer. I think I added, as I certainly did on one occasion to the doctor himself, what a mercy it was that at least the doctor was skilled in adjusting the tube into the throat. The governor made no reply but listened to all I said.

It was on the afternoon of this day, Friday, that the door of my cell was suddenly thrown open, and the man who stood outside was announced to me as the government inspector. I asked, had he come from London? "Yes."

He inquired in a hurried way, as if he had a train to catch, had I any complaint? "Yes," I replied, "first of all about being fed by force."

He said, in a hurried and insolent manner, all in one breath, so that it was scarcely intelligible, "Are you refusing to take your food—If so, the remedy is in your hands, you have no reason to complain—Any further complaints?"

I hesitated for a moment, then, as it seemed to me my complaints against the doctor would certainly in this man's estimation come under the head of grievances easily remediable by the surrender of the hunger-strike, I answered, "No, I suppose not," upon which he abruptly left me.

On this day, Friday, the governor before he left me had suggested that under certain conditions he would allow me to write a letter. "For instance," he said, "if you had a mother you were anxious about, perhaps I could give you leave to write to her." I had so arranged matters before being arrested that I knew my people, if they had traced me, would conclude that by this time my hunger-strike had been superseded by forcible feeding; that those most dear to me had implicit faith in the reasonableness of all officials, that if at any moment they chose to take advantages of the privileges available to them, they could hear all about me; and, finally, that if they were anxious to the point of disregard for those of my principles which they did not share, they could pay my fine; but hastily on these reflections there followed the panic fear that it was my mother who was ill, and the governor was breaking the news to me. He, however, reassured me on this point and he left me.

The permission reeled in my brain. My mother would by this time certainly suspect something. If I could write to her and yet not let her know where I was! The prison paper would alone make this impossible. I thought about it all night. The next day, Saturday, January 22, I determined to eat my breakfast so that I might be in a fit state to write, otherwise my hands trembled and I could not steady my mind to a letter. I told the wardress very early that morning that I would eat my breakfast, and that I should like someone to witness it. The little woman, whom the doctor had told me was a nurse, brought me in a cup of milk and a piece of white bread and butter. It was the most delicious food I have ever tasted; the "nurse" was very kind to me and stayed till I had finished.

Then I wrote my letter; it was only on the slate, of course; I must ask the governor's leave before I was allowed writing-paper. I asked to see the governor, by letter written on another slate. I said that, if it were the same to him, might I go to his room to see him, as there I could stand near the hot pipes, which was a great luxury. He came to my cell, and I told him I would gladly avail myself of the privilege to write to my mother, provided he would grant the same privilege to my fellow Suffrage prisoners. I assumed, too, that he had done the same in the case of Elsie Howey as in mine, omitted to punish her for glass-breaking—I believed, from the sound, that someone besides myself had broken glass—and I reminded him of a remark he had made as to the law being no respecter of persons.

By this time I had an almost certain conviction that he knew who I was. But he would not give me any assurance as to like favours being granted to other prisoners, so I refused to avail myself of the letter-writing privilege. In the afternoon, however, I had decided that I could convey news to my mother without revealing my identity to the officials, supposing that they were not yet fully aware of the truth, and that I had better use every available privilege offered, since I was in the dark as to the grounds on which it was made. I determined to write to the nurse of my sister's children, who lived in Bloomsbury Square, telling her to forward my letter at once to my mother. I asked to see the governor again, but he had left. I was taken before the matron, who told me the privilege would anyhow be conditional, dependent upon to whom my letter was addressed and the urgency of the motive for writing it. I said there was no extreme urgency; she answered I must await the governor's return on Monday morning.

I wrote in my letter on the slate that the forcible feeding was "only pain," and that my mother would think that good for me. I made no other complaint, but said the short sentence would soon let me be with her. My only object was to conceal all that I endured. In the evening I was again fed by force.

On Sunday morning, January 23, the cold was intense. I asked for some hearthstone to polish my tins—they had taken everything of the kind away and the tins were dull and spotted. I hoped to keep some sense of life in my hands and arms by trying to scrub with them. But it did not come. Presently the door opened and the governor appeared; I could not think why he came so early. Then I saw the doctor behind him, and the thought of the forcible feeding blocked my mind. I supposed the governor had come to see it. He was nervous about startling me, I suppose, for he told me the great news twice before I understood. He told me of my release and that my youngest sister, Emily Lutyens, had come to fetch me away. I felt stunned with the quite unexpected shock of joy, it was too good to be true. After ascertaining that my fine had not been paid, but that I had been released on medical grounds, and that it had nothing to do with my mother's health, the chief aim for which I tried to pull myself together was to obtain what news I could of my fellow-prisoners. The governor and doctor, however, left me without giving me any information.

Again I was brought white bread and butter and milk for my breakfast, and the "nurse" stayed with me while I ate it. They brought me my clothes, but the more I realised the news the slower my movements became; all strength seemed to have ebbed from my body. The wardresses knew nothing of the other Suffragette prisoners, whether they were released or not. When dressed I was taken out far away to what was called "the governor's room," but it was not the same one that I had seen before. The doctor came and talked to me, then after a little while my sister came. We greeted each other, of course, by a tremendously warm embrace. The doctor looked away like a witness in a melodrama. I sat there as in a dream talking to him and to the governor, who presently came in.

The doctor said, "I have been kind to you?"

"Latterly you were," I answered, "if you had not fed me. At first you were angry and not kind."

I told the governor that the one thing I wanted to know about was the other Suffragette prisoners, were they fed—were they released? He answered that they were not released, that one of them was in hospital, that they were all quite well. I said that was a curious answer; if they were all quite well, why was one in hospital? He said that he could tell me nothing more. The doctor said they were none of them as bad as I was over the feeding. That was all that I could get from them about the other prisoners. I did not go over again with them the points about which I had protested, while still a prisoner, as to my own treatment. The governor and doctor were courteous to me after my release and to my sister, and the governor's wife had been very kind to her on her arrival in the early morning.

Why we waited I do not know, but in about half an hour we drove away in a four-wheeler. The chaplain was just coming in to the prison as we drove out through the gates; he bowed to me. I went to the station first and got my trunk, or rather my sister got it for me, then we went to the hotel.

We telephoned to Dr. Kerr that I was released and going with my sister to London. She sent her young daughter and man-servant to see us at the hotel, and we left word with them for Miss Flatman, who was not on the telephone and whose Sunday address we did not know.

I had a long bath, which was a tremendous luxury, although my legs were so thin I could not sit down without pain. My dear sister stayed with me the whole time; my voice shook and I could not speak properly. We had a meal before we left.

CHAPTER 14: THE HOME OFFICE

We got into the train for London and I had a long sleep. During the last part of the journey my sister, Emily Lutyens, told how she had heard of me in Walton Gaol. She had a telephone message forwarded to her on Saturday night, January 15, from the Press Association. It was addressed to my eldest brother, who was abroad, saying it was rumoured that I was imprisoned in Liverpool—was it true? She rang up our friend, Mr. Arthur Chapman, who after an infinity of trouble got into communication with Mr. Thompson, one of the Prison Commissioners from the Home Office. In answering the telephone, he welcomed Mr. Chapman gleefully, as having news they had wanted much, he said:

There is a prisoner at Walton Gaol, Liverpool whom they have for some days suspected of being other than her declaration. We have wanted to release her, but have not been able to find out who her people were.

This was a most extraordinary thing for a Home Office official to say. Why had they not released me to the W.S.P.U. organiser in Liverpool, or asked me with whom they should communicate? And why were they more anxious to set me free than the other Suffragettes? They had signed an order for my release. The reason given was loss of weight; they did not mention my heart, since they knew nothing about it! Mr. Thompson recommended that my sister should telephone to the doctor at Walton and he would arrange with the governor to release me. With this news Mr. Chapman went to my sister Emily, who was dining out. They rang up Dr. Price, of Walton, and after communicating with him my sister felt almost sure the prisoner was myself.

Without a moment's hesitation, and dressed just as she was, she caught the midnight train to Liverpool, where she arrived at about six in the morning. She reached the doctor's house at about seven and still was uncertain whether she would find me in the prison. Dr. Price, after some talk, took her to the governor's house. The governor's wife was very kind at that early hour and gave her breakfast. She said she thought it was inhuman to dress the prisoners in such frightfully ugly clothes, she felt only horror when she looked at them; she would have different clothing for them if she had anything to do with it.

Dr. Price told my sister that he had written the report of me to the Home Office. "I said she was spare, very spare, and that she had a nose—I did not say aquiline, but of a somewhat Wellingtonian bend." We roared with laughter at this description of me.

The following is my sister's statement of a conversation which she had with the doctor on arriving at Walton:

After a preliminary conversation with Dr. Price in regard to what had taken place in connection with our telephonic communication with him the previous night, I asked him whether he could tell me anything with regard to my sister's behaviour in gaol and the treatment she had been obliged to undergo. In reply, he stated that she had fasted for four days, that he had begged her to take her food, and explained that if she refused he would be obliged to forcibly feed her. As she had persisted in her refusal, he had been obliged to feed her through the mouth up to the date of her release, with the exception of one meal, which she took of her own accord on Saturday morning.

He further stated that, unlike some other Suffragettes, she had shown no violence beyond refusing to take her food, but that, in all his experience, he had never seen such a bad case of forcible feeding. I asked him what he meant by a 'bad case,' and he said '*She was practically asphyxiated every time.*' I then told him that the medical officers at Holloway and Newcastle reported to us that my sister was suffering from serious valvular disease of the heart, and I asked him if his examination had led him to the same conclusion.

He replied 'Certainly not. My subordinate (or some such word), who is a very clever doctor, thoroughly examined her heart and found no trace of disease whatever,' and I need hardly say that this was a great relief to my mind, as the reports of the other prison doctors had caused us so much anxiety. He further stated that, in spite of the forcible feeding, my sister had lost weight at the rate of 2lbs. a day, and that, consequently, he had been obliged to advise her being released.

Dr. Price several times repeated how much my sister had suffered from the treatment, and, after I had told him about her heart, said that it might possibly have been due to her heart condition, though he had not been able to detect it.

My sister took me to their house in Bloomsbury Square, which we reached at about 8.30 p.m. There was our friend, Mr. Chapman, to whom I gave a brief account of my imprisonment. He went off with it the next day to the Home Office Prison Department, and returned with the news that the officials would be grateful to me if I would make a statement on paper, whereupon they would have it investigated. There were reasons why they would be very glad to have an open inquiry at Walton Gaol.

All that night I woke off and on with cold, and also with terror at the forcible feeding. My sister was most kind to me; she reheated my hot-bottles and at last came and slept with me. I stayed in bed the next morning (Monday, January 24). In the afternoon I saw some of my friends—Mrs. Pethick Lawrence and Christabel Pankhurst. Some days after, when she returned to London, I saw Mrs. Pankhurst. They were all of them content with what I had done and the way I had done it. This was a most tremendous joy and relief to me.

I managed to write a letter to the *Times* and an article for *Votes for Women*. I could only do everything so slowly that I had not finished these until eight o'clock the next morning, after writing all night. I stayed in bed the whole of that day, Tuesday. On Wednesday and Thursday (26th and 27th) I stayed in bed in the morning, but led a more or less normal life after. These days I could hardly sit in a chair, because my emaciated condition rendered it very painful; I ate my meals, very often, kneeling down at the table on a cushion.

On Tuesday, January 25, 1 wrote to Mr. Gladstone, the Home Secretary, to explain that it was not as the newspapers said, to play a practical joke upon him, that I had gone to prison in disguise. It was because of the totally different category of treatment meted out to one set of people from another, and the object of my disguise was to expose this for the sake of bringing such a state of things to an end.

On Monday, January 31, I woke with a blistered heel. I spoke at the meeting at the Queen's Hall, and it was heart-filling to meet all my friends again; the whole audience seemed to understand. I stood for an hour on one foot. On coming home I had to wait about to get a statement finished and typewritten. I had written very carefully for the Home Office of what happened to me in prison. After that I went to bed and stopped there for six weeks. The next day, Tuesday, February 1, the blister on my heel was much worse and my sister wished to send for a doctor. I had always been ill in the country and did not know of one. My sister called in Dr. Marion Vaughan, who from that moment was my doctor, and after she had been to see me I had a nurse. This is her report:—

REPORT OF PHYSICAL CONDITION OF LADY CONSTANCE LYTTON.
Tuesday, February 1, 1910.

21, Thurloe Square, S.W.
February 4, 1910.

I was called in to see Lady Constance Lytton, staying at 29, Bloomsbury Square, W.C., on account of pain, swelling and reddening of right leg and heel; with enlarged tender glands behind the knee, associated with an inflamed blister on the heel. There was cellulitis of the right leg, extending to the knee. Both legs were considerably swollen (evidently due to failing heart), though the patient and her sister. Lady Emily Lutyens, said this was much less marked than on the previous day. The patient's look of extreme illness, malnutrition, and bad colour led me to examine her heart carefully.

This I found to be in a serious condition, considerably larger than normal, with its apex beat in 6th intercostal space, 1½ inches beyond the nipple line; extremely irregular in force and frequency, a marked difference between heart and pulse rate, due to feeble transmission to terminal vessels. The heart sounds were 'trembling' in character. The pulse then (February 1, 1910, at 10.30 a.m.) and now is slow, small in volume and irregular; its rate varying from 48 to 52 per minute. (There is perfectly clear evidence of mitral disease of the heart, with praesystolic murmur.) The most superficial examination of the heart cannot fail to reveal the grave risk to health and life to which the patient was exposed during the forcible methods of feeding recently adopted in Walton Gaol.

> Report by Dr. Marion Hunter (Mrs. Vaughan),
> Plague Medical Officer to Government of India,
>> 1897—1898;
> Plague Medical Officer to British Government
>> in Egypt, 1899;
> Assistant Medical Officer to London County
>> Council (Education) 4½ years.

★★★★★★

The shoes in Walton Gaol were exceptionally stiff, even, as it seemed to me, for prison footwear. They hurt my feet badly and made the heel of my right foot very sore. As I have told, after I broke my gas-jet, the shoes were changed to comfortable slippers, but I think this accounted for the blister after my release, when my foot came to life again.

★★★★★★

On Monday, January 31, Mr. Arthur Chapman wrote to Mr. Gladstone, enclosing the statement which I had made, and begging for an interview, in which he could explain matters to the full; this was refused. On February 4 Mr. Chapman wrote again, appealing for a full and impartial investigation. The following letter was received:—

Please quote 187,986/10,
> and address to the Under-Secretary of State,
> Home Office, London, S.W.

>> Home Office, Whitehall,
>> 9th February, 1910.

Sir,—With reference to your letter of the 31st *ultimo*, forwarding statement made by Lady Constance Lytton, as to her treatment in H.M. Prison, Liverpool, and your further letter of the 4th inst., I am directed by the Secretary of State to say that he has caused careful and detailed inquiry to be made by the Prison Commissioners into the truth of the charges brought by Lady Constance Lytton against the officers of the prison, and as the result of that inquiry he is satisfied that those charges are without foundation and that there is no justification for Lady Constance Lytton's account of her experience while she was in the prison.

The Secretary of State cannot discuss her statements in detail. A single instance must suffice. Lady Constance, with a view to showing that her treatment as 'Jane Warton' differed from her treatment when her identity was known, asserts that, whereas she was thoroughly examined at Holloway and Newcastle Prisons and was found to be suffering from heart disease, no attempt was made to examine her at Liverpool before she was forcibly fed. On reception at Liverpool Prison on the 15th *ultimo*, Lady Constance refused to allow herself to be examined and told the deputy medical officer, who was on duty, that she was quite well. He asked her a second time to allow him to examine her and she again refused.

His evidence on this point is corroborated by that of the wardress who was present, and the matter is placed beyond doubt by the entry 'refused examination' which was made at the time in the medical reception register at the prison. Before artificially feeding her for the first time, the senior medical officer applied his ear to the chest wall and satisfied himself that the condition of her heart was such that the operation of artificial feeding could, in the absence of active resistance by the patient, be performed without any immediate risk of injury to her health. In this connection you will observe that the diagnosis of the medical officers at Holloway and Newcastle, arrived at after thorough examination, is fully confirmed by the report of Lady Constance Lytton's own medical attendant, which you have been good enough to forward.

'Jane Warton's' foolish conduct in refusing to allow herself to be examined and the deception which deprived the medical officers of all knowledge of the medical history of her case, must be held responsible for the fact that the true condition of her heart remained undiscovered while she was in Liverpool Prison. When it was found that the injury to her health caused by her persistent refusal to take food could not be prevented by artificial feeding, her discharge was recommended by the medical officer and was authorised by the Secretary of State, and this was done before anyone at the Home Office or at the prison was aware of her identity. The statement that the medical officer was guilty of slapping his patient's face is utterly devoid of truth, and can only be the outcome of the imagination.

In these circumstances the Secretary of State does not consider that any further inquiry as to the truth of the statements made and published by Lady Constance Lytton is called for, and he must therefore decline to accede to your request for further investigation.

I am, sir,

Your obedient servant,

(Signed)   Edward Troup.

Arthur W. Chapman, Esq.,
33, Whitehall Court, S.W.

In this letter it seems to be thought that it does not matter mis-stating things, provided the misstatement is a small one, then the small things can be added together. Even supposing everything to be true in this letter, no mention is made of calling in the other doctor five days before I was released, on purpose to test my heart. He did so with a stethoscope on the heart itself, though anything but carefully, and pronounced it quite sound.

Eighteen days after my release I called in Dr. Anders Ryman, of 4, Wetherby Place, to give me Swedish treatment. He found that my heart had regained its normal size, but he thought my condition too critical for any but the very mildest form of treatment; insisted on my being kept entirely in bed, absolutely quiet, and forbade all visitors or letters being brought to me. He would not let me be moved to the country for another four weeks, and, even after that, urged me to exert myself as little as possible and only walk upstairs backwards. He seemed to be alarmed at the great fluctuations between the heart beat when still and when I moved or spoke.

During my imprisonment, the side of the jaw on which the gag was used became painful and the whole mouth very sensitive, but five or six days after release all swelling had subsided and pain was only occasional and mild. About ten days after my release, the crown of my artificial tooth broke away entirely. Owing to this and to sensitive-ness in the upper tooth affected, I did not use that side of my mouth in eating, but I was unable to leave my bed to visit the dentist. Some time after I was up the doctors urged upon me that I was still unfit to undergo dental treatment. I went in March, but my dentist thought

I could not undergo any but a temporary treatment of the harmfully exposed surfaces. It was not till April that full treatment was finally given; that is why the date of the report made by the dentist is so long after the release from prison:—

10, Park Crescent,
Portland Place, W.,
April 14, 1910.

LADY CONSTANCE LYTTON.

In order to restore the masticatory efficiency of the left side of the lower jaw, a bridge consisting of one gold crown and two porcelain crowns was constructed. This was attached in May, 1896, and has continued in satisfactory condition until the application of a gag, recently employed in forcible feeding, cracked and broke away the face of the crown of the bicuspid on the lower jaw, also breaking the enamel of the upper natural tooth.

Sufficient force having been employed to occasion this damage, it was feared that the root of the tooth which forms the front anchorage of the bridge was split, but this is not the case, and the inflammatory symptoms have now subsided.

H. Uren Olver.

On February 3 came the news that Selina Martin and Elsie Howey were released from Walton Gaol. I was by this time in bed and received no news and no letters; when the information was brought to me, I felt quite overwhelmed with joy. This release was more than three weeks before their sentence had expired.

By the time the last letter had been received from the Home Office, February 9, my eldest brother had returned from abroad, and he took up the case. All his attempts to have a public inquiry failed. Mr. Gladstone was relieved of the Home Office preparatory to taking up the work of High Commissioner in South Africa, and my brother pleaded in vain with everyone that had to do with the matter. In the meantime, the W.S.P.U. was asked not to take up my case in any way for fear that the authorities would thereupon refuse to listen, and a letter from Sir Edward Troup to the *Times*, in which he said there was no foundation for the declarations against the officials, remained unanswered.

On March 30, my brother had the following letter in the *Times*:—

Sir,—On February 10 a letter was sent to the Press by Sir Edward Troup, relative to a statement made by my sister, Lady Constance Lytton, regarding her treatment in Liverpool Prison, in which he declared on behalf of the Home Secretary that there was no foundation for any of the charges which she had made. I am anxious to explain why this official imputation of untruthfulness has hitherto remained unanswered.

Lady Constance was seriously ill at the time as the result of her prison experiences, and unable to defend herself. I therefore undertook the task of vindicating her veracity. Before making any public statement on her behalf I was anxious to find out what steps had been taken by the Home Office to investigate the matters referred to in her statement, and I hoped by a friendly intervention to secure a full and impartial inquiry into all the circumstances of her treatment by the prison officials.

I have had several communications with the Home Office on the subject, and owing to the retirement of Mr. Gladstone and the appointment of a new Home Secretary, they have necessarily been protracted over a considerable period. My attitude throughout has been entirely conciliatory, and the only claim which I have made was that in the interests of justice, charges of this nature should be submitted to a full and impartial inquiry which would, of course, involve a separate examination of both the parties concerned. This claim has been refused by the Home Office on the grounds that the prison officials have been closely interrogated, and that as they deny entirely every one of the charges made, 'no useful purpose would be served' by granting my request.

In the absence of such an inquiry as I asked for, the matter must be left to the opinion of unbiased minds. I desire, however, to say that nothing which I have been able to learn has in any way shaken my belief in the substantial accuracy of my sister's account. The idea that her charges can be disposed of by the bare denial of the persons against whom they are made, is not likely to commend itself to anyone outside the Home Office, and no amount of denial can get over the following facts:—

1. Lady Constance Lytton, when imprisoned in Newcastle, after refusing to answer the medical questions put to her and adopting the hunger-strike, received a careful and thorough medical examination, which disclosed symptoms of 'serious heart dis-

ease,' and on these grounds she was released as unfit to submit to forcible feeding.

2. Three months later 'Jane Warton,' when imprisoned at Liverpool, also refused to answer medical questions or to take prison food. On this occasion she was entered in the prison books as having refused medical examination, and was forcibly fed eight times. Such medical examination as took place during the forcible feeding failed, according to the medical officer's report, to disclose any symptoms of heart disease, and she was eventually released on the grounds of loss of weight and general physical weakness.

These facts are incontrovertible, and though the Home Office is quite satisfied that in both cases the prison officials performed their duty in the most exemplary fashion, your readers will form their own opinions of the justice of a Government Department which brings accusations of untruthfulness against an individual whilst refusing the only means by which the truth can be established.

I am, your obedient servant,

Lytton.

My brother did not give up his efforts till in April Mr. Winston Churchill, the new Home Secretary, who was well known to him, came to stay at Knebworth, his country place. Mr. Churchill read through the whole case, until he came to the report of the letter to my mother written on the slate. "'Twould be hopeless," he said, "to bring forward any complaint with this letter in the background."

I don't know, of course, what they had made of it, as it had been rubbed out long ago, but I know that I had not told my mother anything of the treatment. I had said that the forcible feeding was "only pain"—so it was.

In the autumn of this year, 1910, I had a slight heart-seizure. I got out of bed in the morning, and was taken with paralysis down one side. I could not move for about an hour, when I managed to crawl back to bed. I had a nurse for six weeks and then it was over.

CHAPTER 15: THE CONCILIATION BILL

On June 12, 1910, I received a letter from Mrs. Pethick Lawrence, in which she told me that I had been made a paid organizer to the union, at £2 a week, and that the committee wished to make this appointment retrospective for the past six months from January, 1910. I felt very much honoured and pleased. It enabled me to take a small flat in London near the Euston Road, so that I was not far from the office at Clement's Lin and close, too, to a good many railway stations. It was quicker for me than having to go home to the country when I was on speaking tours, and also far more convenient for the London work.

In February, 1910, a truce was called after the elections. Mr. Gladstone, made Lord Gladstone, went to South Africa as Governor-General, and he was succeeded by Mr. Winston Churchill at the Home Office. Mr. Brailsford had spent much time and effort negotiating between all the Suffrage parties in the House of Commons, and he as secretary, and my brother. Lord Lytton, as president, negotiated a committee for the "Conciliation Bill." This is the bill in full:—

THE CONCILIATION BILL FOR WOMAN SUFFRAGE.

A Bill to confer the Parliamentary Franchise on Women.

1. Every woman possessed of a household qualification within the meaning of the Representation of the People Act (1884) shall be entitled to be registered as a voter, and when registered to vote for the county or borough in which the qualifying premises are situated.

2. For the purposes of this act a woman shall not be disqualified by marriage from being registered as a voter, provided that a husband and wife shall not both be registered as voters in the same Parliamentary borough or county division.

That is the bill which was slightly modified in 1911, so as to remove any reasonable fear of plural or faggot voting. It looked as if the Concliation Bill had everything in its favour and that it would pass. Ninety city, town and county councils, and thirty district councils petitioned or passed resolutions that the bill should become law. These included the city councils of Birmingham, Bradford, Cardiff, Dublin, Edinburgh, Glasgow, Leeds, Liverpool, Manchester, Newcastle, Nottingham, Sheffield. In 1910 the bill was carried on second reading by a majority of 110. In 1911 it was again read a second time and secured a majority of 167. Among those who voted for it were Mr. Birrell, Mr. John Burns, Sir Edward Grey, Mr. Runciman; Mr. Balfour, Mr. Bonar Law, Mr. Lyttelton, Mr. Wyndham; Mr. Barnes, Mr. Keir Hardie, Mr. Ramsay Macdonald, Mr. Snowden; Mr. Devlin, Mr. Healy, Mr. Swift MacNeill, Mr. W. Redmond. All parties made friends over it.

On Friday, November 18, 1910, Mr. Asquith made a statement in the House of Commons omitting all reference to Woman Suffrage, but announcing the Dissolution for Monday, November 28. On learning that Mr. Asquith had definitely decided to shelve the Conciliation Bill, it was determined to send a deputation to him forthwith. At the head were Mrs. Pankhurst, the founder of the W.S.P.U. and Mrs. Garatt Anderson, twice Mayor of Aldeburgh, who is one of the pioneer women doctors and sister of Mrs. Fawcett. Among other well-known women were Mrs. Hertha Ayrton, the distinguished scientist, Mrs. Cobden Sanderson, Mrs. Saul Solomon, Mrs. Brackenbury, widow of General Brackenbury, over seventy years of age, Miss Neligan, who is seventy-eight years of age, the Hon. Mrs. Haverfield, and the Princess Sophia Dhuleep Singh.

The deputation was composed of 300 women, but was divided into detachments of twelve each. They were not received and were treated worse than any since the conflict between women and the government began. The orders of the Home Secretary were, it appears, that the police were to be present, both in uniform and in plain clothes among the crowd, and that the women were to be thrown from one to the other. The police were guilty both of torture and of indecency. The women were accused of violence and mendacity. Reports were afterwards made by Lord Robert Cecil, K.C., and Mr. Ellis J. Griffith, K.C., M.P., on the women whom they had examined. Lord Robert Cecil writes in his letter to the *Times*:—

All that can be said at present is that the women strenuously deny that they were guilty of any such violence. If they were, it is at least curious that they were not immediately arrested, and that, as I understand, no evidence of any serious assault was offered against any of those who were ultimately brought before the court. . . .

Mr. Churchill accuses them of mendacity. Such an accusation requires more than the *ipse dixit* of a minister to support it. Nor is it in accordance with the principles of British justice to reject without investigation the evidence of scores of apparently respectable women.

In conclusion, may I ask whether anyone thinks that if the deputation had consisted of unarmed men of the same character, their demand for an inquiry would have been refused? Who can doubt that the Home Secretary and the other ministers would have tumbled over, one another in their eagerness to grant anything that was asked? Are we then to take it as officially admitted that in this country there is one law for male electors and another for voteless women?

Yours obediently,

Robert Cecil.

Mr. Ellis Griffith wrote at the end of his letter to the *Times*:—

It is certainly difficult, under the circumstances, to bring responsibility home to individuals, but I am amply satisfied that there was unnecessary and excessive violence used against the women who took part in the deputation, and that they were assaulted in a way that cannot be justified.

Under these circumstances, I strongly support a searching and impartial inquiry. . . .

Yours faithfully,

Ellis J. Griffith.

The Home Secretary refused all idea of a public inquiry.

The morning after the deputation, Saturday, November 19, 1910, those who had been arrested the night before were all dismissed; it was thought bad election tactics to be responsible for the imprisonment of women of good reputation who were merely fighting for their freedom.

Mr. Asquith on Friday, November 18, promised that he would make a statement about the Women's Bill on the following Tuesday. On Tuesday, November 22, accordingly, it was made:

The government will, if they are still in power, give facilities in the next Parliament for effectively proceeding with a bill which is so framed as to admit of free amendment.

The statement fulfilled none of the conditions which had been made by the W.S.P.U. We held that the pledge must be to give full facilities for a Woman Suffrage Bill next Session—next Parliament was a mockery of a pledge. The bill in question must be no more extended in scope than the bill introduced by Mr. Shackle on or the Women's Enfranchisement Bill introduced two years ago by Mr. Stanger. A pledge to give facilities to a bill on a so-called democratic basis would be worthless, it would not have a chance of passing through either House of Parliament.

The House rose immediately when Mr. Asquith had made his

statements. The women waited this pronouncement in the Caxton Hall, and on receipt of it marched to Downing Street, Mrs. Pankhurst at their head, to see Mr. Asquith. Here the detachment of police at first was small and the line was broken by the onrush of the women. But reinforcements of police rapidly arrived and a severe struggle ensued. Many women were hurt who were thrown about the street or crushed, and there were 150 to 160 charged at the police court the next day. In the evening parties of women visited the houses of the Cabinet and threw stones, breaking some of their windows. Mr. Muskett, who prosecuted the next day, withdrew all the cases of "simple obstruction," and only allowed the cases of "stone-throwing and assault." From the day of "Black Friday," as November 18, 1910, was called, stone-throwing became easy to the women—it ensured arrest instead of being assaulted and injured.

This was the eve of the election. The policy of the W.S.P.U. was to oppose all Liberal candidates unless they could get a definite pledge from the prime minister that, if in power, he would allow the Conciliation Bill to be taken through all its stages next Session. The Liberals were returned, still commanding a Parliamentary majority in the House of Commons, and the House of Commons contained an even larger majority of members prepared to vote for a practicable scheme of Woman Suffrage, on the lines of the Conciliation Bill. In May, 1911, this bill was brought in by Sir Alfred Mond; it triumphantly passed the second reading by a majority of 167.

In June Lord Lytton had written to Mr. Asquith asking for assurances (1) that the facilities offered for next session were intended as an effective opportunity for carrying the bill, and not merely for academic discussion; (2) that the week offered would not be construed rigidly, and also that provided the committee stage were got through in the time, additional days for report and third reading would be forthcoming; and (3) that there would be reasonable opportunities for making use of the closure. To this Mr. Asquith replied (on Friday, June 16, 1911):—

My dear Lytton,—In reply to your letter on the subject of facilities for the Women's Enfranchisement Bill, I would refer you to some observations recently made in a speech at the National Liberal Club by Sir Edward Grey, which accurately express the intentions of the government.

It follows (to answer your specific inquiries) that 'the week' offered will be interpreted with reasonable elasticity, that the government will interpose no obstacle to a proper use of the closure, and that if (as you suggest) the bill gets through committee in the time proposed, the extra days required for report and third reading would not be refused.

The government, though divided in opinion on the merits of the bill, are unanimous in their determination to give effect not only in the letter but in the spirit to the promise in regard to facilities which I made on their behalf before the last General Election.

Yours, etc.,

H. H. Asquith.

This letter was further certified in August :—

My dear Lytton,—I have no hesitation in saying that the promises made by, and on behalf of, the government, in regard to giving facilities for the 'Conciliation Bill,' will be strictly adhered to, both in letter and spirit.

Yours sincerely,

H. H. Asquith.

August 23, 1911.

This promise, after the phenomenal majority in the House of Commons, was a solemn pledge made by Mr. Asquith to be fulfilled in the next year. It was a pledge which the friends of women took absolutely in good faith. On the strength of it, the truce was prolonged in 1911 with belief in the guarantee for the following year.

On November 7, 1911, Mr. Asquith announced to a deputation of the People's Suffrage Federation that he was going to bring in a Manhood Suffrage Bill next Session. There was no agitation or demand for more votes for men; this was in answer to the widespread demand of votes for women. The majority already recorded for Woman Suffrage in the House of Commons was composed of members of all political parties. The government's present policy destroyed this composite majority by alienating Unionists and moderate Liberals. In other words, it rendered impossible the non-party solution of the Woman Suffrage question, towards which we had been working for months. We consented to the Conciliation Bill because it gave virtual equality to women with men, and because it made inevitable the equality of the sexes under any subsequent franchise measure. But we absolutely refused to accept the Conciliation Bill as the accompaniment of Manhood Suffrage Bill.

We and many other of the Suffrage Societies were received in deputation by Mr. Asquith, only to be told the case over again. He had not changed his opinion since 1908. The Manhood Suffrage Bill would make no difference to us, who could bring in an amendment!

The leaders of the W.S.P.U. determined to go on a deputation to the House of Commons on Tuesday, November 21, with Mrs. Pethick Lawrence to lead them. I intended to accompany them as a stone thrower; the police on Black Friday (1910) had made the other way—that of going on a deputation—impossible for me, unless I were to see death, and this seemed useless. It was an understood thing that this time, if we were imprisoned, we should not hunger-strike.

Chapter 16: Holloway Revisited: My Fourth Imprisonment

I determined that I would do my work alone. I was afraid that, if I combined with others, I might fail them, through illness, when they counted on me. Some days later Miss Lawless said she would come too, and, as she kindly chose to do the job with me, all was well. I selected a post office window in Victoria Street, on the left-hand side, facing Westminster. I went to buy some stamps there the day before to make sure of my bearings. I studied all the windows where it would be safe, and where not safe, to do the work of smashing without hurting anyone inside.

A friend, Mrs. MacLeod, came to see me the evening before, November 20, 1911. She brought me flowers, lovely lilies-of-the-valley and two bunches of violets. She told me she had bought them in Piccadilly from a girl that was sitting round the fountain. "They are for a friend of mine who is going to fight for the women tomorrow"; she wasn't sure she had said it in a way the girl could understand. "Oh! May God bless her, God bless them all! Here, lady, take this extra bunch of violets for her." She called this out enthusiastically, as she collected the flowers.

This time I had a small hammer as well as three stones wrapped in paper. The hammer, of course, was the safest as well as the most efficient of my tools, but one had to be quite near to the window in order to use it. Another dear friend, Dr. Alice Ker, came to me from Liverpool on the day, Tuesday, November 21. She was coming to the fray in Westminster, but she did not wish to get arrested. Towards six o'clock we took a taxi and went together to the beginning of Victoria

Street. Then we got out and each went our own way. I walked up and down the street, first along one side, then along the other, and I inspected the side parallel streets. Victoria Street I had always supposed was rather a long one, but on this occasion it was infinitely short, and I seemed to pass the same people over and over again.

Once I jumped into a 'bus to go up again towards Westminster, and there I came across many of my friends, who doubtless were going to the preliminary meeting at Caxton Hall. At last when standing, as it seemed to me, for the fiftieth time in front of a door with pillars, which was our trysting place, I met Miss Lawless and soon after Miss Douglas Smith, who had said she would join us for a little, as she had to go to all who were "active" in Victoria Street. We turned into a "Lyons" for some tea, the whole place was full of our friends and a detective or two. A cat was there; she came to lie on my lap and I had to turn her off when we left.

The time was getting near; we were to wait until the clock struck 8; we were none of us to move before and not much later. At last there was a noise of many people coming round the corner of a street; it was Mrs. Pethick Lawrence walking at the head of her deputation, A large crowd surrounded them and cheered them on their way to Westminster. Miss Lawless and I had taken up our position already on the steps leading to the post office we had selected. As soon as the deputation had passed, the clock of Big Ben began striking eight. I said, "I can wait no longer," and I turned and smashed the glass of two doors and one window. I raised my arms and did it deliberately, so that every one in the street could see. Miss Lawless smashed the windows to my right. We were going down the steps and I was afraid no policemen had been near, when two came from over the way. All was peaceable and friendly. My policeman said to me with a smile, "I'll take you this way, lady, see? And that won't inconvenience you."

With that he adjusted his grasp at my elbow. I said to him: "Unless you are obliged, don't hurry your pace more than you can help," and he walked at my pace through Westminster to Cannon Row. He also disarmed me, taking my hammer. In Westminster the crowd was immense and at the bottom of Whitehall, but we got through all right, and Miss Lawless kept close behind me.

Cannon Row was already crowded with women. We stood in a closely packed ring to give our names, and afterwards our names were called out before we went upstairs. To my surprise and great delight Lady Sybil Smith was there. I knew she herself had been wishing to

210

go on a deputation for some time. We were taken into the cells to be searched, but this was not the grim business that it sounds. We were left to walk quite by ourselves; a policeman showed us in and we were put four or five together in a cell. The door was left open, and a wardress asked respectfully if she might search us. We said, "Yes, most certainly," and began to deliver up our stones. The wardress's face was all kindness, and no sooner had the policeman gone away from the door than she burst out with: "Oh! you ladies, I'd be with you tomorrow if it weren't for my child. I am a widow with one child. If only these politicians knew what that meant! They can talk fine about the widow, but when it comes to her earning a livelihood they don't help her." It seemed wonderful, she understood.

Meanwhile she was picking out the stones from our pockets. We were allowed to go back to the central room as soon as it was finished, we left a friend behind us in the wardress. Upstairs, in the policemen's billiard room, we sat in crowds, and everything was noticeably different from last time. All was joy and triumph, and there seemed the echo of these from the street. I felt quite an old hand, and was going about the room collecting telegrams; I had bought a packet of forms on the chance. A policeman was singled out and stood waiting for them in a meek and respectful attitude. One woman, who looked about sixty or sixty-five, had written a telegram but had put no signature; I asked if there was to be none. She hesitated for a moment and then added: "Well—put Mother."

I thought it must be rather trying when it was a "daughter," but much more when it was a "mother," and she getting on in years. There was a girl lying down in the window recess where I had gone with my cough last time; she was ashy pale. I went up to her and asked her if she felt ill. Her face immediately lit up with a radiant smile—"I'm not ill now, but I have been for three months." I said how wonderful was the feeling of the movement, as one realised the difference which a year had made it was impossible that one should feel depressed, though one might be depressed for oneself. "No," she said, "I am never depressed now." Had she a mother? "Oh! mother would be here too, only she is a cripple."

Mrs. Pethick Lawrence had come and was given a great cheer. She looked well and beamingly happy. The Deputation had been much more hustled about than we who had done damage, but still, there was no real roughness that I could hear of, and they had been arrested comparatively quickly. Mr. Lawrence's welcome face came and he bailed us out, though it was a long business this time. When we drove away, every window in Whitehall bore the mark of the women upon it, with the unmistakable smashing, till it looked, as I passed, as though every window smiled.

On Wednesday, November 22, I sent off a telegram, saying that I was arrested, to our organiser at Liverpool for a meeting at which I was going to speak. It was a joint meeting of W.S.P.U., National Unionist and Conservative Suffragists; Lord Selborne was to speak for the Conservatives. It had been arranged when we were at peace with the government; that peace was now at an end. I then went to Bow Street. There were crowds of women; we each took luggage and wraps, for under Mr. Winston Churchill's new rule we were allowed to wear our own day and night clothes, and not obliged to have prison food. There was no difference in being allowed to see visitors or have letters. Books not dealing with current events were allowed, but one could not take them out of prison. At Bow Street we were put into the big room upstairs; again a policemen's billiard room. Large as it was, it was very crowded, and I kept my seat on my luggage in the passage outside.

Amongst others, there was a little American woman, whose husband stuck by her like a man till he should be separated by imprisonment. They had been in India, had heard much there about the Suffragettes, and one lady with whom they had dined had warned him against his wife becoming one of them. I saw there two Hertfordshire members, which did my heart good, when I remembered that a little time ago the whole county was asleep. Whenever I was able, I sat back on my luggage and wrote letters; it was the only way I could escape from talking to everyone, which was most delightful but I was very tired. We waited all day to learn in the evening that we must return tomorrow. I went to my mother from Bow Street who was staying in London at that time.

Three times this autumn, after making a speech, I had been taken with heart-seizure and incapacitated for about a quarter of an hour. On Thursday morning, November 23, I was ill, on waking, with a heart collapse. In spite of my best efforts, I could scarcely hold up my head or speak. Mrs. Francis Smith, one of my dearest friends, had come to my rooms to see how I was, and she determined to call at Bow Street and find out for me if I could not put off going there till the afternoon. She came back, saying that she had had an interview with Inspector A——, who had already shown great kindness to me, and he had said I was not to trouble about the morning, that it would do quite well if I came in the afternoon. I lay down on my bed till nearly 2 o'clock, when I felt much better.

Then I went to Bow Street. The woman who did my room came with me and carried my luggage; she also fetched me milk into the police station. She knew several of the policeman personally, so she managed everything very easily. I went on a deputation with Mrs. Haverfield and Mrs. Mansell-Moulin to Inspector A——, to say that unless the women could be told on leaving whether they would be wanted the next day, they would not go away. As this meant finding cells for all of us—we were 220 women in all—probably we should have to be put four or five in a cell together; it was speedily arranged and we were told that night when we should be wanted; I was one of those who came the following day. I went again that evening to my mother.

The next morning, Friday, November 24, I woke all right and went to Bow Street quite happily. Before our trial we were taken down into the passage next the police court, and put *vis-à-vis* to the policemen who had arrested us, as at my first trial. The magistrate was Sir Albert de Rützen, who was too old for, his work. Miss Lawless was accused with me. The hammers and stones were shown in witness against us, and the damage estimated at £3 15s. Mr. Muskett, the prosecutor, in totalling up my record, mentioned that I had been to Holloway after a deputation to the House of Commons, and in Newcastle I was imprisoned for throwing a stone at a motor car, but he did not mention "Jane Warton "at Liverpool. When I reminded him that he had left her out, he said testily, "Well, I'm very glad if I have."

I said it was quite true that I used a hammer and stones to break windows. I realised that this was the only effective means of protest left to us by a government which boasts of Liberalism and representation where men are concerned, but ignores the elementary principles of representation where women are concerned. Votes and riot are the only form of appeal to which this government will respond. They refuse us votes, we fall back on riot. The wrongs they inflict on women are intolerable, and we will no longer tolerate them Here the magistrate interrupted me; he could not enter into a discussion on the subject, and referred to the fact that Mr. Asquith had received a deputation last Friday.

I said, "I heard Mr. Asquith say he would do nothing in regard to women." The magistrate then advocated peaceful agitation. I answered that this government have said they will do absolutely nothing as a government, and Mr. Asquith is exactly where he was in 1908; all our peaceful agitation has been valueless in his eyes. I said that although we committed the acts alleged, we were not guilty of crime, our conduct being fully justified by the circumstances of the case. "I appeal to you. Sir, to vindicate the fundamental laws of liberty which our country has revered for generations," and with that I concluded. Miss Leslie Lawless said that if to fight for one's liberty was a crime, she was guilty, but she pleaded not guilty, as that was the only protest that this government understood. Our sentence was one of a fine of 40s. and 37s. 6d. damage each, or fourteen days' imprisonment—half the sentence that I had received when I went to the House of Commons, doing absolutely nothing and being mauled by the police.

We were not put into the cells, but again taken upstairs to a room close to the larger one. There was my friend, Adela Smith, with Olive Schreiner's friend, Mrs. Purcell, and Mrs. Tudor, of St. Albans. All these were not among the condemned, but had been let in to see their friends. Towards half-past five Inspector A—— came and told me that presently a taxi would be round to take me to HoUllway, that there would be a policeman inside, but that the other two could be any "fellow criminals" I liked. I at once chose Mrs. Leigh, who had been condemned to two months' imprisonment, though she was said only to have struck a policeman in defence of another woman. I was immensely proud to take her with me. I also chose Miss Lawless. The policeman was in plain clothes and very amiable. Miss Lawless discovered that she had left her purse behind.

We went back for it, and, on arriving at Bow Street, I decided that the constable should get out with Miss Lawless, put her in charge of another policeman, then return and mount guard on us. He was delighted to do this. From the point of view of our safety, of course, nothing could have been more absurd; we were not in the courtyard of the police-station, and nothing would have been easier than to open the door the other side of the pavement and, with the noise of the street, Mrs. Leigh or I could have escaped. But it was understood all round that this was not the game, and we waited quietly for the policeman to return and, finally. Miss Lawless and the purse.

At Holloway all was civility; it was unrecognisable from the first time I had been there. There were no reception cells for us, but we were taken at once to our separate cells in D X, where, after a time the matron, and afterwards the doctor came to see us. Nothing could have been more charming than the matron—another woman than had been there before. She asked me at once after Miss Davison; was she coming this time? The matron had been at Manchester when the hose-pipe had been played on her. This she asked before two war-dresses, and in a voice of sympathetic intonation. I said I did not think she was coming this time, but it would not be long probably before she was in prison again.

Then came Dr. Sullivan. His manner was kind, as it had always been, but I no longer felt the same towards him since he had fed some of the prisoners by force. He said at once, after testing my heart, that I could not stay there, but must go at once to hospital. I said I was much more comfortable where I was than in the general ward, and that I could not sleep there. He said he meant to put me in a cell apart. I was then moved over to the hospital side. There on the ground floor was the superintendent officer I had known before. I smiled, but she looked as if she did not recognise me. She went with me upstairs.

"I believe," I said, as she opened a door, "it is the very same cell I had before."

"No," she answered, "the one next door," and her reserve, to my great delight, broke down. I unpacked my flannel sheets, my flannel nightgown, and my long bed-socks, and made myself ready for the night. It was almost unbelievable to have so much comfort in a place which before had been the very acme of discomfort. They brought me a pint mug of milk and a small white loaf before the night. It was about eight o'clock by the time I got to bed, but the hours, I supposed, were the same as they had been in Holloway before, and besides, I was dead tired.

The next day, Saturday, November 25, I felt ill in the morning. The prison was scarce of food—at least, there were no vegetables; they gave me bread and butter and a pudding for luncheon. The governor came. Dr. Scott, and he was amiability itself, I was only to take care of myself. Since all was made easy, I stayed in bed that day.

The girl who was let in to wash my floor was fair-haired, with a most pleasant and intelligent face. I longed to know about her, but a wardress stood at the door looking on at her work all the time, and I did not once catch her eye. On Sunday, November 26, I felt no bet-ter and again stayed in bed. The second doctor, a new man, who was pleasant in his manner, came to see me. In the morning when I had been let out to the sink, the little prisoner who washed my floor met me coming out. My back was turned for a moment; she patted my shoulder and said, in a tone of voice of utmost comfort, "Cheer up!" By the time I looked round she was off somewhere else and no one would have supposed that she had communicated with me. After that I was determined to get some snatch conversation with her when she was in my cell. When she washed out that morning, I said to her—it was always the first thing—"How long have you got?"

"Three years," was the answer.

This greatly surprised me, for Holloway was not the place for long sentences, but I could not ask her then, there was not time to tell, only time for bare questions and answers. I asked, "What was it for?"

"Stealing my mother's skirt," she said. This was more startling than ever. Where was the mother's skirt one could "steal"?

But the wardress looked in and we were obliged to stop. On another occasion she told me that she had been very ill on first coming to Holloway, and that was why she had been kept there. Another time she slipped this notice under the door, and signalled to me by opening the gas-jet glass from the passage. On one side of the little torn bit of paper was written, "Z— A—, Boardstil Institution, Hailsbray"; on the other side, "I shall be glad to hear from you because I have no friends at all and it will cheer me up." I longed to speak to her, but I did not see her again after this. It was my last morning in prison when she put this paper under the door. After I came out I, of course, wrote to her, thanked her for her cheering words to me, asked if I might go and see her, and sent her a little 3d. book of extracts from my father's poems. I sent these to the chaplain at Aylesbury and asked him if he would deliver them. He sent my letter back, saying that he would not be allowed to give it, for she had already chosen as her correspondent her grandmother or some old lady. I do not know anything of her, of her failings or virtues; I only know that there was no loosening the net that clung round her so tightly for three years.

On Sunday, November 26, in the afternoon I went out to exercise. This was indeed a changed world. All of us assembled were walking about arm in arm, as we liked, in rows facing each other, or round the ground; some of us went apart in a little side-walk, all talking to one another, and all, of course, wearing our own clothes. One or two wardresses were there, but they were smiling all the time and chatted with us. One of them asked me why I had not come to visit Holloway. I told her that they would not allow "criminals" to come back except as prisoners, that I had tried in vain. She said I could come as someone who visited the cooking places, or something of that kind. I was afraid

I was too well known in Holloway, as I had paid rather frequent visits to the governor. I saw and walked with Mrs. Pethick Lawrence, arm in arm, and nothing that we did caused any disturbance.

On Monday, November 27, I stayed in bed again, and at about 11 o'clock the doctor came and offered me vegetable soup from outside, and massage from my masseur-doctor, Mr. May. I said surely that would not be allowed! He told me that of course in the ordinary course of things it was not allowed, but, if I wished for it, he would see what he could do. I refused all these offers, which were not, 60 far as I knew, offered to the others. I heard after my release, how my dear friends had put themselves about to get me all these things, and how my servant had brought soup to the prison every day, which she had made. I had a tin of biscuits sent in to me and some orange sweets. As I was not feeling well, I was unable to eat these, but I managed to give a good many to the girls who washed my cell. I only once got a look into the general ward.

I saw Mrs. Mansel-Moullin, Mrs. Mansel and others, but it did not seem to be the thing for the prisoners from the cells to go into the general ward. That night Mrs. Mansel came in to see me from there. She and some others were to be released the next day. She had suffered from influenza and had a bad time of it while she was in prison. We had a long talk, and she gave me *The Man-made World*, by Charlotte Perkins Gilman, to read, as a wonderful book that had just come out. She was not allowed to take it out with her. The publisher, Mr. Fisher Unwin, had kindly sent me the book, but I had not yet had time to read it. I read it that night and found it all that she had said—a most remarkable book. It is dedicated to a man, showing that the woman's movement has in it nothing, as is sometimes supposed, against men, but only against the vices of some men. In a chapter called "Crime and Punishment," this passage struck me with intense truth:

"Does a child offend? Punish it! Does a woman offend? Punish her! Does a man offend? Punish him! Does a group offend? Punish them! 'What for?' someone suddenly asks. 'To make them stop doing it!' 'But they have done it.' 'To make them not do it again, then.' 'But they do it again and worse.' 'To prevent other people's doing it, then.' But it does not prevent them—the crime keeps on. What good is your punishment to crime? Its base, its prehistoric base, is simply retaliation."

On Tuesday, November 28, I felt much better and went out to exercise in the morning. While there I was summoned to see the governor. He told me that my fine had been paid anonymously and that I was free. Among my friends there is none that I can think of who would have paid my fine; my state of health, I suppose, after the forcible feeding, was "dangerous," and it was thought safest to pay the fine "officially." To my great surprise, the superintendent came with me to my flat. She was very dear but quite "official." As I had packed up my things rather quickly, I felt ill and not inclined to talk much. She told me how very overworked the superintendent officers had been with the 220 Suffragette prisoners there were this time, she herself sometimes not getting to bed till one or two in the morning. She looked very tired and I felt very sorry for her. It seemed hard that, when they made us prisoners, so much extra work should fall upon the wardresses. When we reached the Duke's Road, I did not like to ask her into my rooms, not knowing who would be there, so I said goodbye to her, kissed her, and begged her to take back the taxi at my expense. This, however, she refused to do; she preferred to go home by omnibus, and we parted at the front door. I went upstairs and found three of my friends. We were delighted to see each other, but they soon went away, and I rolled wearily into bed.

I frequently had to lie up during the winter and spring months that followed. On May 6, 1912, I had a stroke and my right arm was paralysed; also, slightly, my right foot and leg. I was taken from my flat to my sister Emily Lutyen's house, and for many long months she and my mother and Dr. Marion Vaughan were kindness itself to me. From that day to this I have been incapacitated for working for the Women's Social and Political Union, but I am with them still with my whole soul.

And what is this which yet comes to us from the prisons? The torture of the "Cat-and-Mouse" Act and of forcible feeding! Oh! if only people could know what these things signify! But surely they must understand that they are barbarous practices such as we have not tolerated for long in our prisons. "Cat-and-Mouse" Act—what does it mean? The prisoner does not eat or drink, nothing to pass the lips; it may be three days, it may be a week, it may be nine days. Then the prisoner is let out, watched day and night, and taken back to prison, back to hunger and thirst, till she is again at death's door. This they do twice, three times, four times, five times, till life is all but out. Not yet have the government admitted that they will stop the "Cat-and-Mouse" torture short of death itself. And the forcible feeding—what is that? The only possible excuse for it is that it prolongs the prisoner's sentence by so many days, so many weeks, and that is all. But heed what it is. I have described it exactly as it was done to me.

See what it has meant in the recent case of Mary Richardson. It took eight wardresses and one man to overcome her. On two occasions it was said: "Twist her arms—the only way to unlock them." They held her feet by pressing in the hollow of her ankles. Occasionally the doctor pressed her in the chest to hold her down. He announced that he was going to use the stomach tube. As he could not get through her teeth, he put his fingers to the extremity of her jaw, and with his finger-nail deliberately cut her gum and cheek until her mouth was bleeding badly. He then inserted the gag and stomach tube, but she was so choked by the process that he stopped the feeding, and said he would return to the nasal tube. This is inhuman, like the feeding of a beast—no, of an insentient thing. Where is the gain? A week or several weeks more of imprisonment, and you have let in torture to our form of punishment; yes, and repeated torture, for these prisoners are let out by the "Cat-and-Mouse" Act, and, on those ghastly terms, the police will mount guard on them to seize them again if, according to their judgment, they have regained sufficient fitness.

And why are these women imprisoned? Because they and many thousands, or rather several millions, of women with them, have asked for the vote, but the government would not give it to them. For forty-five years women have supported their demand in Parliament for enfranchisement with ever increasing vigour. Petitions, processions, meetings and resolutions all over the country were infinitely greater in number than have been achieved for any other reform. When the Conciliation Bill was framed, women waited to see what the government would do for them; the vote on the second reading of the bill, for the second time, was immense. Women listened to the pledges of the government and they seemed to hold out a certainty of the vote. Now, when these promises have all been broken, women have taken to burning empty houses, railway stations and stacks, though they have respected life and refrained from wounding, as men would do for far less a cause. Yes, and they will burn buildings until they are treated rationally as an equal part of the human race.

I hear the cry go up from all parts of the country, "How long? How long?" The time is fully ripe, when will women be represented in Parliament by the vote, equally with men?

Pages from the Diary of a Militant Suffragette

Why Working Women Want the Vote.

Because as long as women cannot vote for Members of Parliament they are not asked what they want, and they are treated like children who do not know what is good or what is bad for them.

Because only those who wear the shoe know where it pinches, and women know best what they want and what they don't want.

Because Members of Parliament must attend to the wants and wishes of those who have votes, and they have not time to attend to the wants and wishes of women who have not got votes.

VOTES FOR WOMEN

The Women's Social and Political Union.

Head Office: 4, CLEMENTS INN, STRAND, W.C.

Atrocities in an English Prison.

Two Englishwomen, unconvicted prisoners on remand in an English prison, (Walton Gaol, Liverpool,) are been assaulted, knocked down, gagged, led by force, kept for consecutive days and nights in cells. Two Women has been **frog-marched**. Frog-marched? What does that mean? Read the story.

The Facts.

On December 20th Miss Selina Martin and Miss Leslie Hall were arrested in Liverpool, and were remanded for one week, bail being refused.

Accordingly, while still unconvicted prisoners, they were sent to Walton Gaol, Liverpool. There, contrary to regulations, (prisoners) with their friends, was denied to them. As unconvicted prisoners they refused to submit to the prison discipline or to take the prison food. Forcible feeding was threatened and Miss Martin thereupon barricaded her cell. The officials, however, effected an entrance, fell upon her and handcuffed her, dragged her to a punishment cell and flung her on the floor, with her hands tightly fastened together behind her back.

Contents

WINDOW BREAKING
AND
INCITEMENT
TO
MUTINY.

For Breaking Windows as a Political protest, Women
are now in H.M. Gaols serving sentences of
Four and Six months imprisonment.

For Inciting Soldiers to Disobey Orders, a much more
serious crime, known to the law as a felony, and
punishable by penal servitude, the Publishers of the
" Syndicalist," were sentenced to nine months hard labour,
and the Printers of the paper to six months hard labour.

The Government under the pressure of men with
votes reduced this sentence on the Publishers to
Six months imprisonment without hard labour.

and the sentence on the Printers to
One month without hard labour.

IS THIS JUSTICE TO
VOTELESS WOMEN ?

Pages from the Diary of a Militant Suffragette

PROLOGUE

The Prison

And I saw a gaol lifting its grimy walls to heaven. And they that passed by looked at it askance, for they said: "It is the abode of Sin."

And to them the broad sky and all the earth was fair to look upon, for they saw the early buds opening, and heard the birds that had come back from the south, and they felt the sun which was new warming the hearts of beast and plant.

But within the prison, and behind its cold, thick buttresses, and its small, round, triple-barred windows, that looked like tunnels, they heard faint groanings and sighings and much lamentation, and they said: "It is most just, for it is the abode of Sin."

And I heard a voice saying: "Woe to the cause that hath not passed through a prison!"

And I looked again, and I saw in the gaol those deliverers who in each age have saved the world from itself, and set it free, and gyves were on their wrists and ankles.

And I saw Israel in the house of bondage before it came forth to preserve Duty for mankind.

Woe to the cause that hath not passed through a prison!

And I saw the Praetorian Hall and One that was bound therein, and the soldiers bowed the knee before Him and mocked Him, and then led Him away to proclaim Love to the world.

Woe to the cause that hath not passed through a prison!

And I saw within the gaol them that gave liberty to the slave, and them that unbound the mind of man, and them that strove to free his conscience, and them that led onward to Freedom, and Justice, and Love.

Woe to the cause that hath not passed through a prison!

And I saw also, those in our own time who have counted themselves as nothing if they could but point out God's way unto their brethren; and there were many, too, of the prophets who are still to come, and these were also in bonds.

Woe to the cause that hath not passed through a prison!

And lo! the sky became clouded, and night fell, and there were no birds nor blossoms, but a chill came upon the earth, and they that passed by shivered and trembled; and I beheld, and saw that they were not men, but that they were really wolves, and apes, and swine.

And within the gaol was a great light, and a pleasant warmth came from the barred windows; and I heard a burst, of triumphant song.

And the gyves fell from the limbs of the prisoners, and there was great joy.

And they that passed by would come in, but they could not; and now within was freedom, and without was captivity.

And the hosts within held up their arms, and the marks of their shackles were upon them.

But I hid my hands behind me, for there was no mark on my wrists.

Woe to the cause that hath not passed through a prison!

Ernest Crosby.

The Diary

February 4th, 1909

While I was out this morning doing some shopping, I met a Suffragette! It is the first time that I have seen one, owing to the fact that I have been living abroad; but, of course, I have read about them in the papers. This one was not one bit like what I should have expected.

Obviously a lady, and most becomingly dressed in a white costume with a green hat, and wearing a large bunch of violets at her waist, she was standing at a corner of the street in the busiest part of the town endeavouring to sell papers to the passers-by.

"She's a Suffragette," said a small boy beside me, in tones of contemptuous scorn, to a still smaller companion.

There was a slight drizzle of rain, and I noticed that most of the people to whom she offered the paper brushed it angrily on one side and walked on. Being greatly impressed by her cheerful indifference alike to the state of the weather and the attitude of the public, and marvelling much that any woman should have so much moral courage, I paused for a moment to look at her.

Instantly she walked up to me. "You are wearing our colours," she said, smiling; "Are you interested in our Cause?"

I happened to have on a green coat and skirt with a white blouse and a purple motor scarf. "What are your colours?" I asked.

"White, Purple, and Green. They stand for purity, courage, and faith."

"I did not know," I replied; "and I am not particularly interested in the Cause. However, I am extremely interested in you. I want to know why you are doing this. I would not be in your place for thousands of pounds."

The Suffragette laughed. "Will you buy one of our papers?" she suggested. "When you have read it you will understand why. Later on perhaps you will be doing it yourself."

"Never," I replied, "that I can guarantee; but I will buy a paper."

On my return home I read it straight through with the greatest interest. It is a weekly paper, called *Votes for Women,* and costs one penny. I have said for years that women ought to be allowed to vote if they want to, just as I think they should do any other thing they like, if they are able to. It is ridiculous to debar a person from any sort of profession or occupation, which she is capable of pursuing, simply because she happens to be a woman, as if that in itself were any disqualification; but what I fail to understand is why they want a vote. Personally I have no desire for one, and cannot see what advantage it would be. However, there must be some reason, so I have decided to investigate the subject without further delay. I see in this paper that there are weekly At Homes here, so I shall certainly go to the next one, and hear for myself their side of the story.

February 6th.

I managed to find my way to the Suffragettes' At Home this afternoon, and am extremely glad that I did so. I have never heard such good speeches, or been so much entertained before. It is not my intention to write a dissertation on Woman's Suffrage, but I wish to record in my diary the fact that I have made three discoveries today.

(1) That this is not a sex war. The women who are members of this union have no desire, I find, to neglect their homes, or to become like men; they are simply fighting against an overwhelming force of prejudice to bring in what to them seems the biggest reform of modern times. Moreover, I am convinced that they will succeed, because they are fighting with the weapons of loyalty, faith, and love for humanity, and the best men in the country are on their side. They realise, as Tennyson has said, that

Woman's cause is man's; they rise or sink
Together, dwarfed or godlike, bond or free.

(2) I have discovered why they want the vote. They look upon it merely as a symbol of citizenship—in other words a latchkey, which will open a very big door. It seems a small and insignificant thing—a latchkey—but when one considers that there is no other way of getting into one's house, *i.e.*, of bringing in certain reforms, which, in their opinion, are of vital importance to women, except through political power, one begins to understand why they go through so much to get it.

My third discovery is that I have been a Militant Suffragette all my life and never realised the fact until just now.

It was not only the extremely clever speeches which impressed me today, but the personality of the women who constituted the audience. I talked to several while we were having tea, and before leaving the hall I joined the union as a member.

"I want very much to help you," I said to the girl who was in charge of the membership cards, "but I am afraid that I shall be of no use."

"We all feel like that at first," she replied; "but there is a great deal that you can do. For instance, there is a bye-election next week. Workers are badly wanted. If you will come to our Committee Room on Monday, the organiser, Miss M., will find plenty for you to do," and she gave me the address. She then introduced me to a sweet-looking girl who was buying some literature at a large table in a corner.

"This is Miss E.," she said; "she has been in prison."

I looked with interest at the ex-prisoner. She seemed so fragile and dainty that I could not picture her fighting with a policeman.

"Why were you imprisoned?" I inquired; "What had you done ?"

"I am sorry to be so uninteresting, but as a matter of fact I did absolutely nothing. I was walking in one of the deputations to the House of Commons, when I met rows of policemen, who refused to let me pass. When I tried to push through, a man in the crowd struck me, and then two of the policemen arrested me. The charge brought against me was that I had assaulted the police."

I could not help smiling. "Was it very bad in Holloway?" I asked.

She laughed lightly. "I did rather miss my hot water bottle," she admitted; "the cells are not kept too warm. I am quite ready to go back, however, if I am wanted. The worst thing of all, really," she added, seriously, "is the opposition one has to contend with from one's friends. I know that many more women would volunteer if they could give a *nom de plume*, and feel sure of not being found out by angry relatives. It would not be quite playing the game, though, and one does want to stand by these women openly."

"My difficulty," explained a woman who was sitting alongside us, "is that I have got a baby of ten months old. I really do not feel that I ought to leave him for a month. I should not be able to get even a line all that time, telling me how he was."

"Your duty is with the baby, of course," we both exclaimed together. "That is quite clear. There are plenty of others who can go to prison."

"The fact of the matter is," observed another woman, who was selling the literature, "that in this country women are oversexed. I come from Australia, where there is adult suffrage, and what struck me most when I came over here was the different attitude of men towards women. Out there it seems quite natural that men and women should walk together to the polling booths to register their votes. In every way there is much more comradeship and equality between them. I wonder how long it will take to make people realise that the right to vote is not a question of sex but of ability."

"Exactly," said the ex-prisoner. "If in order to be qualified as a voter it were necessary to possess a certain income, or to pass a stiff examination, or something of that sort, we should not mind being too stupid to vote or too poor. What we resent is that sex should alone be held as a disqualification; coupled with crime and insanity, it is a poor compliment to womanhood."

I have bought a good deal of the literature which I intend to read during my leisure moments, and meanwhile I shall go to this committee-room on Monday, and see what there is to be done.

February 8th.
Immediately after breakfast, this morning I went to the Suffra-

gette's committee-room. They have taken a shop in the central part of the town, and decorated it beautifully with purple, white, and green flags. On a counter I saw piles of leaflets, pamphlets and Suffragette literature, also very pretty little brooches in the colours, one of which I bought and intend always to wear.

The organiser was there, busily arranging the leaflets, and apparently quite oblivious of the fact that a crowd of small boys kept opening the door and throwing things in. She looked up to ask me if I would take a bundle of the pamphlets and distribute them to passersby in the street. I promised that I would, but asked her first if she would explain to me clearly what the militant methods consisted in, as I felt a little ignorant about it, and might be questioned.

She did so in a very few words.

(1) We go in deputations to the prime minister. Men do so constantly, and are received; but in every case where women go, they are refused, and when they persist, are arrested.

(2) We interrupt Cabinet Ministers' speeches by asking for an answer to our question. This policy was started because in the first place two girls asked this question most constitutionally in question time and were thrown out of the hall. It seems to me obvious that when our petitions are overlooked and our deputations not received, the only possible thing left for us to do is to ask our question at a public meeting. When one reflects further that men constantly heckle and interrupt political speeches with impunity, although the constitutional weapon of the vote is not denied to them, one begins to realise the importance of securing political power.

(3) We work against the government at bye-elections. This serves a double purpose: that of reducing the enormous majority of the Liberals, and at the same time of educating the people to the real meaning of this agitation.

"Two more questions I want to ask you," I said, "and then I will go out and distribute these leaflets. (1) Have any of the women thrown stones, thus endangering life? (2) Why did two Suffragettes chain themselves to railings?"

The organiser smiled:

The reason that the women chained themselves to the railing was in order to be heard when they made their protest. Finding that as soon as they began to speak they were seized and roughly thrown out of the hall, they determined that when next they spoke the audience would have a chance of hearing what it was they were asking for. Accordingly, they took chains which they passed round their waists and through the railings, and having padlocked them, the stewards were unable for some time to release them. The women did this at very great risk to themselves, but in the short time thus gained, they made a most effective protest and converted a considerable number of people to the cause.

As regards your other question, two girls did throw stones once. They were young, and carried away by the injustice and insolence of Mr. Asquith's attitude towards Woman's Suffrage, they threw two stones at the kitchen window of his house in Downing Street, as a political protest. They were careful to hurt no one, and the sentence they got was two months in the second division, without the option of a fine; yet for days afterwards women kept coming to us saying they wished to resign their membership on account of the fact that violence was being resorted to! That is what the government is relying on," she added, thoughtfully, "that women, as a whole, are so opposed to violence.

Having satisfied myself on these points, I collected my bundle of papers and went out, not without many misgivings. As I stepped into the street an interested crowd surrounded me.

"Here you are, Miss, here's a young man what will vote for you," called out a boy; while others shouted: "Here's a Suffragette! Votes for Women!"

The first man to whom I handed a leaflet tore it in pieces and threw it on the ground at my feet. I shall always be grateful to him for having done that. It was just what I needed to give me courage. Instantly all sense of nervousness left me, and I was conscious only of a feeling of indignation that any man should dare thus to treat the question of women desiring to be counted as citizens. I walked on, handing the papers to everyone I met; occasionally stopping to discuss the subject or to defend the methods. On the whole, though trying to the nerves, it is interesting work, and as an opportunity for studying types of humanity almost unique.

One man came up to say that he thought we were very brave to fight for the vote as we were doing, and that he admired our pluck. I did not mention that one week ago I had not even met a Suffragette.

When I had finally disposed of all my literature, I returned to the committee room, where I found several women discussing the work for next day. I have volunteered my services for three hours tomorrow. I am not exactly looking forward to it, but one must do something.

February 11th.

Thank goodness, there are only two more days before the polling takes place. Not that I mind this work nearly so much now, but it is very tiring, and the weather has been horrible. Besides distributing the leaflets in various localities, I have assisted at several open-air meetings. This is what happens: The speaker arranges to hold a meeting in some convenient place for working men, either outside a factory or distillery, during their dinner hour or out in the street, in the evening.

She hires a lorry to serve as a platform, and hitherto my part in the programme has consisted in accompanying her to the place and walking about among the crowd, handing leaflets, selling the *Votes for Women* paper, and discussing the subject with questioners. It is quite wonderful how the attitude of the public has altered within the last few days, since the open-air meetings began. Crowds of interested men surround the lorry, listening attentively, and asking intelligent questions. Instead of telling us to go home and look after the baby, they now ask whether we will vote Tory, whether working women will get the vote, and so on.

It is a little difficult to make them understand why we oppose the Liberal candidate, irrespective of his views with regard to women's suffrage. One man called out:

"You should be working for the Tory this time, miss; he's in favour of votes for women, and the Liberal isn't. You don't know what you are doing."

It takes them some time to grasp how little the pledges of private members count as against the opposition of the government to which they belong, and that our fight is against the government in power until we are enfranchised, and not a party question at all.

"Look here, miss," said one loafer, addressing me; "if we gives you this vote, what are you going to do for us?" One would have supposed from his tone that the vote was a thing he had in his pocket, and could hand to me if I made it worth his while.

"When we get the vote," I replied, "we shall do as much for you as you are doing for us now; we shall look after ourselves."

"You can do that well enough without the vote, it seems to me," put in a man, who had strolled up. "You have plenty of indirect influence."

"Which would you rather have, direct or indirect influence?" I asked.

"Direct, of course," he replied, promptly.

"Well, so would I."

"Women are different," he explained, and I think he felt that he had logically settled the question.

Among other things, we have been asking the electors to sign postcards, addressed to Mr. Asquith, informing him that although they are Liberal, and have always voted Liberal, they are voting against the Liberal candidate this time, on account of the way the government has failed to carry out Liberal principles, in its treatment of women, and a great many have done so.

I am beginning to understand why the cause has been so enormously helped by the fact that nearly four hundred women have gone to prison for it. Whatever fashionable women may imagine about prison in the second division, to these working people it is evidently a stern reality. They know what it means, and they realise perfectly that the women, most of them ladies by birth, who went there must have had some very strong reason for doing so. When they find that it was with a view to securing political power for the protection of the working women, and remember what they did themselves, in order to procure the vote, their attitude towards the question alters entirely.

I mentioned this to the organiser as I was leaving the Committee Room today. "It has helped more than anything else," she assented.

"I do hope," said a lady, who came in at that moment, "that a deputation will not go from here. I should feel so ashamed not to go with them."

"Then why not go?" I inquired.

"My husband is very much against my going to prison," she explained, "and he has been so good about letting me help in other ways that I do not feel it would be right to do it."

At this point an elector, who had evidently been dining not wisely but too well, strolled into the shop and leant up against the counter.

"I'll vote for the women this time," he announced, with a friendly smile. "I've always voted Liberal, but I'm for the women this time. Why shouldn't they vote just the same as us?" and he looked round vacantly.

"Will you sign this postcard, then, to Mr. Asquith?" asked the organiser, holding one out to him.

He regarded it doubtfully.

"I'm not just very well today," he said. "I'm thinking I couldn't sign it right. Maybe the wife will, though," and taking it in his hand, he lurched but into the street. We looked at each other in silence.

A moment later an errand boy opened the door to call out: "Votes for women, votes for donkeys, votes for dogs!" Then we laughed.

February 13th.

I woke this morning with a feeling of distinct thankfulness that the last day of the bye-election week had come. It certainly is most trying work, and to make things worse, it has been snowing hard, and we have felt horribly cold standing about. I do think the women are wonderful. One girl came into the Committee Room yesterday and said she could give from 8 a.m. to 8 p.m. if they let her have half an hour off for lunch. I was feeling dreadfully ashamed of myself at the time, because I had just refused to go with another woman to chalk pavements advertising open-air meetings.

I had made some excuse about not having time, but in reality it was because I had not sufficient courage to do it, so when this girl came in prepared to do anything they wanted, and for any length of time, it made me feel worse.

I only volunteered to give four hours' work today at one of the polling booths, and I had expected that to be comparatively simple, as we merely have to hand leaflets to the electors on their way in, asking them to keep the Liberal out.

While occupied in doing this I was much interested In watching a girl who was endeavouring to persuade the electors to sign a petition to Mr. Asquith, requesting that qualified women should be enfranchised. She was a sweet-looking girl, and evidently was feeling very tired and cold. She stood just outside the door of the polling booth, beside a table on which there were some writing materials, holding this petition in her hand, and as each man came out she said rather nervously: "Will you sign this petition, please?"

Hardly a man did so. They either ignored her completely or made some contemptuous reply and hurried on. I watched these proceedings for a long time with a growing sense of anger, until finally, half an hour before my time on duty had expired, I saw one of our women approaching. I begged her to take my place while I went over to help the girl with the petition.

"You can't do that," said the Suffragette. "She belongs to the National Society, and they disapprove of our militant methods."

"Nevertheless, I intend to try," and I handed my leaflets to the newcomer, who said she would watch and see how many signatures I got.

The girl smiled pleasantly when I came up and offered to help her. "I wish you would," she said. "I am so tired of standing here, and they do not seem to want to sign."

I do not believe for a moment that these petitions do any good, but I was determined to make some people sign, so I stationed myself at the outside gate, just in the entrance. Instantly a policeman came up.

"You Suffragettes have no right to be here at all," he said; "you can't stand there blocking the thoroughfare, you must get further back."

I stepped back instantly, recognising the importance of keeping in with him. "How am I to stop these people and make them sign that paper if I do not stand at the entrance?" I asked, pleasantly.

"You can't stop them," he replied, shortly.

"Do you not think that women should be allowed to vote ?" I asked.

"There is no reason why they should not vote," he replied, "but they've no call to chain themselves to railings."

"Well, after all, it is ourselves we chain," I observed. "We take all the risks in this fight, and we do not kill other people as men did when they wanted the vote. What I want to know is this: What are *you* doing to help the women to get this enfranchisement, which you think they ought to have?"

He looked at me for a moment. "What do you want me to do?" he asked.

"Only just to look the other way," I suggested, "while I go forward a step or two and speak to these electors. I will promise not to hit anyone," I added, as he hesitated.

The policeman smiled. "Right you are, miss," he said, and walked on.

An oldish gentleman had just looked scornfully at the lady with the petition, and was about to pass me, when I laid my hand on his arm. "Why did you not sign that woman's petition?" I asked, in my most militant tones. "Do you understand what it is about?"

He turned round angrily. "Madam," he said, looking me up and down, "I understand perfectly what it is about. What I fail to understand is, why you women should be satisfied to throw away your privileges for the sake of rights."

"I will gladly make you a present of all the privileges I have ever received," I replied, "in return for the most elementary justice of being considered a citizen and a person in the eyes of the law."

The old gentleman hesitated for a moment. "What do you want a vote for?" he asked.

"What do you want one for yourself?" I retorted.

He straightened himself. "I am a man," he explained, "and politics are a man's work. Your place is in your home, and that is where you should be now," and he walked on.

I smiled at the policeman, who was standing near, and then turned my attention to business again. A gentlemanly-looking man was approaching.

With a feeling of diffidence I touched him on the arm. "Why did you not sign her petition?" I asked, reproachfully. "Do you also believe that qualified women are not fit to vote, while all these men are?" and I glanced at the mixed crowd round us.

He stepped aside to let the others pass out. "Women are above politics," he said, thoughtfully. "I do not think they should touch them; it would tend to degrade them."

"On the contrary," I exclaimed, "women would raise politics. What has woman's influence been everywhere?"

"You are right," he said, quietly; "woman's influence might raise politics."

"Then you will sign the petition?"

"Yes, I will sign," and he walked back to the table. Encouraged by this success, I intercepted the next man. He looked at me and laughed.

"By Jove! you are not a Suffragette, are you?" he inquired.

"Yes," I replied, "I am a Suffragette. I should be ashamed to be anything else."

"Not a militant Suffragette?" he persisted.

"Yes, a militant Suffragette. Why not?"

"You do not look like one," he explained.

"Have you met many?"

"No, none, but I have read about them, and that is enough for me. As for signing that paper—I am a Liberal."

"All the more reason why you should approve of Liberal principles, which are that taxation and representation should go together. Can you give me one logical reason why qualified women should be disfranchised on the ground of sex only?"

"I see no reason why they should not have votes," he admitted, "but I object to your way of asking."

"It is surely not much trouble to sign your name," I said, "and I thought I had asked you very nicely. You do not want me to go down on my knees, do you, with all this snow on the ground?"

"You know quite well what I mean," he said, impatiently. "The militant methods are what I disapprove of."

"The word 'militant,'" I observed, "is a strangely misleading term. We all learnt in our grammar books the difference between 'I eat,' or 'I am eaten,' 'I beat,' or 'I am beaten,' etc. Our so-called militant methods consist solely in having things done to us; we hurt no one—at least, so far we have not," I added, cheerfully. "I have great hopes that in the near future we shall improve upon our present methods."

"Is it not something to have scratched and kicked policemen?"

"Do I look as if I would scratch a policeman?"

"No," he admitted; "but you do not deny that some of them have done so."

"I deny it absolutely, because I know that they have not. Will you sign that petition, or will you not?"

He hesitated for a moment. "Yes, I will, if you really want me. to."

"Thanks, awfully," I said, with genuine gratitude, as he retraced his steps; and I had just time to stop a man who was hurrying past.

He looked me up and down, insolently. "Why should you wish to take an interest in politics?" he inquired. "You should get married—that is the best thing for a woman to do."

"I am married," I explained, "but I fail to see what that has to do with the case."

"You are married, are you? Well, if I were your husband you would not come here and do this sort of thing, I can tell you."

"No doubt," I replied, "I should be too much taken up with my own troubles under those circumstances to be philanthropic about other women's, but Fate has been kind. Though I have not as yet got a vote, I have been spared that."

Though I smiled pleasantly as I said this, I wanted dreadfully to hit him, and I am sure he felt much the same. Anyhow, he did not sign, but gave a stiff bow, and walked away, just as a middle-aged man, wearing a big rosette of the Liberal colours, waved aside the petition and approached the gate. I touched him on the arm.

"Why did you not sign her paper?" I asked.

"Because I do not approve of every woman having the vote," he explained, in a loud voice. "For women qualified as men are it is all very well."

I pointed out that that was all we were asking for, but he still hesitated.

"Oh, do please sign," I said. "It will only take a minute, and you would if you knew how tired I am of arguing and how cold it is standing here in the snow."

"It must be," he said, sympathetically. "I do not think you should stay any longer."

"Oh, never mind about me; only sign that petition before you go," and he did.

The next man whom I questioned remarked that women were not interested in politics, and would certainly not use the vote if they got it.

"In that case there can be no harm in letting them have it," I observed, "so you may as well sign the petition."

"That is true," he admitted, and went back.

When half an hour later the time came for me to go I had secured the signatures of nine men, all of whom had passed the table in the first instance, besides having some interesting discussions during the intervals with the policeman and a man who was standing outside holding a note-book and asking the electors as they came out for their voting numbers. I succeeded in entirely converting the latter to the necessity for militant methods.

"Your voting number, please, miss?" he inquired of me with a grin as I was leaving.

"Nineteen hundred and nine," I replied, "for we are going to get it this year."

"I hopes you will, miss, I'm sure," he said.

When I got home I had barely time to change my frock and hurry off to a tea-party at a friend's house. As it was I arrived late.

"I want to introduce you to Mr. S——," said my hostess, in a whispered aside; "there he is sitting on the sofa; he is a virulent 'anti-Suffragist,' so you can have a nice discussion. Convert him if you can, only do not come to blows over it," and walking across the room with me, she introduced him, and left us together.

At first he talked about ladies' frocks and whether large picture hats were becoming or not. He was the type of man who always speaks to a woman as if he were addressing a child, coming down to the level of her understanding. So long as he did that it was all right, but presently during a pause in our conversation we heard a very pretty girl, who was sitting not far off, remark to the lady next her that she had been going round to all her friends with an anti-Suffrage petition, collecting signatures, and had been most successful.

"Several of the people refused at first," she explained, "because they had already signed for someone else, but I persuaded them to do it again. I did so want to get thirty signatures on my paper."

Involuntarily I turned to my companion. "That was a good plan of hers, wasn't it?" I said, drily. "If everyone were to sign twice it would help enormously."

Then, of course, we started discussing "votes for women." I asked him to explain to me why he disapproved of woman's suffrage, and he did. In spite of my recent experiences at this election, I was surprised at the things he said to me. I do not suppose he really meant to be insulting. Anyhow, after having done his best to prove that women have no intelligence, and are only fit to do the cooking or to bring children into the world, and adding that any woman, if she were attractive enough, could make half a dozen men vote any way she chose, he concluded his remarks by saying: "Those are my views on the subject."

I purposely drank a little tea before making any reply, because I find that if one answers without a moment's reflection one is apt to be rude, and I did not want to be.

"I was expecting arguments of that sort," I said, quietly, "but I had hoped that you would have spared me the 'Mind the baby' one. Even the cabmen and loafers have almost outgrown it. You see, married women would not get the vote unless they were earning their own living, in which case their work would keep them away from their homes all day, anyhow. As for indirect influence, it seems a pity that intelligent male electors should be influenced in their decisions by the fact that a woman happens to be attractive or pretty."

I could not look at him as I said this, because my eyes were full of tears from having swallowed the tea too hot, and he did not make any remark for quite a long time, so I could not tell at first how he was taking it.

"Dear me," he said at last, with a return to his "come-down-to-your-level" manner, "we are very much in earnest. With your views, Mrs. Brown, you ought to be a member of the 'Women's Social and Political Union.'"

"I am a member," I replied. "These are our colours," and I showed him my Suffragette brooch. He examined it critically.

"Very pretty," he said; "charming. And do you drive about in a wagonette decorated with purple, white, and green flags? I should not go to Holloway if I were you. The excitement and notoriety are all very well, but the prison clothes are not at all becoming."

"That settles the question then, of course," I said, laughing, and endeavoured to change the subject, perceiving the futility of pursuing it.

He persisted, however, in discussing woman's suffrage, and nothing else.

I have neither the time nor the inclination to record all the things that he said. As for convincing him, one might as well have tried to convert Mr. Asquith. I think, however, that I am glad I have met him, otherwise I should never have supposed that there were men who had those views about women. At last he rose to go.

"Mrs. Brown," he said, "I will give you a word of advice before I leave. Women are very charming when they keep in their own place. Just stay where you are."

I made no reply, and perhaps he felt that he had been rude, for after saying goodbye to the hostess he walked back to where I was sitting and said playfully: "You must not mind me, Mrs. Brown; being only a mere man, I am very obstinate and pig-headed."

"Please do not trouble to explain that," I said. "It is the only one thing you had made quite clear to me already."

The moment I had said it I was sorry, particularly as he walked away without replying. It was horribly rude, and worthy of an "Anti." If I ever meet him again I shall apologise.

March 6th.

I had a most interesting time yesterday stewarding at a meeting for Mrs. Pankhurst. This is the first time that I have heard her speak, and I enjoyed it thoroughly. For quite an hour she kept the audience spellbound, and the constant applause was most encouraging.

I had rather a busy time before the meeting began, showing people to their seats and taking the tickets, but there were a good many of us stewarding, so we each took a certain part of the hall. The place was crowded, at least two thousand people were there, and when question time came a large number of questions were asked, all of which Mrs. Pankhurst answered immediately and convincingly in the amazing way that all these women do.

I have been very much struck by the gift of the Suffragette speakers for light repartee; it has a wonderful effect in appealing to a crowd.

I was present at an evening meeting for working men a few days ago, where it seemed as if the audience were going to be extremely rowdy. Men and boys at the back were singing and stamping or playing musical instruments, and when the speaker, quite a young girl, stepped on to the platform I could not help wondering how she would manage.

To my surprise, she smiled sweetly at them all, and said that if the gentlemen at the back would be so very kind as to allow her to be heard she would be glad to answer any questions afterwards which they cared to ask her. Quite soon there was not a sound to be heard, with the exception of one man who was drunk and persisted in interrupting, much to the indignation of the others, who wished to turn him out, but the speaker interposed.

"Oh, please don't," she said, "we never turn people out of our meetings for asking questions; we leave that to Liberal Cabinet Ministers."

When the meeting, which proved to be a most successful one, was over, I had a few moments' conversation with the speaker.

"How splendidly you answered them all," I said. "Do you like this work.?"

"I love it," she said. "I have given up my professional career to devote my whole time to it, because I can see no other way of bringing in the reforms we want than by securing political power for women."

"When we get the vote you will miss having all this sort of thing to do."

She laughed as she tied a purple, white, and green scarf round her neck.

"Our real work will begin then," she said, quietly.

March 8th.

I have undertaken to promote the sale of the *Votes for Women* paper here. The work consists in getting the names of girls who are willing to sell it in the streets, and arrange with them the days and hours they can spare and the locality in which they will work, also to see that our paper is exhibited at the station, and to interview newsagents and endeavour to persuade them to sell the paper and show it in their window.

Hitherto, I have secured three sellers and one newsagent. I feel that I ought to go with these women myself, but somehow I cannot summon up sufficient courage to do it. The idea of chalking notices on the pavement, or standing at a street corner wearing the large regalia and selling the paper to passers by, simply terrifies me. I may be able to some day, but at present the very thought of it makes me feel cold all over. However, I am seriously contemplating going to prison.

I hear that a deputation is going to the House of Commons on the 30th inst., and after that the organiser is anxious that some of us should volunteer for a later one. The leaders would like members from every part of the country to be represented, and so far none have gone from here.

My only difficulty is what arrangement to make for the boys during my absence, but I dare say something could be managed. The more I think of it, the more I feel that I ought to go to prison. When I realise what other women are doing in this movement, I am ashamed. Yesterday a hospital nurse came to me and said she got two hours off every day and could give that time for selling the paper, if I liked. I know what work in a hospital means, and how vitally important it is to rest during those short two hours. So I thanked her very much and said we had enough sellers at present.

March 14th.

I have definitely decided that I shall go in this deputation to the House of Commons, so, this morning, I went to the committee room and gave in my name to the organiser. Miss M———.

To my surprise, she seemed to hesitate for a moment.

"Do you quite understand what going to prison means?" she asked.

"I think so," I said. "Anyhow, I know this much, that about 400 women have gone already for this Cause, and where they have been, I can surely follow. I admit that I dread the crowd, rather, and having to force one's way through, but as regards prison, is it so very bad?"

"There are many people," she said, slowly, "who think that because our women come out of Holloway with smiling faces, are unwilling to talk of what they have suffered, and profess themselves ready to go back a second and a third time, that prison life must be easy and almost comfortable, but you see. Suffragettes are afraid of having the movement side-tracked on to prison reform, so they keep to the point. They do not complain of insufficient air, bad food, dirty prison clothes, plank beds, and damp, cold cells. They know, because it has been proved, that going to prison does help as nothing else does, so they go again. If you are prepared for all that prison means, with its solitary confinement, no communication with the outside world for a month, and no conversation with anyone except a wardress with the special prison voice, then I will send in your name to Christabel Pankhurst as a volunteer for the deputation next month."

I could not help smiling at the "special prison voice." "Are the wardresses always disagreeable, poor things?" I asked.

"Well, not always. Things have altered wonderfully since our women first went to prison. Many times when they were leaving the other prisoners have said: 'God bless the Suffragettes. They have brought sunshine into Holloway,' or words to that effect. No one ever seems to have smiled or looked happy there before."

"Well, I am prepared for all that prison means, so that is settled," I said. "Can you tell me when the deputation is likely to go?"

"The date is not fixed yet, but it will probably be at the end of April or early in May. This first one goes on the 30th of March, and there will be at least a month before another is sent, so you will have time to make the necessary plans."

I am glad of that, for there will be a good deal to arrange.

March 16th.

I have been today to an anti-Suffrage meeting. It is a thing I shall never do again, but I almost think I am glad that I went.

To me it would always seem a pitiable and deplorable spectacle to see a woman trying, however ineffectually, to retard the progress of other women, but I would never have believed it possible that any educated, intelligent person could deliberately bring herself to stand on a platform and talk the nonsense that that woman talked for the space of nearly an hour. Having begun her speech by assuring us that the world would be a better and a happier place if women remained in their own homes, attending to their duties, instead of lecturing on platforms about "rights" (a sentiment which, in her case, I for one fully endorsed before the meeting ended), this lady proceeded to explain to the audience that women had not sufficient intelligence to understand or take any serious interest in political questions, adding that they already had an immense indirect influence and were always able to help men enormously by canvassing for them at elections. (Why an intelligent male voter should allow his decisions to be thus influenced by a person admittedly incapable of understanding a political question she did not say.)

A portion of the audience, who evidently approved of backstair influence, applauded feebly. Encouraged by this, the speaker went on to say that in England women are in the majority, and that as Adult Suffrage would be bound to follow eventually if qualified women were enfranchised, the feminine vote would outnumber the male by a million, which, in her opinion, would evidently mean the fall of the Empire. In Australia, where there is Adult Suffrage, the fact that there are a million more men than women has never to my knowledge been used as an argument against men being enfranchised. Be that as it may, the audience again seemed feebly gratified by this suggestion of the "dangerous majority," even when the lady added triumphantly that if the vote were given to women more than half of them would never use it!

I heard a Suffragette behind me say in a whisper to her companion that as all the logical arguments were on our side, it seemed a pity not to have had at least a speaker on the other, adding that she could have made a much better "Anti" speech herself. I smiled at her, glad to catch one understanding eye. The speaker then proceeded to explain that she admired women. She enlarged on their charm, and usefulness in the home, and of course managed to introduce the "physical force" argument that women could not fight for their country.

I always think that "antis" fail to make the most of that physical force argument, which seems to be the only real one they have. Instead of pressing the point that women are not soldiers (considering that history and recent events have proved that many women could and would fight if they were allowed to, not to mention the fact that soldiers do not have the vote) it would be better to state the case as it really stands. They should say:

> Custom has hitherto given the Parliamentary vote to men only, and men are physically stronger than women; logically we admit that you are entitled to it, but practically we refuse to give it to you; take it if you are strong enough.

But no; this lady meandered on about men being men, and women being women. She informed us that their spheres were separate, that their points of view were different, not seeing that all this was only another strong argument why the woman's point of view in the country required to be represented as well as the man's.

I was very glad when she stopped, because I was feeling so ashamed for her. In a speech of Forbes Robertson's on this question I heard him say that if anyone among the audience was still unconverted to the case for woman's suffrage he would recommend them to go to an anti-Suffrage meeting, where their last doubts would be dispelled.

It might, of course, be argued on the other hand, that if a woman is capable of making such a speech as the one I have just heard, clearly women are not qualified to vote, but I must admit the fact that practically all these same contradictory arguments were used by the "anti" man whom I met at tea on the polling booth day.

There was not much applause and no enthusiasm. The speaker did not tell us what we ought to do to avert this impending catastrophe of woman's suffrage. Perhaps she is still of those who believe that signing petitions will be sufficient, or possibly she would consider it unwomanly to do anything except talk.

Two people at the door were standing taking a collection. I saw 3d. put in as I passed. Outside in the street were a man and a woman selling pamphlets. Simultaneously they offered me one.

"For or against woman's suffrage?" I asked.

"For," they both answered together.

"Yes, please, I will take two. I was afraid it might be 'anti,' and I can't stand any more tonight."

They laughed with the cheerful optimism of the Suffragist as I took one from each, but my cheeks are still hot with the sort of horrible ashamed feeling one gets when a woman has made a fool of herself in public. It is like seeing a woman drunk. It always seems so much worse than if it had been a man, I don't know why. If a man had made that speech tonight I *think* I could have laughed. As it is, I only feel hot.

March 28th.

I decided to buy a copy of *Votes for Women* from the railway book-stall this morning, as I had been told that our poster there was not properly exhibited, and no effort made to show the paper.

When I reached the station I found this report to be only too true. It was some time before I could find the poster, which was almost hidden in a corner, and there was not a copy of the paper to be seen on the stalls. I handed a penny to the man who was selling papers, and asked him if he had a copy left of *Votes for Women*.

He stared at me blankly, then searched for a few moments on the ground behind the bookstall, and fished out a paper, which he threw on to the counter in front of me. His manner could scarcely be called an advertisement for the cause.

I asked him quite politely if he would mind leaving a copy where it could be seen, and also requested that the poster should be placed in a more conspicuous place, explaining that we wanted the paper advertised.

He replied that the poster would do well enough where it was, and there was no room on the stalls for the paper. "Them that wants it can ask for it," he said, "and as for advertising of it, I should think you Suffragettes could do that well enough for yourselves."

I manfully (or should I say "Suffragettefully"?) resisted a strong desire to hit him, and contented myself by placing the copy I had bought in a conspicuous position on the stall, after which I left the station.

On my way home I met a girl selling pamphlets, so I stopped to speak to her. She told me she was a member of the Freedom League, so I asked her wherein lay the difference between their methods and those of the W.S.P.U. to which I belonged. "You disapprove of militant methods, don't you?" I asked.

"Oh, no! I am going to prison next month," she explained, cheerfully. "We go on deputations the same as you do, only we do not interrupt Cabinet Ministers' meetings."

"Why not?" I inquired. "Surely you do not disapprove of that?"

"Not at all," she said, laughing. "Personally, I think, as a policy, it is excellent, but I do not wish to be killed."

March 29th.

A funny thing happened today. A friend of mine, who was very anxious to have her hand read by a palmist, and had been strongly advised to visit a clairvoyant here who is said to be wonderful, asked me if I would accompany her, which I did, as I was curious to hear what would be said. When we reached the house, however, the woman refused to have us in the room together, so finally we both had our fortunes told separately.

It really was rather extraordinary, for of course the clairvoyant had never seen me before, and there is nothing about my appearance to suggest that I am a criminal. I was not even wearing our colours, and yet, after looking into her crystal, she said: "You will be in prison."

I hurriedly explained that I contemplated going in a deputation to the prime minister, and I presumed that would be the result.

She gazed steadily into the crystal. "No," she said, slowly, "it will be for something else later on."

"Please do not infer," I begged, "that I shall be imprisoned for theft."

The clairvoyant smiled. "No, it is for something in connection with this work. You will go in a very big deputation, much larger than has ever gone before, you will be roughly handled, and will be in great danger from horses. You will be arrested, but I do not think that you will go to prison this time."

"That is impossible," I interrupted. "Everyone that has been arrested has always been to prison. You surely do not mean that I would pay the fine?"

"I cannot tell what will happen," said the clairvoyant. "I can only tell you what I see. The government will do something quite unexpected. Later on I see a great disappointment for you; also you might go in a still larger deputation next year. I see a flag, which means triumph in the end, but it will not be for some time yet."

Of course, she must be wrong, but it is strange that she should have seen the deputation in the crystal.

March 31st.

At breakfast this morning I read the description in the paper of yesterday's deputation to the prime minister. It made me feel hot and cold all over. I still feel it when I think of all the people who must have read that account. To relieve my feelings I went to the Committee Room at 10.30 to discuss the subject with Miss M——.

She was talking to a stranger. "This is a prisoner," she announced, as she introduced her to me. "She will be able to tell you what to expect in Holloway."

"I don't care *what* happens in Holloway," I explained. "I never have minded the idea of prison. I only wish I were there now, and the deputation over. That is the part I can't bear to think of. Have you read today's paper?"

"Yes; wasn't it splendid? "she said, her cheeks glowing with pride, her eyes sparkling. "Really, Mrs. S—— is wonderful. She got through them all."

"You call it splendid!" I exclaimed, in amazement. "Well, I think it is horrible. If that is what a deputation means, I fail to see what good it can ever do to the Cause."

Miss M—— glanced at me. "You mean that you have changed your mind about going in May?"

"I have given in my name for the next deputation," I replied, "and of course I shall keep my word, even if I have to struggle with policemen and knock off their helmets; but picture it to yourself. The paper says: 'For hours the women fought desperately, kicking and struggling in their efforts to overcome the police.' As for this Mrs. S—— whom you call splendid, this is how she is described: 'Hatless, breathless, and dishevelled, clutching a broken banner in her hand, she staggered on to the steps of the House of Commons.'"

With one accord Miss M—— and the prisoner sank on to two chairs, and laughed, till I thought that they would never stop. "The papers always write that sort of thing," they explained, when they were able to speak.

"But, is it not true?"

"Surely, surely," said the prisoner, reproachfully; "you did not for one moment believe it to be true?"

"Of course I did, when the paper said so. If it is a lie someone must write and contradict it at once."

"The letter would not be inserted. The Press is boycotting this movement, and nothing is put in unless it is sensational. Shall I describe Mrs. S—— to you? I know her very well. She is an elderly lady with white hair, gentle and sweet, almost early Victorian in her views about what is womanly. She is not strong, though she has such amazing courage. I hope she was not much hurt."

"Have you ever been in a deputation?" I asked, turning to Miss M——.

"No," she said, "not yet. I have asked for permission often, but the leaders won't let me go. I am required outside as a speaker, and they cannot afford to have many speakers and organisers in prison. We must obey orders, of course, and do whatever helps the Cause best," and she sighed.

"Have you ever heckled a Cabinet Minister?"

"Oh, yes, several times. You must do that if one comes up here to speak. Afterwards you will feel that you don't mind anything else."

"Tell me what happens."

"It is very simple. You go to the meeting, and the first opportunity you are given in the Cabinet Minister's speech you stand up and ask your question, 'when he means to carry out Liberal principles by giving women the vote,' or something of that sort. The audience does the rest. Great excitement always follows. Half a dozen stewards rush forward instantly and throw you violently out of the hall. A few moments later, when quiet is restored, another woman gets up in the same way, and the scene repeats itself."

"But you do not hit people with umbrellas on the way out?"

Miss M—— smiled. "It is a rule of the union that we never take an umbrella with us, even if it is raining we carry nothing in our hands."

"But do the stewards really hurt the women?"

"Hurt them? Of course they do. One woman I know nearly lost the sight of both eyes, several sustained internal injuries from kicks or blows. I have seen one woman who interrupted before my turn came kicked by six different men on her way out of the hall, though she was held by two others, and walking quietly. Generally they are thrown down the steps into the street below."

"Do not tell me any more," I begged. "It makes me feel sick, and I must go now anyhow, as I have shopping to do."

"Will you post a letter for me as you pass the pillar-box? It is to a prisoner; I hope it will catch her before she goes to Holloway."

I promised to do so, and took the letter almost reverently.

On my way home someone came up behind me and touched me on the arm. I turned round, to see a girl I have spoken to occasionally at our meetings.

"Mrs. Brown," she said, "I hear you are going to prison. Don't go; it is not worth it."

"Why?" I exclaimed. "Do you really think it does not help the Cause?"

"These small deputations are useless. We have gone on too long hurting ourselves and not others. I believe nothing will get us the vote but a fight— sticks, stones, and violence. You take my advice and do not go to prison. It is horrible; I have been there."

I could not help laughing as I walked on. This is the first Suffragette I have met who advocated violence, even jokingly, which only shows what astounding patience women have got.

April 2nd.

It was suggested to me the other day that a good way of increasing the weekly sale of our paper would be to dispose of copies in the evenings at the queues of theatres while people are waiting for the doors to open. The woman who made the suggestion stated that she had done this in London with great success, and sold eighteen copies in quite a short time.

Accordingly I wrote notes to the three women who have been selling the paper, asking them to come here and discuss the new plan with me, adding that I had decided to accompany them myself in future, which I feel was very brave of me. They came last night, arid really they were most amusing.

One is quite a young girl, who works all day in a post office help-ing to support her mother, and spares her "off duty" time on Saturday morning to sell the paper. She regrets bitterly not being able to go to prison, but says that her mother will not hear of it.

I asked her what she thought of the new suggestion.

"I do not believe it will work here," she said. "The movement is not sufficiently understood, and it is horrible standing outside theatres at night selling the papers to people who do not understand."

"It must be," I assented. "Then I suppose you for one will not do it?"

"Oh, yes! Of course I'll do it. After all, it is not so bad as having to heckle a Cabinet Minister."

"No, indeed," joined in another young woman. "There have been days when I have wakened in the morning with a sort of sick pain, afraid to open the paper lest I should see that a Cabinet Minister was going to speak, and it would be my duty to interrupt his speech. That was when I lived near the seat of war. It is dreadful that these things have to be done."

"Yes," said the third woman, "one feels before one stands up to say, 'Why don't you give women the vote?' that one's heart is not only going up and down, but round and round. After the suspense of an-ticipation it is a positive relief to be knocked down and thrown into the street."

At this we all laughed. "Have you ever heckled a Cabinet Minis-ter?" I inquired of the post office girl.

"No; but I once made a speech. I am sure nothing could be worse than that."

"Tell us about it," we all exclaimed, simultaneously.

"It was not a good speech," she explained, "but it served this pur-pose, that I have never been asked to make one since. I was persuaded to accompany one of the organisers, who was going to hold an open-air meeting for working men, and I imagined that all I had to do was to carry the papers for her and help in that sort of way. However, when we had reached a street corner in a rather slummy part of Lon-don and had deposited a very shaky orange box on the pavement to serve as a platform, she insisted that I should 'take the chair' and say a few words while a crowd collected.

"With feelings which I shall never forget I stepped on to the rick-ety platform and gazed for inspiration at the handful of dirty children and loafers who represented the audience.

"'Friends,' I began, 'we have come here today as representatives of the Women's Social and Political Union to explain to you our by-election policy.' At this point the organiser pulled my sleeve and whispered that there was no by-election, with the result that I nearly fell off the orange box, and hurriedly concluded by saying: 'And Miss M——— will now tell you all about it.' I have never quite lived down that speech."

Of course, we were much entertained, and several anecdotes followed before we discussed the business in hand.

It has been finally settled that on Monday evening we shall go, two of us to one theatre, and two to the other, to try our luck. We are going to take eighteen papers each to sell, and the post office girl is to be with me. I am not much looking forward to the experience, but one must help.

April 4th.

I went today to an "At Home" given by the National Society for Woman's Suffrage, as I thought it would be interesting to hear their point of view. The meeting was not inspiring, and I felt dreadfully bored.

The speakers argued well as to the reasons why women should be enfranchised, and gave statistics about the petitions signed and meetings held in this connection within the last forty or fifty years, but that was all. They suggested no means by which we might hope to secure this Parliamentary vote, but insisted on the importance of constitutional methods, after Having proved them to have been useless so far.

With all due deference to the astonishing patience of these ladies, and the good they have doubtless done in the way of spadework, I must admit that I have no desire to join their Society.

As I walked home I sympathised vaguely with the feelings of the Irishman in the story whose little girl went up to where a crowd had collected and said: "Please, is there a fight going on? because, if so, father would like to be in it."

April 5th.

I have just returned from selling papers at the queues of theatres, and having partaken of a light meal and a strong drink, I now feel equal to recording our experiences before retiring to bed.

It was much worse than I had expected. Clearly this place does not understand yet. Counting the people outside the theatre, and those we passed in the street on the way there and back, I suppose we offered papers to sixty or seventy persons tonight, out of which number barely a dozen were even civil.

The post office girl kept assuring me that it was all right on Saturday mornings, and the mistake was in coming at night. It is mistake which I, for one, shall not repeat.

Almost every woman to whom I offered the paper stared at me coldly and waved it aside, or made some scornful remark. The majority of the men seemed to be under the impression that we were doing it for fun, and either made jokes or insulting remarks.

"What is your name, dear? Are you Christabel?" asked one; while others would inquire, "Which would you rather have, a husband or a vote?"

It was just when I was wondering whether to give it up or not, and my companion had crossed the street to intercept anyone passing on the opposite side, that I noticed a gentleman coming towards me.

"Will you buy our paper, *Votes for Women*, one penny," I asked, walking on slowly as I spoke. He stopped, however, and held out his hand for a copy.

"I have got one already at home, but I may as well take another; I can give it to a friend. I think it is so brave of you all to do this work," he added, pleasantly.

"Oh, how nice of you to understand," I could not help exclaiming. "They think, all the others, everyone we meet, that we do it for fun; that we like doing it." And I gave the sort of laugh that one gives when one has to laugh, so as not to scream.

He understood, perfectly.

"Never mind the others," he said, as he gave me a penny and took the paper, "it really does not matter in the least bit what they think."

I described, briefly, our experiences this evening.

"Why do you do it?" he inquired. "There must be plenty of others who could sell the papers."

"If war were declared and your country needed you for active service you would not sit at home, comfortably, and say: 'There are plenty of other men.' Now that I understand what this movement really means, I must stand by these women. I should be so ashamed afterwards if I had not helped."

"That is true," he admitted. "I should feel exactly the same in your place; and of one thing I am certain. Woman's Suffrage will come, and before very long, but do not forget that every great movement for reform has evoked opposition similar to this, and try to have patience for a little longer."

With these words he raised his hat and walked on.

From that moment my luck seemed to turn somewhat. First a labourer came up.

"Look here, miss," he said, "are you prepared to do a man's work?"

"Certainly not," I replied, "are you prepared to do a woman's work? Would you like to change places with your wife, for instance?"

I do not believe this side of the question had ever occurred to him before. He considered for a few moments, then he said, slowly:

"Well, no, I can't say that I should. A woman's work is never done, as you might say, what with the bairns and all." Then he bought a paper, "Just to see what it was about," as he expressed it.

After that, my companion joined me again, and we walked slowly homewards, selling papers here and there on our way. Just as we were approaching the Committee Room we noticed a cab with a gentleman in it, waiting in front of a large house. I walked up and offered him a paper. Then, for the first time, I noticed that he was drunk, and that a rather sweet-looking girl was sitting facing him.

"Are you a Suffragette?" he stuttered.

"Yes," I replied.

"Well, I'll give you a bit of advice," and he lowered his voice to a confidential whisper. "You get married. That is the best thing for you to do. Get married."

I looked beyond him at the girl, and she held out her hand for a paper.

"How much is it?" she asked.

I told her and she gave me the money, with a pleasant smile.

"I shall enjoy reading it," she said. "I am sure it must be very interesting."

On our arrival we found the organiser patiently awaiting our return.

"We are not going to do this again," I announced, as we deposited the remaining papers and the money on the table in front of her. "If selling these papers at night here really helped the Cause, it might be worth while to be insulted by every man one meets and looked at with contempt by every woman; but I don't believe that it does."

The organiser said that she thought she agreed with me. That in London it was different; but perhaps here it would be as well to content ourselves with selling them in the mornings.

So that experience is over anyhow, and I am going to bed.

April 7th.

At last I have chalked pavements! It is wonderful how, in this movement, one gradually keeps on doing a little more. I daresay I shall heckle a Cabinet Minister before I have finished.

Yesterday, I went with two others by train to a neighbouring town to do what they call pioneer work. Having provided ourselves with some chalk and a good supply of Suffragette literature, we met at the station and started our journey in very good spirits, if with some inward misgivings. On arrival at our destination, we proceeded to chalk on the pavements of the town at intervals:

"Votes for Women. Meeting at Corn Exchange, 1.30 p.m., today."

It was not so bad as I had expected. Of course, pieces of the chalk would break off, and one's back ached from stooping. An interested crowd always collected at once to watch the proceedings. Occasionally a spectator would rub the first word out with his foot before the second was written, but as a rule they contented themselves with remarks, such as:

"They're Suffragettes." "Oh, it's Votes for Women they're wanting," etc.

When this work was finished, we hired a lorry, to be placed at our disposal in the Corn Exchange—a large square capable of accommodating as big a crowd as we wanted. Then we visited two newspaper offices, to ask for an account of our meeting in the local paper, strolled into a newsagent's to request a *Votes for Women* paper, and express great surprise on being told that they had none in stock, finally presenting the shopman with a copy and persuading him to exhibit the poster in his window.

After this, having found a confectioner's shop, we partook of a light lunch, and retraced our footsteps to the Corn Exchange.

A large crowd had already collected round the lorry, most of them having evidently come out of idle curiosity. My share of the work consisted in walking about among the audience selling *Votes for Women* and pamphlets to anyone who wanted them, and discussing the subject with those who were too far away to hear what was being said by the speakers.

They were standing on the lorry, and each spoke for about half an hour. I made several converts, and found the people most interested and sympathetic. They were principally farmers who had come in for market day, and had never had the subject explained to them before.

One man strolled up to me with an amused smile and asked me if it was a vote I wanted or a voter. For one moment I failed to grasp his meaning, and replied that what we wanted was that women qualified as men are should have the Parliamentary vote. He changed his tone at once and began to discuss the question, so I explained the policy and views of the W.S.P.U., with the result that he gave me a shilling for the Cause.

Ten minutes later, when another man to whom I offered a pamphlet, called out: "It's no use, miss; I'm a married man," the other told him that he was a fool, and began to argue hotly for woman's suffrage, finally persuading him to give a shilling also!

The speeches were a great success, and we sold quite a lot of literature. After that we were only just in time to catch our train back, and returned, feeling much pleased with the result of the day's work.

During the journey home we discussed the Votes for Women question with the other occupants of our carriage, and produced a distinct impression on one man, who bought a selection of pamphlets.

A girl seated next to me remarked coldly that it was possible to look after a baby without being a Member of Parliament, after which enigmatical remark she gazed beyond me out of the window. I was too much taken aback to make any reply. She might just as well have said: "You can go for a walk without learning to play the piano." It reminds me of another occasion, when I discussed the woman's suffrage question with a man at dinner, who really seemed interested, and just as I was congratulating myself on having put all our strongest arguments clearly before him he remarked thoughtfully that it seemed to him it would be a mistake to abolish marriage. These people make one feel as if one were Alice in Wonderland talking to the Caterpillar.

April 8th.

I was darning stockings in the most domesticated way this morning when the maid came in and announced that a lady had called who wanted to know if I would sign an anti-Suffrage petition. "I told her it was no use," she added, apologetically, "but she said she would call again."

This sounded interesting. I had never seen one of these petitions, and I wanted to meet a militant "anti" off the stage, so to speak. Accordingly I instructed the maid to show the lady in when she returned, and to tell her that I wanted to speak to her.

Admiration for the woman's courage in going to people's houses with the paper gave me a sort of sympathetic feeling. "Probably," I reflected, "the poor thing really does think she is doing good."

It was in quite a friendly spirit that I rose to meet the "anti" when she arrived about an hour later. She was carrying a roll of paper. I pointed to an armchair near the fire, and asked her to sit down, which she did, and proceeded to remove her gloves while I tried to decide what type she belonged to.

Certainly not the "indirect influence" sort, who are afraid of chivalry being killed; she was too unattractive looking, and not a bit helpless. Clearly not the sweet womanly kind who adore housekeeping and babies, and seem to think that enfranchisement will abolish both. On the contrary she looked hard and rather bitter. "Evidently," I decided, "she must be of those who think women are not clever enough to understand politics."

Having settled this point, and noticing that my visitor had unfolded her document and was unscrewing the top off a fountain pen, I remarked pleasantly that I was very glad to meet her, as I wanted to hear a logical argument against woman's suffrage. "At present, I am a Suffragette," I explained, "but I would like so much to hear your side of the question."

She stared at me. "You are a Suffragette!" she exclaimed, in the tone she might have used if I had said I was a Nihilist. "If I had understood that I would not have come here. Your maid clearly said that you wished to see me."

"So I did. I wanted to hear your side. Have you ever been to one of our 'At Homes' to hear "ours?""

"Never, and I do not wish to." She was rapidly folding up the roll of paper.

I was a little taken aback by her manner. "But how can you discuss the subject and persuade people to sign the paper if you do not hear both sides of the question? How can you even feel sure that you are right?"

She rose and looked at me coldly. "I do not discuss the subject," she said, "and I do not intend to." With which words she walked out of the room and banged the door behind her.

I do not suppose that many "antis" are like that. I hope not, anyhow. But what are they thinking of to let her take the petition round?

April 9th.

I have just been told that the plans for the deputation have been altered. Instead of a few women going this time, there are to be over

100, consisting of representatives from all over Great Britain, and the date is to be June 29th. This gives me plenty of time for making arrangements. There is a good deal to be thought out and settled, as I do not intend to tell people that I am going. A friend has already offered to keep the boys for me and take care of any letters which come during my absence, so I shall, just say that I am paying visits, like the man who left a piece of cardboard in his window with the words "Removed to larger lodgings" when he went to prison.

In the meantime I had been spending my time doing fancy work for the Cause and knitting motor scarves in purple, white, and green for a stall at their bazaar. Truly in this movement there is work for the most constitutional among us. And yet it was only the other day that a man asked me why we did not hold meetings. This about a union which has held as many as 1,000 in a month!

April 14th.

At last I have succeeded in making some headway about getting our poster properly exhibited at the railway station. Finding after repeated efforts that it was quite useless to appeal to the man at the bookstall, I decided to go to headquarters, and having secured the address, went there this morning and requested to see the manager.

I was informed that he was busy, and offered a substitute. However I explained that I was in no hurry and could wait indefinitely, with which announcement I sat down patiently and waited.

After some time the manager came in, and looked at me with evident surprise. I explained the position to him, pointing out that we wanted our paper advertised and not hidden. "It was through reading one copy of this paper that I became interested in the Cause myself," I explained, "and now I am an active worker."

He was not very sympathetic. "What do you want me to do?" he asked. "The poster is exhibited, is it not?"

I explained once more that it was barely visible, and that each time I had asked for a paper the man had had to search somewhere on the floor for a copy, which he gave me with evident reluctance. "Evidently that man at the bookstall is a Liberal," I observed.

"No such thing," said the manager, gruffly. "There is no party feeling about it at all. Probably he had been already asked for it by a great many other ladies."

"That would be natural," I observed, "when there is such a demand for the paper."

The manager smiled. "Everyone complains," he said, "that their own paper is not sufficiently exhibited. We can't show all the papers on the stalls."

"Well, you see, it is not a matter of vital importance to the country that *Ally Sloper* and that sort of thing should be exhibited, but with this paper it is."

"That," said the manager, drily, "is a matter of opinion."

"Couldn't you let a boy walk along the platform beside the principal trains selling them?" I suggested. "Passengers starting on a journey would be sure to buy one out of curiosity, seeing the cartoon on the outside, and, having read it, would become interested in the Cause."

"Certainly not; we could not possibly allow that."

"Very well, then," I said, resignedly, "I suppose I shall have to do it myself. Walking along a platform beside a train will not be any worse than selling them in the street."

The manager looked at me with interest. "We have the monopoly of the station," he explained, "so you could not do that. But would you really be willing to?"

"In this movement," I said, "it is expected that every woman will do her duty, and if a thing of that sort would help it would be a duty. We do not always like the things we have to do, but it is a big Cause."

The manager looked thoughtful. "I can't understand why you do it at all," he said. "I have often wondered."

"Well, I cannot understand why you will not do this little thing I am asking. It is uphill work getting votes for women," I added slowly, as I rose

"I am quite sure it is," said the manager, kindly. "But I'll do what you want, miss; you may depend on me for that. I'll go this very afternoon and give orders that the poster is to be well exhibited and a copy of the paper always to be seen." I thanked him warmly and left the office.

May 7th.

I want to make a note of an amusing parody I read in today's *Votes for Women*. Knowing that Mr. Birrell was to take the chair at a meeting of the League for the Tax of Land Values, in Colston Hall, Bristol, the other day two of our members contrived, during the afternoon, to slip in unobserved and hid in the organ, in spite of great precautions having been taken against Suffragette disturbances, the hall having been searched by stewards and policemen before the meeting. As the poem shows, they succeeded in making an effective protest.

AN ORGAN RECORD.

Seated one day in the organ
We were weary and ill at ease;
We sat there three hours only,
Hid, 'midst the dusty keys.
We knew not if they'd be playing.
And to us what would happen then,
But when we heard Mr. Birrell,
It was then we protested, then.

Our voices rang out from the twilight.
But nowhere could we be found;
They looked from the floor to the ceiling—
Then stewards came searching round.
We asked for votes for women.
And that justice should be done;
But Birrell he could not answer,
And the audience made such fun.

He said he had come from Asquith,
And to him they must give ear;
But a voice rang out still louder,
Making our question clear.
It may be that Mr. Birrell
Won't speak in that Hall again,
And it may be never in Bristol,
Until the vote we gain.

Vera Holme.

May 10th.

I was introduced this morning to one of our London speakers.

"So you are going to prison?" she said, cheerfully, when we had shaken hands.

"I am going in a deputation to the prime minister," I replied. "I may get into the House of Commons."

She laughed merrily. "I daresay you will if you are stronger than twenty or thirty policemen."

"That is the part I dislike," I explained. "I do not mind the idea of prison if I could get into a cab and drive straight to Holloway."

"That would be very simple, wouldn't it?" she replied. "However, I am afraid you will not do it so easily as that."

"Do you think," I asked, "that there is any chance of Mr. Asquith receiving this deputation in preference to imprisoning over one hundred of us.?"

"No, I do not, but it is possible that before the 29th of June he might give a government pledge to the Suffrage Societies who advocate constitutional methods. You see, he under-estimated the strength of this movement to start with, and we can scarcely expect him to climb down now and admit that he has been compelled to grant the franchise to women against his will."

"But, in that case, everyone will imagine that the vote was got through constitutional methods, and in spite of the militant women, not because of them."

She laughed again. "Of course they will, but that does not matter in the least. We do not care what the public think so long as we get the vote."

They really are wonderful, the leaders of this movement, always so optimistic and happy, so absolutely indifferent to criticism, so ready to sacrifice everything merely for the sake of benefiting other women. And yet there are people who really believe that they do it for notoriety, which, being interpreted, means misrepresentation, and magistrates are under the impression that they punish them by giving them a month or six weeks in Holloway, while most of them, like myself, look forward to the imprisonment with equanimity and indifference as compared with the horrible ordeal of having to make the protest, which will inevitably result in them being sent there. When one reflects for a moment that punishment was primarily intended to diminish crime one begins to realise the absurdity of the position which the government has taken up.

June 28th.

I have had rather an eventful day, so must scribble a few lines in my diary before retiring to bed. I can hardly realise that tomorrow I shall take part in a raid on the House of Commons and the following day shall be in prison. I do not suppose I shall be allowed to write a diary there, but on the other hand I shall probably remember very clearly what happens during my sojourn in Holloway.

I have been invited to stay in London with a member of the W.S.P.U. who has a flat not very far from the scene of action. I have never met her, but she offered to put up a member for the deputation; such is the *esprit de corps* of the rapidly increasing family party who serve under the purple, white, and green.

I had lunch today with a friend, who evidently invited me for the sole purpose of dissuading me from my intention of going in the deputation. She pointed out to me that there was every chance of being killed or seriously injured, and said that it was not fair to my husband and the boys.

I wish she had not talked like that; it has made me feel unsettled and worried, without doing any good, and after all, one might just as well be killed in a railway accident as in a deputation.

After leaving her house I went to the Suffragette Committee Room to say "Goodbye" to the organiser. She wished me luck, and so did one or two others who were there.

"Do not forget," said Miss M——, "that at five o'clock every afternoon we shall all be thinking of you. One of our prisoners told us it helped her wonderfully, that she does not think she would have got through the two months without it, just knowing for a few moments every day that her friends who understood were thinking of her. You will know when it is five o'clock in Holloway, because a bell rings then."

I shall certainly remember. How kind they all are!

I let the boys sit up later than usual, on account of it being my last night, and told them stories partly to distract my own thoughts. About half an hour after they had gone to bed the maid came in looking rather alarmed to say that two policemen had come, and wanted to see me.

"Surely," I reflected, "even a Liberal Government cannot arrest one beforehand because one contemplates going in a deputation."

She had shown them in the dining-room, so I walked in there, trying to look unconcerned. They explained that the boys had been firing a toy pistol through the back garden, and some of the pellets had struck the window of a doctor's house opposite, so he had sent a complaint to the police station.

The relief of finding that their visit had nothing to do with political agitations made me treat the incident of the shooting as a good joke, particularly as no harm had been done, the pistol in question being a toy air-gun. I said I was very sorry, and that I would see that the gun was not used again except in the house, adding that I hoped none of the doctor's patients had been killed while they were waiting in the consulting-room.

"No one was hurt, madam," said the policeman, quite solemnly, "as the pellets did not break the window." Clearly he had a small sense of humour.

After a few moments' pleasant conversation, they said "Good evening," and left. What an excellent story this would make for the "antis."

"While a Suffragette woman, who ought to have been looking after her home, was occupied with politics, her neglected boys were spending their time risking their own lives and those of the neighbours, by shooting peas from a two-and-sixpenny rifle."

Oh! I do wish it was the day after tomorrow. Meanwhile, I shall go to bed.

June 29th.

I am almost ashamed to admit the fact, even to my diary, but I am feeling horribly frightened. I positively dread the prospect of this deputation tonight. I am sorry to be so cowardly and unworthy of the splendid women who will be my companions in the fight; but when I think of the London crowd and the mounted police I feel cold and a little sick with apprehension. However, I shall not dwell on my feelings, but will briefly relate the events of the day. As Miss M—— has so often impressed on me:

In a movement of this kind what one feels does not count.

I arrived at St. Pancras in time to drive here, have a short talk with my hostess, and go off to a meeting held by Mrs. Pankhurst for members of the deputation only. I find that my hostess, besides being a member of our Union, is a theosophist and a keen anti-vivisectionist, so if I were staying here longer we might have many interesting talks.

She had a business engagement this afternoon, so, during her absence, I am sitting in my room writing. A charwoman, who comes twice a week to do the rough work of the flat, has just been in and had a little talk with me. She bitterly regrets not being able to join the deputation herself, but explained, apologetically, that as she had to support her husband and children she could not afford to lose her place, and the people she worked for would not employ her again if she had been in prison. She wished me luck, and expressed the hope that I would not be very badly knocked about.

"It will be a rough crowd, miss, I fear," she said, by way of encouragement; "you will not wear a dress you mind about getting torn."

I assured her that the dress I intended to wear might be sacrificed in the interests of the Cause, but added that I, too, sincerely hoped it would not be so very bad.

"They do say," she observed, "that the government have sent to Wales and Whitechapel for the roughest set of policemen they can find for tonight, because most of the others know Mrs. Pankhurst too well now and are on her side, so the Suffragettes gets arrested too easy. Anyhow, I hope as how no one will be killed."

Having cheered me up with these few words of encouragement, the woman has now gone off to finish her work, so I will try to describe the meeting for members which I attended this morning.

When I reached the place, I found a long. queue of women waiting outside for the door to be opened. I was much struck by the splendid organisation. Although there were at least 140 of us, each one received typewritten instructions explaining most clearly exactly what we were to do. I will not try to describe Mrs. Pankhurst's speech, beyond saying that I shall remember it always, and the strange impressiveness of the scene. She told us that a new stage in the women's agitation had now been reached. Hitherto, the Suffragettes had quietly submitted to being treated as common criminals for political offences (if, indeed, they could be called offences at all). Now, however, we were to make a protest against this, for the sake of political prisoners in the future. The opportunity was a good one, for there would probably be over 100 of us in Holloway tomorrow, and unity is strength.

She told us exactly what she wanted us to do. We were to refuse to wear prison clothes or to scrub out our cells, and as a protest against insufficient air in the cells we were to wait till a bell rang at 1 p.m. the first day, and then each of us must carefully, with the heel of a shoe, break a pane of glass in her window. She explained that, on our arrival at Holloway, we must stand together and refuse to go to our cells until we had seen the governor. If we were forcibly taken to the cells, we must refuse to be medically examined or to wear the prison clothes. If undressed by force and our own clothes removed, we must undress and get to bed. She made it very clear that we were to be polite always to the wardresses and everyone with whom we came in contact, that having always been our policy, that our strongest weapon was passive resistance and endurance, whatever the cost to ourselves.

Each detail was thought out and carefully explained. I could not help being struck by the fact that though everyone knew it would be very much easier to quietly submit to second division treatment, yet all were ready to do as she wished.

"We shall be given solitary confinement," said Mrs. Pankhurst; "we shall be put in punishment cells, probably in different prisons. As for me, I don't know where I shall be put, but wherever we are, whatever happens, in spirit we shall be together."

As I looked round the room at the bright, happy faces of the women, such sweet, womanly, gentle women—a great sense of pity came to me, for the blind obstinacy of the prime minister who thinks to check a movement of this sort by physical force, tyranny, and misrepresentation.

"Why," I reflected, "could he not have received this one deputation courteously as he receives deputations of men, and thus obviate the necessity for all this?"

Before leaving the hall, we were each given type-written instructions on a sheet of paper. Mine are as follows: At 6 p.m. tonight I am to find my way to certain offices in Parliament Street, the address of which is given, where I am to remain in seclusion until 8.40 p.m., when, in company with five other women, whose names are given on the paper, I am to leave, by the Parliament Street entrance, walk towards Parliament Square, and endeavour to force my way through the carriage entrance to the House of Commons.

It has been arranged on this occasion that we are to go in a series of deputations, not one of which is to exceed eight in number, as in accordance with the Bill of Rights; thus deputations, numbering from six to eight delegates, will start from different directions at intervals of about fifteen minutes during the evening, the result of which should be somewhat baffling to the police. We are to carry nothing in our hands except the resolution to the prime minister. There is also a note to say that if arrested we shall be bailed out for the night by Mr. Pethick Lawrence, and advising us to find out the most direct route home from Westminster.

I talked to several of the women while waiting for my instructions. They all seemed quite prepared for the fact that they may be killed to-night, quite happy just to be helping the Cause, and cheerfully ready for the extra ordeal of the revolt in prison.

Women of all ages were there and of different types. What impressed me most was their mutual love for each other and for the leaders of the movement, also the expression in their eyes, which I cannot describe better than the "Suffragette eyes," the look of people who are seeing beyond what is happening around them. University girls, hospital nurses, women who had spent their time and money working among the poor and fallen till the conviction came to them that until women could claim the rights of citizenship little could be done in this direction, and so threw in their lot with the W.S.P.U.

One old lady of 79 interested me particularly by her conversation.

I shall not write any more now, as I want to collect my things. Mrs. Pankhurst told us to bring a small bag to the police court tomorrow, with a change of clothes, in case of first division treatment. The rest of my belongings I shall leave here until I come out of prison. 2 a.m.

I have been bailed out for the night. Tomorrow at 10 o'clock I must be at Bow Street to answer to a charge of obstructing the police.

It really is very funny, and I cannot get away from the ludicrous side of it; but oh! how thankful I was to get arrested. I must quickly scribble down what happened and get to bed, for tomorrow night I shall be In a cell. I can hardly realise it.

To begin at the beginning, my hostess accompanied me as far as the office in Parliament Square. On the way there she remarked how brave she thought I was to go on the deputation. I am sure she would have felt less admiration for my courage if she had known how dreadfully frightened I was feeling, though I managed to conceal the fact. As we got near the battlefield, although it was not yet 6 o'clock, lines of policemen and mounted police were to be seen everywhere, and fresh relays coming along the street. I heard the 'bus conductor say to a passenger: "It's on account of the Suffragettes. There's going to be a big row tonight."

There were placards up in several places:

Serious warning to the public. Grave danger in coming to Parliament Square tonight.

When we reached the office I found it already half full of extremely cheerful-looking Suffragettes. We had to speak softly and keep away from the windows in case of attracting the attention of the police, who, if they had suspected our presence there, would have surrounded the house and prevented us from getting out.

If there is one thing that I find more trying than another it is anticipation, and the prospect of remaining in that room for nearly three hours was too much for me, so I persuaded one girl to go out with me for a stroll. We did not wear our colours, so were allowed to walk about, though watched suspiciously if we got too near Parliament Square.

To help to pass the time we had some tea in a shop. "I am feeling dreadfully hot," observed my companion. "It comes of wearing all this cotton wool."

"What, cotton wool?" I asked, in surprise.

"Well, you see, I have padded myself well with cotton wool and put cardboard outside that. I have been in deputations before, and I do not intend to get my ribs broken this time."

"Good heavens, surely it is not so rough as all that!"

"Wait till you try it," she said, as she calmly spread some butter on a roll.

"You have been in prison?" I said. "Did you mind it much?"

"Oh, no! You will get through that all right. It is the crowd I dislike."

By this time I was feeling rather cold, possibly with apprehension; besides, I was not padded.

"Look here," I said, "will you go arm in arm with me on the deputation? Let's hold on to each other, and not let go. I should not like us to get separated in that crowd."

My new friend "laughed bitterly," as the *Daily Mail* would express it. "Separated! Of course we shall get separated. We may start together, but after the first few moments none of us will see each other again till we meet in the police court."

I did not answer. The crowd was every moment getting bigger. Presently we returned to the office, which was now quite full. The blinds were drawn down, and two men who were with us warned us not to approach the window. I shall never forget that time. One man, who had a watch in his hand, told each deputation when the time had come for them to go, whereupon they would start, with the whispered good wishes of us all.

It seemed as if our time would never come. "I think your watch must have stopped," I said once. "It seems hours since the last deputation left."

The man smiled and said the watch was all right.

"It will be a blot on English history," he remarked presently, "the way the British Government has treated the women who were asking for the rights of citizenship."

The noise in the street increased, till I felt as if I were taking a part in a scene from the French Revolution. One could hardly realise that it was real. Occasionally someone would peep through the blind and exclaim softly: "The mounted police are clearing the street! Oh, someone is hurt! No, it is only an arrest." And so on.

"I am thankful that some have been arrested," said my companion. "There was a report that the government had given strict orders they were not to arrest us, in which case, of course, the chance of not being seriously hurt would be small. However, I daresay the police are afraid of the crowd tonight. It has been so well organised for weeks that nearly all the people are with us, and there are a great many."

Suddenly I thought of the old lady whom I had spoken to in the morning, so fragile, but with so much courage, alone out there. Kneeling beside the window, I shut my eyes and prayed that no harm would come to her. A few moments later I heard someone exclaim: "The old lady has been arrested! She is all right!" After that all sense of fear left me, and I was only conscious of a longing to be in the fight doing something to help. From where I knelt I could see through the window by raising the blind an inch or two, and one after another I watched the prisoners being marched between two policemen and surrounded by two or four others towards the police station. No one seemed to have been much hurt.

At last our turn came. Someone pressed my hand and whispered "Godspeed" as I passed.

Silently we wended our way down the narrow staircase and into the street, my friend and I who were last holding each other tightly by the arm, determined to stick together as long as humanly possible. The crowd round the door was so dense that we had a little difficulty in forcing our way out. Instantly a shout went up as the colours were recognised; cheers and encouraging remarks greeted us. "Here are some more Suffragettes! Go on, miss; you're all right; get through them," etc., while one woman's voice pleaded: "Don't go, miss. You'll have a rough time there."

On we went. The crowd was enormous. It almost took one off one's feet. For some moments I clung tightly to the arm of my companion, the others being already lost to sight; but her prediction proved only too true. A force which we were powerless to resist tore us apart, and I saw no more of her or any of the others till we met in the police court.

Meanwhile I moved on towards Parliament Square, helped by the pushing, eager crowd, until I saw a line of mounted police advancing towards me and stretching right across the road from one end to the other, including the pavements. As they came they cleared the streets before them, sweeping the crowd backward on to us—the crowd but not the Suffragettes. One and all those women must have forced their way through, for there were none among the people being forcibly driven back on to us.

Noticing a small space between two of the horses, I ran forward and attempted to push through. Instantly they closed on me, and another horse barred my way. I seemed to be wedged between prancing, backing horses, evidently bent on trampling me to death, though in reality I daresay well trained to act their part.

I kept my face towards the House of Commons and struggled on conscious only of one fervent prayer to the Power at the back of the universe to protect and keep my brave companions and bring them all safely through this night.

Presently two rows of police on foot, who were following up behind the mounted men, pressed forward. I felt my arms seized on either side by very strong hands, and forcibly I was dragged almost off my feet right through the horses back to the other side. For a brief moment I thought that these policemen, seeing my peril, had done this to save my life, but as they kept a firm hold of my arms I realised with a feeling of inexpressible thankfulness that we were walking in the direction of Cannon Row Police Station.

To make sure I addressed the man who was holding my right arm. "Have you arrested me?" I asked him, very politely.

"Yes, miss," he replied, "and a good job too, to get out of that crowd. You wasn't hurt, was you?"

"Not at all. I have only been in there quite a short time." I wanted to say how very grateful I felt to him for having arrested me like that at sight, but did not quite like to. The irony of it all is that the papers will probably report that I struggled, bit, and scratched in order to escape. It will always be a mystery to me why the public have so long believed those reports. When I remember how absolutely powerless I felt in the grasp of two exceptionally big and strong men, backed by three or four others who walked alongside, how worse than useless it would have been to attempt to move, far less struggle, on account of the way my arms and wrists were being held. When in addition to this one reflects that a Suffragette's life practically depends on the protection of the Metropolitan police, and that her ambition invariably is to get arrested as quickly as possible, the absurdity of supposing that she would be so foolish as to strike or kick the man who, apart from the fact that he is her best friend, is so very much stronger than herself, is surely too obvious to require further comment.

"Are you on our side in this Movement?" I asked, as we walked along.

"On your side, miss?" exclaimed the man on my right. "Of course I am on your side; we all are. Didn't I hear Miss Christabel at Peckham? Is she here tonight?"

"No," I replied. "We can't all go to Holloway; and she is too badly wanted outside. A good many of us are here, though—one hundred and fifty or so, I think."

"Well, there's five or six thousand of us, anyhow," he observed, "so it will be all right."

"I'm wearing your colours, miss," said the man who was holding my left arm, "the badge, I mean; it's inside my helmet."

On our arrival at the police station we entered a large room filled with Suffragette prisoners cheerfully discussing politics with the policemen who had arrested them. The place reminded me somewhat of a custom house abroad. We all had to walk in turn past a table, at which a man was sitting with a pen in his hand making a note of our names, ages, and addresses, also of the charges brought against us.

Clearly he had not much sense of humour. A sweet-looking and extremely fragile little girl with fluffy hair, who gave her age as 21, though she looked less, was passed not long before me.

"What is the charge?" he inquired, gruffly, of the very tall policeman who accompanied her.

"The prisoner assaulted me and knocked off my helmet," said the man, solemnly.

At this point I caught the eye of the little girl, and we both laughed. It was so very funny.

She made no remark when a paper was filled in charging her with having assaulted the police. Perceiving that this was the sort of evidence they were all giving, I asked the little girl why she had not denied the charge.

"It is a sort of understood thing," she explained, "that if the police will help us by arresting us on sight, as they have been doing tonight, we will not contradict anything they may say as an excuse for having done so. They do help us splendidly now that they understand," she added, "and it would never do to annoy them in any way. Besides, what does it matter what people believe?"

I walked up to my policeman, who was discussing the advantages of *ju-jitsu* with another prisoner, and asked him if he would do me a great favour.

"Yes, miss, of course I will," he said, pleasantly.

"I want you to promise not to say that I scratched your face or knocked off your helmet. Of course you must say something, but please not that."

The officer of the law reflected for a moment. "Very well, miss, I'll not say that, if you like."

When my turn came I wondered for a moment whether my friend would keep his promise, and if so, what he would accuse me of.

"The prisoner refused to turn back when told to," he announced, "but forced her way through, and seizing one of the horses by the bridle, led it towards the House of Commons."

I was too much astonished by this story to make any remark, when the man at the table observed that it was a serious charge and an extremely dangerous thing to do.

Having passed through this "custom house," we were all taken to an enormous billiard-room upstairs, where we remained until Mr. Pethick Lawrence came to bail us out. Anyone would have supposed it was a big "At Home," and Mrs. Pankhurst the hostess. We sang Suffragette songs and compared notes as to our experiences.

Outside, thousands of police were collecting and preparing to disperse. One girl leant out of the window and called: "Three cheers for the Metropolitan police!" which were heartily given.

I soon discovered that, although there had been no serious casualties owing to the splendid behaviour of the majority of the police, comparatively few of the women had got off quite so easily as myself. Many were covered with bruises; some had been repeatedly knocked down owing to having been in a hostile part of the crowd or having come in contact with the new policemen who "did not understand," as predicted by the charwoman. It was very late before we were all bailed out. I was one of the last to receive a piece of paper, which I shall always keep, summoning me to appear at Bow Street tomorrow to answer to a charge of obstructing the police. Quite near Parliament Square I was lucky enough to meet a belated hansom, which I hailed and drove home. Thus has ended the most alarming experience I have ever had in my life.

June 30th.

It still seems quite incredible, but here I am back again. Our case has been remanded for a week. I shall briefly record the events of the day, as the hour is late and I am looking forward to a good night's sleep. My hostess accompanied me to Bow Street, the route being as yet unfamiliar to me, and we started in good time. I was carrying a small bag, as per instructions, containing a change of clothes, etc.

When we were settled in the 'bus I remarked to my friend that on this occasion anyhow the papers could not possibly say anything against our behaviour or describe us as disorderly.

"Oh, yes, they will," she said, smiling. "They always do. The women were no more disorderly last time than this."

Scarcely had she said the words when my eyes fell on a poster outside a newsagent's shop. On it was written in large letters:

RAID OF THE FURIES.
DEMENTED SUFFRAGETTES RUSH
THE HOUSE OF COMMONS.

We both laughed. I do not know why I did. I was not feeling amused. A sense of the hopelessness of ever making people understand came over me like a sort of wave. A lady sitting opposite to us was reading a paper. I glanced at it and could see the same headlines.

"When you have finished," I said, gently, "I wonder if you would be so kind as to let me read that paper? I am one of the 'Furies' who raided the House of Commons, and I would like to see myself as others see me."

She laughed, and handed it to me. "They do put a lot of nonsense in the Press," she remarked. As I went on reading I felt my face getting crimson. "You know this is not true!" I began, hotly. "You know we did not do these things!"

"Yes," she said, quietly, "I was there."

Then we all three talked shop comfortably for the remainder of the drive, oblivious of all other passengers.

Outside Bow Street a crowd had collected, and the prisoners were standing in a long queue waiting to be admitted. It was a strange sight. A man with a camera who was taking snapshots asked me to point out the old lady to him, but I could not see her.

After some delay we were admitted, but not actually into the police court; we remained either in the hall, which we almost filled, or in the courtyard outside, and there we spent the greater part of the day.

It was a most interesting scene. Inside the hall the women either talked in groups or scribbled farewell notes, while husbands, brothers, and friends, some of whom had come in motor-cars, arrived to say "Goodbye" or to take letters to the post. In the courtyard were to be seen groups of women, some singing in chorus the pretty Suffragette songs, while others talked to policemen, for everywhere were the police watching the proceedings with friendly interest. Outside the police court Black Marias were waiting to convey the prisoners in relays to Holloway, while crowds of interested spectators thronged the streets ready to cheer at the sight of the colours.

I was again very much struck by the attitude of the police, and made a point of talking to as many of them as possible, for there was plenty of time, and I was anxious to get the views of as large a number of them as possible. Among all those I spoke to only one was an "anti." He remarked drily: "Well, I can't say that I admire your methods."

I replied that we had not come here to agitate for his admiration, but for the vote.

"Well, do you suppose you will get it by doing this sort of thing?" he asked.

"I daresay we shall have to do considerably more," I admitted, "but we certainly will not get it by doing less."

Every other man was friendly. One said: "Who do you reckon is your worst enemy in this movement, miss?"

"Mr. Asquith, I suppose," I replied.

"Well, it's not him, it's the Press. The papers never tells the truth about these deputations."

Just then I noticed Mrs. Pankhurst talking to Inspector Jarvis, who appeared to be extremely friendly. "The papers say that she assaulted him," I said, glancing in their direction.

The policeman laughed loud. "That is just what they would say," he remarked. "It would have been an honour for him if she had," said another.

Hours passed, and still we were not summoned for trial.

"When do you think our case will be heard?" I asked of a tall policeman who was guarding the door.

"Can't say, miss. I'm tired myself. It's night and day duty for us when you ladies has these raids; but you'll be in the cells before long now, for sure."

"I'm very sorry," I replied; "but anyhow, you don't have to go to Holloway when it is over."

"You're right there, miss, and I don't mind telling you I would not go to prison in the second division for a month not for any Cause, and I can't think how you ladies comes and does it again and again."

"In the meantime I would like very much to go out and have a cup of tea," I said, pleasantly. "Don't you think I might go, just for a short time?" He glanced at me, and hesitated. "I am a Suffragette," I added. "You know what Suffragettes are like. I will not run away."

"That's true, miss, and there is a shop of Lyons's just a few doors down the street on your left."

I thanked him warmly and hurried off. As I entered the restaurant I perceived that the tables seemed almost all taken, and the place full of people having lunch. I stood for a moment in the doorway, hesitating.

Instantly every man and woman stood up and cheered, the men in most cases waving their hats, and all looking straight at me. Much embarrassed and presuming that I had been mistaken for Mrs. Pankhurst or someone else, I hastened to a small empty table with two chairs and sat down.

A few moments later, however, another prisoner came in, and exactly the same thing happened, so I realised that they knew by our colours that we were members of the deputation and were expressing their sympathy.

The newcomer, who sat at my table opposite me, informed me that our case would not be heard for another hour, so when we had finished our repast we decided to go for a short walk down the Embankment.

"I wonder why they are delaying so long over hearing our case?" I said to my companion.

"Well," she replied, "I hear that most of the morning has been spent trying cases of petty thefts which occurred last night in London during the absence of the whole police force, which was occupied in protecting the Cabinet Ministers from us."

That solution of the problem had not occurred to me.

A boy was selling papers as we passed out of Lyons's shop. He held one out. "Full account of Suffragette prisoners at Bow Street," he shouted. "Scenes in court."

"We are two of the prisoners," I explained, "so we know what they are doing, which is very little so far."

As I said this, two men who were near took off their hats and stood with them in their hands till we passed. It was the same most of the way along. We met smiles of encouragement and saw handkerchiefs waved by all classes of people as they caught sight of our colours, and knew what they meant.

On our return to Bow Street we were informed that Mrs. Pankhurst and Mrs. Haverfield were being tried, so our turn would come soon now. We waited for some time longer, and then were told that the case was to be adjourned for a week, as the Magistrate wanted time to enable him to reply to some points raised by Mrs. Haverfield's counsel.

Accordingly we were all allowed to leave the court, the further hearing of the case being fixed for Friday, July 9th, at 10.30 a.m.

I was much impressed by the fact that without bail, without even taking down our addresses, the Magistrate dismissed us all, taking the word of one woman, Mrs. Pankhurst, that we would not fail to appear for trial on the appointed date. I hurried to the nearest Post Office and telegraphed to a friend at Hastings that I would arrive next week and spend a week.

As I passed some carts with fruit and vegetables for sale, an old woman standing behind one, seeing my colours, stopped me to ask anxiously what the Suffragettes' sentence had been.

"The case has been remanded for a week," I explained.

"I'm glad of that, anyhow," said the old woman.

A man standing beside her took a clay pipe out of his mouth and said: "This government is mad, that's what it is." After which announcement he continued to smoke placidly.

On my return, I was received with rejoicing by my kind hostess, and we discussed the political situation at great length. Now I really must go to bed.

July 4th.

I am having a splendid time with my friends in Hastings, enjoying the respite of a week off duty by the seaside, not to mention motoring and picnics. When I say off duty, I must not overlook the fact that I have sold five dozen copies of *Votes for Women* along the Parade.

It took three days, but I have disposed of them all. As is inevitable when employed in this sort of work, I encountered many "antis" and much criticism and contempt, but on the whole I did not have a very bad time, once I had got over the first horrible ordeal of walking through the town carrying an armful of papers and wearing the regalia of purple, white, and green.

As I passed the General Post Office an old gentleman hurried out with a handful of letters. He paused a moment at sight of me, so I held out a paper, showing the cartoon on the outside.

"Will you buy a copy of *Votes for Women,*" I asked. "Full account of the deputation to the prime minister; one penny."

He glared at me.

"Madam," he said coldly, "I consider that women are women when they remain in their own place, and that is in their home."

With these words he walked on and posted the letters, feeling, I am sure, that he had crushed me and the entire movement with the force

274

of his logic. At that moment I caught the eye of a cabman who had overheard the conversation. He did not exactly wink, but he somehow conveyed to me by his expression that he shared my views, both as regards Woman's Suffrage and the old gentleman, for which I felt really grateful.

It would take too long to record all the conversations I held with my various customers, considering that for every person who bought a copy, at least ten met my request with more or less disdainful refusals. In many cases I found myself ready with a suitable and crushing rejoinder, but as a rule I received jeers or criticism in silence.

Not so my friend, Mrs. R——, who accompanied me one morning to the extreme discomfort of my opponents. I shall never forget her comments, always made in a clear and loud voice. When an old gentleman waved my paper aside with an irritable "Votes for Women, indeed; we don't want any more women"; she exclaimed:

"Evidently this person supposes that to give votes to a few women would create others; that is at least a new light upon the subject."

A few moments later a girl informed me that she did not vote for women, whereupon Mrs. R—— asked her whether she voted for men, adding that she was glad to hear that she had a vote, anyhow. Once, when a man told me to "go 'ome and look after the biby," she remarked:"There is no use in offering the paper to trippers; do talk to people with some signs of intelligence."

As Mrs. R—— (who is not a Suffragette) was not wearing the colours, none of these people had connected her with me, though we were walking alongside most of the time, so were all the more taken aback by her scornful remarks, and generally remained staring after us in silent and open-mouthed amazement.

A gentleman who was leaning back on a deck chair on the Parade held out his hand for a paper as I passed. When I handed him one he remarked that I ought not to charge a penny but should give it to him for nothing if I really wanted to help the Cause. I replied that as I was already giving my time and the greater part of my income and the whole of my reputation to help this Cause, I had felt that he could give a penny towards it.

"However," I added, "since you cannot afford it, I will very gladly buy this copy myself and give it to you."

He said nothing, but he handed me a penny.

The next man to whom I offered the paper remarked that he had no desire to read anything about Suffragettes; what he saw in the papers was quite enough for him.

"But," I explained, "the papers write about things which we never did, whereas this will give you an accurate account of our deputation to the prime minister last Tuesday. It is very interesting, and I know it is true, because I was there."

He looked at me contemptuously.

"I'd rather believe the papers," he said, shortly.

The extreme insolence of his tone made me angry. So after looking him up and down for several moments in complete silence, I said, slowly: "Yes, I should imagine that you most probably would."

I was glad to see him crumple up a little.

The women, on the whole, were worse than the men; but obviously from ignorance of the whole subject. One old lady informed me that she disliked Suffragettes, so I smiled, pleasantly, and asked her why.

"Because I think women ought to stay at home; it's their place," she replied.

"Then are you prepared to support the millions of women who have to leave their homes to work for their living, also to give homes to the others who have none?" I inquired. "Because if not, how can they stay at home, even if they want to?"

She turned her back on me and walked away, which can scarcely be called an argument.

A few moments later I offered a paper to a man who seemed to want one, explaining that it contained a full account of the deputation, adding that I could vouch for the truth of it as I was one of them and was now on remand.

"Are you?" he said. "Well, I hope you will get three months."

I could think of no suitable reply to this, so smiled pleasantly and walked on.

I am glad they are all sold, as I can now enjoy life peacefully till next Thursday.

July 8th.

I wish that the people who imagine the cause of Woman's Suffrage is being retarded by the militant methods could have been present in the St. James's Hall tonight. I returned from Hastings in time to attend the evening meeting there, as I had received a letter from Clement's Inn asking me to come, if possible, and to wear white. I was seated in the orchestra behind the platform along with the rest of the prisoners, all except those who were working at the Cleveland Election and could not get away in time. We almost completely filled the seats.

It was a wonderful meeting. I certainly have never seen such enthusiasm before. The hall was absolutely packed, so that an overflow meeting had to be held elsewhere for several hundred people.

When Mrs. Pankhurst stood up the cheering and clapping was so prolonged that I feared she would never be able to speak at all. When at last they stopped, she explained that she had just returned from working at Cleveland, and that she had heard Mr. Samuel, the Liberal Candidate, allude to the members of our deputation as the "Wild Women of Westminster," whose behaviour was putting back the Cause. "These," said Mrs. Pankhurst, indicating the orchestra, where we were all seated, dressed in white, with the purple, white, and green regalia. "These are the Wild Women of Westminster. What do you think of them?"

Instantly the cheers and clapping began again louder than ever, and men stood on their seats waving their hats.

Just before the meeting began Mrs. Pankhurst had received a letter from Miss Wallace Dunlop, the girl who was sentenced to one month's imprisonment in the second division for stamping on the walls of the House of Commons with indelible ink an extract from the Bill of Rights: "It is the right of the subject to petition the king, and all commitments and prosecutions for such petitioning are illegal."

This was her third imprisonment, and she decided to try the effect of a hunger strike as a protest against second division treatment for political offences, with the result that she was released today, after ninety-one hours' starvation,

Mrs Pankhurst read her letter aloud. It described how they tried to make her eat by offering her tempting food. Finally, the doctor threatened to feed her through the nostrils, and she said:

"You may do so for a month, but supposing you get 108 women in here on Friday, all requiring to be fed through the nostrils, your hands will be full."

"At this," she wrote, "the doctor's face was a study."

She ended her letter by wishing us all luck, and regretting her inability to be with us tonight on account of feeling rather weak.

If it had been possible to exceed the enthusiasm shown before, the audience would have done it now; and when Mrs. Pankhurst asked for three cheers for the bravest woman in England, they were given in such a way as almost to have persuaded Mr. Asquith even that there are some people in favour of Woman's Suffrage.

I will not attempt to describe the speeches. Suffice it to say that the net result of our deputation last week has been an added membership of ninety-three women, the sympathy and support of a large number of men, who confessed to having taken no interest in the movement before they saw what happened in Parliament Square on June 29th, also subscriptions amounting to £1,300 in one week, and the sale of the paper raised from 25,000 to 50,000 copies. One person after another stood up to offer so much money for the Cause for each of the 108 prisoners.

When the time came for questions to be asked, one man protested against all the prisoners who were on remand till tomorrow having to follow Miss Dunlop's example and go through the ordeal of a hunger strike, adding that in his experience the women he had met did not want the vote.

There were shouts of "Then I'm sorry for you," and "Sit down," from men among the audience, and when quiet was restored Mrs. Pankhurst explained that such a course might not be necessary, but if it were, we were all prepared to follow where Miss Dunlop had led the way.

With that exception, there were no protests or criticisms of any sort, and as I left the hall in company with my hostess, the hospitality of whose flat I am once more enjoying, I realised more than I have ever done before the underlying strength of this Movement and the futility of attempting to stop the militant methods by treating as common criminals women of gentle birth and high ideals, who look upon imprisonment in this Cause as the highest honour they could obtain.

July 9th.

In this world it is generally the most unexpected thing which happens. After another long day, spent at Bow Street Police Court, I am once again back in my hostess's flat.

This time, for some reason or other, the police refused to let us break the monotony by going out. I tried to persuade one to let me pass, by saying that I was hungry and wanted some lunch, but he "wasn't taking any," and replied that a man from Lyons's shop was coming in for orders, and I could get what I wanted inside. Meanwhile, the case against Mrs. Pankhurst and Mrs. Haverfield was being heard. But as the prisoners were almost sufficient in number to fill the Court, we had to remain in another part of the building, where we could not hear what was going on.

At last, just as our patience was becoming exhausted, Christabel Pankhurst came in and explained the situation to us. The magistrate, she said, had passed a provisional sentence on Mrs. Pankhurst and Mrs. Haverfield of a fine of five pounds or a month's imprisonment in the second division. He had, however, consented to state a case for a higher court, as suggested by Lord Robert Cecil, in view of the importance of the constitutional issue, on a point of law raised by the defendants, namely, the right of the women to present the petition to Mr. Asquith.

The result of this decision is that we shall all be on remand until the further hearing of the case, which may very probably be postponed till November or December. She assured us, however, that we should find plenty of work for the Cause waiting us outside, which I do not for a moment doubt. Meanwhile, we are free to go our several ways, all, that is to say, except fourteen women, who were accused of throwing stones in addition to obstructing the police. Their case is to be tried on Monday.

I spoke to one or two of them today, as I wanted to hear their point of view. Personally, I think that stone-throwing is a mistake, and prefer the policy carried out till now of hurting no person or property; but far be it from me to judge anyone, least of all women who are members of this union. The day may come when I shall consider stone-throwing right and justifiable. If it does, I shall record the fact in my diary.

The woman I asked about it was extremely unmilitant looking. No one would have supposed that under any circumstances she would have done such a thing. She explained, quietly, that she had already been in prison for this Cause, that she felt the time had come for a further protest, and ever since windows had been invented, men had looked upon breaking them as a very mild form of political protest. One of the Cabinet Ministers has said to us: "Do you think to succeed with a policy of pin pricks. Use weapons that hurt."

"Men break bakers' shop windows," she added, "when they make protests, whereas we only broke Government windows, which our taxes are paying for, and we are prepared to take the consequences. I am quite ready to do three months with hard labour, if necessary." And she smiled.

The others whom I questioned said much the same thing. They had wrapped the stones in brown paper the day before, to show that it was thought out and not done on the spur of the moment.

279

As I was leaving the Police Station,, having said goodbye to the policeman who had arrested me, and who asked for my ribbon badge as a souvenir, I noticed one of the stone-throwers. She was tying her shoe-lace.

"If you are imprisoned," I said, "carry on the agitation for first division treatment. Do not give in, whatever happens."

She looked at me in surprise, as if she wondered whether I could be in earnest.

"Give in," she repeated, and laughed lightly, "I do not think you will find that any of us will give in."

July 15th.

This afternoon I have made a speech. Anyone who remembers doing so for the first time will understand how I felt. To describe it would be quite impossible.

On my return from London to home duties and constitutional agitation for the Franchise, I was informed by the organiser that it was my plain duty to speak at the first weekly At Home, because the others would want to hear about my experiences on the deputation. I explained to her that I should probably be unable to say a word when the time came, and that there was nothing I could think of which I would dislike more. But she waved aside all objections.

"Wait till you have heckled a Cabinet Minister," she said, "that is very much worse."

I made a few notes of what I wanted to say, and when the time came it was not quite so bad as I had anticipated. At first it was horrible, but soon I forgot that I was speaking, or that there was an audience. I seemed to lose sight of myself, somehow, and only to be filled with a longing to adequately describe the Woman's Movement, as it had impressed me when in London.

I do not remember what I said, but I was surprised to find how words came; and as I described the events of June 29th, I felt that I had the audience with me.

When I had finished a lady came up to speak to me.

"I do not know you," she said, "but I want to shake hands and to thank you for your speech. You made the others laugh with your little anecdotes, but I could not laugh, because there was a lump in my throat and tears in my eyes all the time, from the way you described the real meaning of the Woman's Movement."

I explained that I was not a speaker, but that there was something about the atmosphere of the W.S.P.U. which made one ashamed to refuse to do anything at all that might help.

As I was leaving the hall the organiser told me that a lady was anxious to give an At Home next week in her own house, and invite about thirty friends who were either "antis" or opposed to the militant methods, and wanted me to be the speaker.

I was naturally very much taken aback.

"But I could not, really," I exclaimed. "To speak to people like this, who are friendly, is bad enough; but to 'antis' would be impossible."

"You will find it much easier," she replied. "The mere fact of knowing that they are against it will help you to stand up for the Cause. All you have got to do is to defend the methods, and you can manage that. Mrs. W—— particularly wishes you to be the speaker, because she says she has never heard the militant methods so well explained as by you this afternoon."

Of course, I had to consent, and the date is fixed for Thursday of next week.

In this movement there is no retrogression. I can see that the day is not far distant when I shall heckle a Cabinet Minister. Well, it is a great Cause!

July 17th

This morning, as I was selling papers in the street, a man whose face I felt I had seen before came up to me and, holding out sixpence, asked for a copy of *Votes for Women*.

"Do you not recognise me, Mrs. Brown?" he asked, smiling. And suddenly I realised that he was the "anti" I had argued with at tea after my day at the polling booth.

"Yes, I remember you well, now," I said, "and I have often wished to meet you again to say how sorry I am that I was so rude to you that day. One wants to be worthy of the colours, and Suffragettes are never rude."

The "anti" looked perplexed.

"You must be making a mistake," he said. "I am quite sure that you have never been rude, certainly not to me. I have no recollection of anything but a most interesting conversation with a very charming lady. Oh, no, I do not want the change. Keep it for the Cause." And, raising his hat, he walked away.

Of course, he remembered perfectly. I wish now I had said nothing. I had barely recovered from this interview when a middle-aged man with a very red face walked up, smoking a cigar. He stopped to inform me (without troubling to take the cigar out of his mouth) that he had always advocated Woman's Suffrage until the commencement of the militant methods, but owing to them he was no longer in favour of the Movement.

I am really getting very tired of this weak argument, and just then I felt as if I could not stand it again, so I told him that I had always believed in Tariff Reform, and felt sure it would lessen unemployment and benefit the country, but that recently I, too, had been compelled to change my opinion, and was now advocating Free Trade, owing to the fact that one or two men had interrupted a Liberal political meeting and heckled the speaker about Tariff Reform, even going so far as to create quite a disturbance. This, to my mind, proved conclusively that their policy was a wrong one, and many others shared my view.

The middle-aged man rose to it at once. He got very excited, and explained that Free Trade was ruining the country, and the only hope for England was Tariff Reform.

"If these men heckled the Liberal speakers they were perfectly right to do so," he exclaimed, "what else should they do ? Did I expect them to sit still and say nothing? As for a person who could change his policy because of what any man chose to do, it only proved that he never wanted Tariff Reform to start with."

"Precisely," I said, "and anyone who strongly believes that Woman's Enfranchisement would be a benefit to the country would scarcely change his views on the subject because of the behaviour of what he takes to be a handful of quite unrepresentative people. On the contrary, he would" exert himself more than ever to retrieve the damage that they had done to the Cause. That is my point. I am so glad you have seen it."

"It is not a parallel case," he stuttered, angrily. "The fact of the matter is that women can't argue; their place is in the kitchen or the nursery."

Having settled this point, he walked away, fuming with indignation and wiping his forehead with a large pocket-handkerchief.

I have no doubt some woman will marry that man if one has not already done so. It is a strange world.

Soon after he had gone a young woman, wheeling a perambulator, stopped to tell me that she would rather have her baby than a vote.

"Well, you have neither at present," I explained, cheerfully, "for by law you are not recognised as a parent. That is to say if you are married," I added, as an after-thought. She seemed puzzled, and merely repeated her former statement.

"Well, I daresay when we get the vote," I said, soothingly, "it will be quite possible for you to have a baby as well. It seems to me improbable that the extension of the Franchise to qualified women will result in the population ceasing. It does not appear to have had that effect in Australia and elsewhere."

She looked at me with evident interest.

"How much do they pay you for selling them papers?" she asked presently.

"What would you do it for?" I asked.

"Not for nothing you could give me," she replied, emphatically.

"Exactly, that is how we feel about it."

At that moment a lady, wearing the colours, came up to buy a paper, and when she had walked on I turned to find that my friend with the perambulator had gone.

On the whole I had a successful morning, for I sold all the papers.

July 22nd.

My second speech really was a success, "though I says it as shouldn't."

I arrived at Mrs. W———'s house to find a large drawing-room filled with ladies who were having tea as a preliminary entertainment. Of course, I was wearing the colours and the badge. My hostess introduced me to the assembly as "the speaker who has just returned from London."

It was decided that Mrs. W would take the chair and say a few words, then I was to make a speech in defence of the methods, after which questions could be asked by the audience. Six questions had already been written on pieces of paper by some of the ladies and placed on the table in readiness for me. I do not believe that a single woman in the room was really an "anti." They were principally people who knew little or nothing of the subject and a few who strongly disapproved of our methods as unwomanly, having read and accepted the newspaper accounts. Anyhow, by the time I had finished speaking, I asked if any women who still felt that we had gone too far would hold up their hands, and not one did.

"I am glad to see," I remarked, "that no one here has any fault to find with the militant methods. Personally, I have got one—that they are not militant enough."

I then proceeded to read out and answer the written questions, as follows:—

I have kept the papers so as to remember.

(1) Admitting, as everyone must, that many laws as they now stand are unfair to women, why should you blame men? I am sure they are just as anxious as we are that laws should be just.

Answer. We do not blame men. *Tout au contraire.* We blame the fact that men have to make laws referring to women and the home without any woman's point of view being represented.

(2) As the laws which are unfair to women were made many years ago, when social conditions were different, is it not likely that any new ones will be made equally fair to both sexes without women having the vote?

Answer. Certainly not. John Burns has been trying to bring in a law to prevent married women from working, the inevitable result of which, if it passed, would be that they and their children would starve. This law was to help the solution of the unemployment problem; "unemployed" being evidently a masculine term. I could quote several laws passed recently with the best intentions, which are extremely unfair to women.

(3) I have met more women who were against Woman's Suffrage than men, which proves that the majority do not want it.

Answer. Of course, men are less opposed to Woman's Suffrage than women because they understand political economy better, and realise how vitally important the political vote is to any class or sex, and how impossible it will be for women to better their conditions without it. If men had not realised this fact they would not have fought as they did to secure it for themselves. All the women who understand want it—the medical women, the University women, the working women.

(4) If Adult Suffrage were to follow later, would there not be a majority of almost a million women voters over men?

Answer. Yes, but women as a sex would never combine on any question. Why, even this extremely personal question of votes for women has men in favour of it and women against it.

(5) If women are not satisfied with man-made laws neither will they be satisfied with woman-made laws.

Answer. Of course not. But who ever suggested having woman-made laws? That would be as ridiculous a mistake as the present arrangement. We want the use of a left hand as well as a right, not instead of it.

(6) Are not the militant methods retarding the movement and putting the hands of the clock back.

Answer. Militant methods have advanced the hands of the clock beyond the hopes of the most sanguine of the Suffragettes. Whoever heard of Votes for Women before the militant methods began, although these same women had been agitating constitutionally for years. A movement that can raise £50,000 and which can number thousands of members in a space of a few years is a progressive movement.

After the questions had been answered, we all discussed the question at great length, and to my surprise I found no opposition at all. Many of the women said that they would certainly join the union, and all the literature I had brought with me was sold at once.

July 23rd.

The fourteen women who were sent to Holloway for throwing stones on June 29th have all followed Miss Dunlop's example and adopted the hunger strike. Twelve have been already released, and the other two will probably follow. I see that some of them were without food for as long as six days and six hours.

This is a wonderful union. And to think that I asked one of them to be sure not to give' in.

I have received a letter from the organiser asking me to become a regular speaker. She is particularly anxious that I should. This is the result of having got carried away in my defence of the methods. I shall write back that I could not possibly do such a thing.

It is a great Cause, but there are limits to what one can bear. Prison is all very well. A hunger strike even I could contemplate with comparative equanimity, but for the present I cannot be a speaker.

July 29th.

An opportunity for heckling a Cabinet Minister has come and gone.

A political meeting, to which women were not admitted, was held here yesterday about the Budget; so, of course, a protest meeting was held outside by members of the W.S.P.U.

Really, the precautions taken to protect members of the government from the attentions of the Suffragettes are getting more ridiculous every day. It would be difficult to believe if one had not seen it for oneself. Plain clothes detectives, mounted police, and policemen on foot thronged the street, while large crowds naturally collected to see what would happen.

The speaker, a small and fragile-looking girl, was standing in a wagonette addressing an interested audience. Presently she stepped down and walked towards the door of the hall, followed by several other Suffragettes and a crowd of friendly sympathisers. Instantly the police hurried to the rescue.

A tall man in the crowd, who was watching the proceedings with ill-concealed amazement, walked up to a constable and said drily: "Don't you think it would be safer to send for the Territorial forces as well if you really hope to arrest that little girl?"

Sarcasm was unheeded, however, and the speaker was soon to be seen walking away between two tall policemen, with whom she was conversing in a friendly way.

It was some time before a cabman could be persuaded to drive them to the police station, one of them exclaiming that he was a Suffragette himself and would not do it for a thousand pounds.

Finally, one consented, and they drove away, the speaker well pleased with the success of the protest. Two or three other women were also arrested in exactly the same way.

The account in last night's paper was as follows:

Struggling, kicking, and biting, the women were dragged through the street, and from there were driven to the police station."

Clearly, the next step to be taken is to persuade the Press to report things fairly. I should like to interview an editor on the subject.

I pointed out the absurdity of the newspaper description to a man this morning, and he remarked that it was rather hard lines on policemen to be scratched and kicked because women wanted a vote. I explained that I knew from personal experience that those things were not done, and that no one realised the fact better than the policemen themselves, who were our best friends, and most of them on our side now.

"Oh, it's that way, is it?" he said, laughing. "Aren't the cooks and housemaids getting jealous?"

It was not a loafer outside a public-house who said this to me, but a gentleman; yet he evidently presumed that if we were not scratching policemen's faces we must be kissing them. I refrain from further comment.

August 2nd.

I was carefully arranging purple and white flowers with plenty of green in the drawing-room vases this morning when a Suffragette friend, Viola Green, looked in to ask me to have tea with her tomorrow. She explained that she particularly wished to introduce me to a charming girl. This girl, she felt sure, would be an asset to the Cause, if it were properly explained to her, because she had money and was independent with plenty of leisure time at her disposal, besides being clever and interesting and sweet to look at.

"Have you discussed Woman's Suffrage with her?" I inquired.

"No, I have not had a chance yet. I only met her the other day, but I liked her awfully, so I have asked her to tea, and I am depending on you to secure her as a member."

"So you want me to convert her. Why not try yourself.? You know as much as I do about the subject, and once the facts are put plainly before her, or anyone else, '*She that hath ears to hear, will hear what the spirit of the age is saying to the women.*'

"But I want you to meet her, and I would much rather listen than talk."

"Very well," I agreed. "I am disengaged tomorrow, so I will come and do my best. In the meantime, will you kindly admire these flowers, and note the fact that my room is now entirely furnished in the colours—cushions, curtains, and everything."

"There is another thing I wanted to say," continued Viola, absolutely disregarding my remark. "I want you, if possible, not to be rude to her. She may be against our methods and that sort of thing, so do promise not to make her angry and spoil it all."

I could not help laughing.

"I promise," I said, and gathering up the remaining flowers I bunched them together and handed them to my companion, who thanked me and pinned them carefully into her frock.

"You *will* remember about not being rude to her?" she repeated, anxiously, as she rose to go.

"Good gracious! What do you take me for?" I exclaimed. "Am I an 'anti' that I should be rude, or a Member of Parliament that I should break a pledge?"

Viola sat down again with a gesture of despair.

"There you are, that is just what I mean. You will say something of that sort, and probably she *is* an 'anti'; people who know nothing about it so often are. And most likely she has a brother or someone who is a Member of Parliament."

I managed to calm her fears and promised to be careful. If I find this girl is an "anti" I shall just change the subject to a safer topic.

August 3rd.

When I got to Viola's flat this afternoon the girl had not arrived, so we had a few moments' conversation as to the best way of opening the attack. Just as we had decided that I might begin by saying quite casually, "Are you interested in Woman's Suffrage?" the door opened to admit the visitor.

She was, as Viola had said, a sweet-looking girl. As we rose to greet her I perceived that she wore a white costume with a green straw hat and a purple scarf. Then, simultaneously, our eyes fell on the lapel of her coat. On it there was pinned a Votes for Women Badge. We stood still, staring at it in silent amazement.

The girl laughed lightly.

"Do not be shocked," she exclaimed. "I may as well confess at once. I am a Suffragette, and, moreover, I approve of militant methods."

Of course, we got on splendidly at once. We explained that I had come for the express purpose of converting her, to which she replied that had she guessed that she would have hidden the badge and pretended to be an "anti," to draw me out. She is only here on a visit, so I may not see her again; but her account of her work in London was most thrilling and amusing. Like every Suffragette I have met so far, she has a keen sense of humour, extraordinary courage, and an optimism which makes one feel that the fight is almost over and victory in sight.

Three times I have tried to interview the editor of that evening paper, and three times I have failed. I suppose it was my own fault for wearing the colours so conspicuously when I first called. On each occasion I was told that he was out or too busy to see anyone.

Yesterday I wrote him a very polite letter saying that I was anxious to speak to him on a matter of business, and would be greatly obliged if he would make an appointment, as I could come at any hour, on any day which would suit best, and would not detain him for more than a few moments. I have this morning received his reply.

A short note in the third person to the effect that the editor regrets he will not be able to have a personal interview with Mrs. Brown, but if she will write what she wishes to say he will give the matter his attention.

I put on my hat, and with his note in my hand went at once to the Committee Room. The organiser was busy doing accounts. I handed her the letter.

"What shall I do next?" I inquired, when she had read it through. "What sort of bricks shall I throw at him?"

She laughed. "They always write like that," she explained, cheerfully. "There is no use doing anything more."

I am leaving tomorrow for a small seaside place, where I have taken lodgings for myself and the boys, it being their holidays, so I really have no time anyhow for a further attack on the editor.

August 6th.

It is hopeless by myself to attempt any propaganda work here where I am staying. As an artist whom I met yesterday, and who is interested in our Cause, remarked when I consulted him on the subject, "This place is asleep and scarcely worth awakening." I have decided not to try.

The other day, however, I received a letter from Miss M——, to whom I had given my address, informing me that there is to be a meeting next Monday at a town about half an hour's journey by train from here, and that she is there with a helper. Miss P—— , working it up. Lady Constance Lytton is one of those who is going to speak, and they are having some open-air meetings, and Canvassing to sell the tickets, as they are very anxious that the hall should be filled.

She wants me to go over tomorrow and help them by calling on the residents and persuading them to buy tickets, so I have promised that I will. I shall be interested to meet the helper, Miss P——, as she has taken part most successfully several times in heckling Cabinet Ministers, and quite recently did the hunger strike.

August 7th.

Having reached my destination, and with some difficulty found Miss M——'s lodgings, I was informed by the landlady, an amiable-looking, fat woman with red cheeks, that my friends were out, but she was expecting them back at any moment, and would I please come in and be seated.

I accepted this invitation and followed her into a large sitting-room, where a fire was burning brightly, and Suffragist literature was scattered freely over the table and on the mantelpiece. Moving aside a large bundle of *Votes for Women* papers, I seated myself on a sofa.

"Where have they gone?" I inquired of the landlady. "Perhaps I might go out and join them."

"Oh, they'll be back in a minute; they only just stepped round to the cleaner's."

"The cleaner's!" I repeated, in surprise.

"Well, you see, mum," she explained, "they held one of their open-air meetings last night, and the young men they threw such a lot of rotten eggs and flour at them that their skirts was really spoilt like, and wanted cleaning. It's lucky they had others with them to change. Not but what it was a good meeting," she added.

A few moments later they came in, both looking a little tired but supremely happy. Miss M—— welcomed me warmly, and introduced me to her companion.

"Let's sit round the fire and talk for a little," she suggested, "then we can go out and do some canvassing."

Miss P—— is quite young, and, like most of the women I have met in this union, charming and very attractive. She has the Suffra-gette eyes of course, and the Suffragette smile. Somehow these women always make me feel a little bit ashamed of myself.

"Tell me about your hunger strike," I said, presently. "Did you feel very bad?"

"Oh, no, not very. I am quite prepared to go through it again. The prison officials were kind; they are beginning to understand now in Holloway. The last night was the worst; they put cocoa beside me, and I was so weak and so very thirsty. I had to keep my eyes shut and just pray for strength not to drink any. After a while I lost consciousness, and afterwards I was released."

"She is going to prison again on Monday," announced Miss M——, "so I must get another helper. I wish that you could stay."

"Or come with me," suggested Miss P——. "A Cabinet Minister is going to speak on the Budget at Dundee, so I am going up there to make a protest. It is only a case of saying a few words; and I hear that the Dundee prison has much nicer cells than Holloway."

"Do you think that you ought to do a second hunger strike so soon? "

"I do not mind the hunger strike. What I dread is that they may feed us forcibly. Some lawyers say it is legal, and of course they will if they can. If only a great many women would go to prison now all ready to carry out this protest it would help so much."

"I hope you will believe me," I said, "when I tell you that I am very much sorrier than you are that I shall not be able to go with you on Monday; but I have got two small boys, and I can't possibly leave them alone in lodgings for weeks."

"Of course not," assented Miss P—— readily. "Home duties always come first."

Half an hour later we started, all in different directions, each carrying a list of names and addresses of residents, and a packet of tickets for the meeting, having carefully divided the names into three lists so that the same people should not be visited twice. There were 1s. tickets, 2s. ones, and 2s. 6d. ones.

I wonder whether anybody who has never done it can possibly realise what it feels like to ring the front door bell of a stranger's house with no better excuse for calling than that you are a Suffragette, not having the remotest idea whether the occupier is a sympathiser, a disinterested onlooker, or a virulent "anti"?

Having with a great effort summoned up sufficient courage to do this, I inquired of the maid whether her mistress were at home, and on being told that she was I gave my name, with the request that I might see her for a few moments. The maid showed me into a dining-room, where, with the feelings of a child waiting in a dentist's room, I sat down in a large leather armchair.

Presently the door opened to admit a timid-looking, rather sweet little fluffy woman, of the clinging type, who looked at me in evident surprise. I rose to my feet.

"I must apologise for intruding like this," I began, with some hesitation, "but I called to ask whether you are interested in Woman's Suffrage—I mean in votes for women," I added, as she looked puzzled. "I thought perhaps you might care to attend a lecture on the subject next Monday. Lady Constance Lytton is coming to speak for us, and there will be one or two others also."

The little woman smiled quite pleasantly. "Won't you sit down?" she said. "I don't know anything about votes for women, and I am not sure whether my husband would care to go to a lecture like that. I should have to ask him first. It's about Suffragettes, isn't it?"

"Yes."

"You do not approve of them, surely? Those hooligans who do such dreadful things," and she gave a little shiver.

"I do approve of them," I replied. "I am one myself, you see."

"Now you are joking, of course," and she laughed merrily. "But tell me about them. I can't understand why women should wish to rule men."

"Do they? I have never met one who expressed that desire."

"Oh, well, those Suffragettes want to be exactly like men, anyhow."

"I am sorry to seem to be contradicting you again, but I have never met one of those, either. I certainly have no wish to be exactly like a man. I admire my own sex so much more."

My hostess leaned forward. "Are you really a Suffragette, or were you joking just now?"

"I am really a Suffragette, and moreover, a militant one. I am 'on remand' at this moment."

"On remand?" she gasped. "I do not quite understand."

"I took part in what the papers describe as a 'Raid on the House of Commons' on June 29th. Our case has been adjourned to a higher court."

She looked at me in amazement. Then she burst out laughing. "I am so glad to have met you," she said. "I never saw a militant Suffragette before. You look quite different though to what I should have expected."

"You thought I should have short hair and large feet, and wear smoke-coloured glasses?" I suggested.

"Yes, I think I did. Would you mind if I were to fetch my husband? I am sure he would like to talk to you."

Without giving me time to answer, she ran off and returned in a few moments, followed by exactly the sort of man I would have expected her to have married, the type who talks loud and dictates to everyone, and never realises that he is being 'managed' skilfully by a small, fragile person who appears to be giving in to him.

He looked at me hesitatingly, and then glanced in the direction of the window. There was a cracked pane of glass.

"I did not break that," I said, meekly. "I do not happen to have any stones with me today; besides, you are not a Cabinet Minister."

He perceived that I was making fun of him.

"Precisely, madam," he said, stiffly. "I am not a Cabinet Minister. I should therefore be glad to know to what I am indebted for the honour of this visit."

Without giving me time to reply, he went on to explain that for years he had been strongly in favour of Woman's Suffrage; had, in fact, always advocated it; but now, after reading of the outrageous be-

292

haviour of a few hysterical women, he found himself compelled to withdraw his support.

When he had stopped speaking I asked him what he had done for our Cause during all those years before he had changed his views.

"I spoke in favour of Woman's Suffrage," he said, impatiently. "I gave it as my opinion that qualified women should be allowed a Parliamentary vote. So long as they contented themselves with womanly methods it was all very well; now it is quite a different thing."

"The sole difference between our methods and those of the non-militant Suffragists is as follows: We all ask for precisely the same thing, namely, the elementary justice of citizenship, but whereas the others remain good and happy, signing petitions which will not be read and holding meetings which are never reported in the Press, we of the W.S.P.U. having discovered that the vote will never be secured in that way, have volunteered to pay the necessary price. You do not surely suppose that we like doing it, that we are the class and type of people who are in the habit of breaking windows for fun?"

"I consider that you ought to be ashamed of yourselves. This behaviour on the part of the Suffragettes is destroying all chivalry."

"Well, I am *not* ashamed of myself," I retorted. "On the contrary I am ashamed of you. I think I have always admired my own sex most, but I had many illusions about men. I trust that before we get this vote they may not *all* be shattered. I was brought up to believe that Englishmen were brave, chivalrous, and strong, ever ready to protect the weak, that they respected women; but what do I find? Our open-air meetings broken up with violence by hooligans who admit that they have been paid by 'Liberal gentlemen ' to do it; our women, ladies by birth, assaulted, even knocked down and kicked, while hardly a man steps forward to interfere (if one does he is subjected also to brutal violence and looked upon as a fool for his pains). This is not a sex war. It is the men and women of the future, against the men and women of the past, but it seems we shall have to do the fighting part alone. As for the men of England, what are they doing to help us? How many of them have sacrificed themselves for this Cause, as women would so gladly do for them if it were necessary.? What did *you* do while yet you approved of us? Did you offer to hold open-air meetings for us and sell our papers in the street so that we might be womanly and sit comfortably at home? Oh, the argument that we are destroying chivalry makes me reel sick. As if real chivalry could ever die! Like love, it is immortal. Why, it lives in this Movement, if nowhere else. As for the artificial chivalry which you allude to, take it back, keep it, we do not require it, we can open the door for ourselves."

I rose and walked towards the door as I spoke, for I felt that perhaps I had said too much. The little wife stared at me in amazed silence, but her husband walked after me.

"What would you like me to do?" he asked, quietly.

"To buy these tickets, please," I said, handing him two of the 2s. 6d. ones, "and go on Monday to hear what these women have to say. Listen with an unbiased mind, and afterwards you will decide how to help them best. Everyone can do something, and you will want to so badly. You, also," I added, turning to the little wife, "you will not be able to resist the spirit of the age. You need not go to prison, of course. There are other ways of helping."

She glanced at her husband as if uncertain how to reply. He gave me 5s., and put the tickets in his pocket. "I shall go to this meeting," he said, "because I always like to hear both sides of a question. '*Live and let live*,' is my motto, and no one can accuse me of being prejudiced, but I won't have my wife lecturing on platforms or fighting with policemen in the street, so don't you think it."

I burst out laughing. Somehow I could not help it. "Deny and Toms have charming hats in the colours." I observed; "they are really most becoming."

"What are the colours?" asked the wife, with interest.

"Purple, white, and green. They stand for purity, courage, and faith."

As I walked away I could not help wishing inwardly that I had more of the courage and even a little faith.

My next experiment proved less successful. The lady opened the door herself, and informed me that she was a widow, and did not go out much. When I explained my errand she drew herself up.

"Suffragettes, indeed!" she said, angrily. "I won't have any hooligans in my house."

"Then perhaps I had better go away," I suggested, "since I am one?"

"I think you had," she replied, and banged the door in my face.

At the next two visits I drew blanks. The ladies were out. I hope the maids who answered the door did not notice the relief with which I received this intelligence.

"Things always go in threes," I reflected, as I approached a house with a large garden surrounding it. "This woman will be out, too."

However, she was not. I was shown into a charming drawing-room, where a smartly dressed woman was seated, doing some fancy

294

work. She did not appear to resent my visit, and at first, though she admitted having signed an anti-Suffrage petition some months ago, I really felt that she might become interested. However, I was doomed to disappointment. She was of the type who, on the whole, are most difficult to deal with—the kind who, as soon as they realise that a reform will in no respect benefit themselves personally, cease to feel any further interest in the subject. I can remember a woman of this type once saying to me: "My husband does not drink, so why should I take an interest in temperance reforms?"

After a few moments' conversation I found myself discussing babies and the servant problem. It was very much easier, and we parted on good terms.

I then proceeded to interview in turn an "anti," who was comparatively civil but "not taking any" as regards tickets; two indifferent women, who were also polite, but who thought they had engagements that evening and preferred to leave it open; and lastly, a bright little woman, who became mildly interested and consented to buy two of the 1s. tickets.

After that I returned to the lodgings, where I had only just time to have some tea while we compared notes as to our experiences, and then I had to run all the way to the station to catch my train.

The others disapproved of what I said to the fluffy woman's husband. They insist that all the best men are on our side, and that they do help the Cause as far as they can. If this is so, I tender my apologies to the men of the country, but I wish that some of them had gone to prison.

I cannot help feeling horribly ashamed that I am not going there myself on Monday with that sweet girl, but it is quite impossible to leave the boys alone now, and like the Irish Member of Parliament, "I am not a bird that I can be in two places at once."

September 24th.

This morning I read in a comic paper an article entitled "When we are Suffragetted." It purported to be a letter written by a man to his wife after women had secured the vote. He complained of having to bath the baby, and cook the dinner, etc., while she spent her time at the polling booth or in Parliament. It is a strange thing that no one has ever depicted harassed wives of doctors having to prescribe for patients while their husbands vote, or lawyers' wives preparing legal documents and interviewing clients in their husbands' absence at the polling booth.

Evidently it is considered quite possible for a man to attend to his duties, even though he be the breadwinner, and at the same time possess a Parliamentary vote, but in the case of women the exercise of the vote would occupy the whole of their lives, to the detriment of all other duties. I should very much like to hear the reason of this explained, for it is the commonest argument against Woman's Suffrage, if the most futile. One never sells the papers without hearing the same thing over and over again. "Who will cook the dinner? Who will look after the baby." "What about the washing?" One is compelled to wonder whether there is such a thing as family life and homes in Australia.

Another point which these critics seem to entirely overlook is that so far as the law is concerned the home is the one place where a woman has no power at all—less, in fact, than anywhere else. "The husband has the power to select where the home shall be, and how it shall be conducted. In the eyes of the law he is the sole parent of the child so long as he is alive, and the decision as to the child's upbringing rests entirely with him. Whether the husband be good or bad, the wife is by law entirely subservient to him. She has no legal right to any share of the husband's income except in the case of actual desertion; and if, while continuing to live with her, he refuses to pay her a single penny of his wages, she cannot obtain such payment except by breaking up her home and going into the workhouse. Short of this she and her children can starve, and yet she cannot claim the protection of the law to obtain maintenance from her husband. Finally, in the event of either party to the marriage being guilty of definite immorality, there is a total difference in the treatment accorded to husband and wife."

The fact that the majority of men live above the law and do not take advantage of this state of affairs does not make the legislation any fairer, and it seems reasonable to me that if a woman is to look upon marriage as her real *raison d'être* she should be accorded *some* rights in her sole legitimate sphere, the home.

September 28th.

There was a very amusing, poem in one of the *Votes for Women* papers, referring to the occasion when Mr. Asquith was intercepted on his way home from church by two of our women, who asked him the usual question, to which there is no reply. I must copy it into my diary while I have the paper. It runs as follows:—

In church he sat, with contrite air,

And sweet, stained-glass emotions,
And chastened mood:
A halo fluttered o'er his hair
And lightened his devotions:
He felt quite good.

He passed outside with stately stride,
When (exit exaltation)
Those women stood,
Importunate! The sanctified
One burned with indignation:
They were so rude.
"My breakfast, lunch, and dinner, too,"
He said, "bring indigestion:
I cannot sleep.

In fact, life wears a sultry hue
Since first this deuced question
Made my flesh creep.
My nerves, thanks to your most abrupt,
Unwomanly gyrations,
Are far from strong.
Women, how dare you interrupt
My pious meditations?
Damme—It's wrong!

C.L.E.

The incident to which this poet refers has considerably incensed many good people, notably an "anti" lady and her husband whom I met yesterday at a friend's house.

They both said what a shocking thing it was that these dreadful women had no respect even for Sunday, or a place of Divine worship. One would have supposed from the way they spoke that the Suffragettes had addressed him inside the church or interrupted the sermon.

I succeeded in deriving a little amusement from this couple, however, who, on hearing that I was a Suffragette, talked the usual nonsense about chivalry dying out if women had equal rights with men, and the fact of the militant methods proving that we were not qualified to vote, etc. "Lawbreakers," announced the husband, solemnly, "should not be lawmakers."

"Prison statistics prove," I replied, "that twelve men break the law to every two women, in spite of the fact that women predominate considerably in Britain. Nevertheless, men are at present the sole law-makers."

"I wish you had brought the boys with you," said my hostess at this moment, as she came up to hand me some tea. "I got sugar cakes and chocolates on purpose for them."

This remark fortunately diverted the conversation, and the lady asked me if my boys were fond of cakes. I think they were both rather surprised that a woman with children should under any circumstances be a Suffragette.

"I never give them cakes," I replied. "If they ask for them I say, 'Those who ask shan't have,' and, of course, if they don't ask, that proves they do not really want them. It saves a lot of useless argument."

My new friends looked puzzled and unconvinced. Neither of them made any reply.

"How many children have you got?" inquired the husband, after rather an awkward pause.

"I have got two boys and two girls. They get on so well together. I must tell you the plan I have about their pocket money. I give the boys 1s. each every Saturday, and it is an understood thing that they always give a part of it to their sisters, or else buy them some little present. Yesterday the eldest girl actually asked me to let them all have 6d. each instead. She said they would much prefer it, as they could then buy what they liked. Both girls complained that they seldom got exactly what they wanted, and that when they did they felt it did not properly belong to them. Of course I was very much annoyed at such a ridiculous suggestion. Why should they want any money of their own? Surely a boy has as much sense as his sisters with regard to what to buy for her. As I pointed out to the youngest girl (who complained that the week before last her brother would not buy her anything because he wanted all his money for a school feast and this week got her a toy cradle for her china doll, which was too small, when she had particularly wanted a ball), it would never do for girls to have money of their own, as they could scarcely expect to be treated with any consideration or kindness by their brothers unless they were dependent on them. Besides, of course, a girl should always find her greatest pleasure in being unselfish."

"I do not agree with you at all," exclaimed the "anti" lady, hotly, "and I call it a most unfair arrangement. I wonder that you, who advocate equal rights, should make so much difference between your girls and your boys."

"I am so glad you agree with me about that," I said, pleasantly. "I intended it as an illustration of the government's attitude towards women."

"And yet you employ for your own children the very methods you profess to disapprove of in others!" sneered the lady.

"Just like a woman," observed her husband, feebly.

"But that was part of the illustration," I explained. "As a matter of fact I have got no daughters."

I have never seen people look more surprised. "You mean," said the lady, coldly, "that what you have been telling us all this time is untrue."

"Yes, if you prefer to put it that way."

Simultaneously they rose to go. "I think it is a very good thing that you have not got daughters," observed the husband, as he bowed stiffly.

"I have got two sons, however," I replied, laughing.

"I trust," said the lady, "that you will teach them to speak the truth!" and she walked away.

It really was very funny.

I can see, however, that I shall have to be more careful after this what sort of jokes I make to people "whose yea is yea, and their nay nay." I have actually been told by two friends that I am reported to have advocated the use of bombs in our warfare against Cabinet Ministers. Fortunately this is not Russia, so I shall probably not find myself in Siberia."

October 1st.

I have just read in today's paper that the Suffragettes now in prison have been forcibly fed. The article was headed, "Collapse of the Hunger Strike." They make out that only one woman was subjected to this treatment, and that the others then consented to take food. The *Votes* paper will not come out for days, so there is no way of finding out the real facts. I do hope it is not true. Somehow I feel that the other women would not have given in. One thing is quite plain—if it is true we must all go to prison. The only way to stop a thing of that sort is by unity and large numbers, as Mrs. Pankhurst said when the protest against second division treatment began. I do hope they will convict us when our case comes off next month. Ninety-five prisoners all requiring to be forcibly fed would give the doctors some work.

October 9th.

I have undertaken to take part in a Woman's Suffrage demonstration of a peaceful nature in Edinburgh two days hence. The object of this demonstration is to wake up Scotland a little to the need of, and the desire for, the enfranchisement of women. Like everything else undertaken by this wonderful union, it is being splendidly organised, and the work done in preparation beforehand has entailed an enormous amount of propaganda work all over Scotland.

The procession is to include an historical pageant, representing Scotch women who have distinguished themselves in various ways, and it is as one of these characters that I am going to join. I have secured the necessary costume, and am looking forward with some interest to the experience, never having taken part in a demonstration before. It is rather tiresome having to travel all the way to Edinburgh and back, but that cannot be helped. I shall go tomorrow, so as to have a night's rest there before the day of the procession. I only hope it will not rain.

October 9th.

I had a most interesting journey yesterday, and did not find it a bit tiring, owing to the fact that I made friends with two travelling companions *en route*. When we started there were several people in the carriage of the type who look angry if anyone else gets in, and who insist on shutting both of the windows; but seated opposite me was a very nice-looking girl, who presently unfolded a paper she was holding in her hand and began to read it.

One glance was sufficient to show me that it was a copy of *Votes for Women*. I had secured one myself to read on the journey, so I took it out of my bag and smiled at her as I held it up. She smiled also, and a few moments later leaned forward to ask me if I were going to Edinburgh to take part in the procession. I replied that I was, and we then began to compare notes about our experiences when working for the W.S.P.U. She was most apologetic about not having been to prison, and explained that she was not at all strong, having a weak spine, and that her people absolutely refused to consent to her taking part in a deputation.

I sympathised deeply. I think it must be dreadful to want to go and not be able to manage it. After about an hour the other passengers got out, and a man came in who soon joined in our conversation, being very much interested in the Suffrage question. He was a doctor, and disapproved of women having a vote, though he admitted that logically we were entitled to it, and that ultimately we were quite certain to get it. With regard to militant methods, he said that undoubtedly they were necessary, but that we should have to go further than we had done; breaking a few government windows was not sufficient. Men, he explained, had always broken windows ever since windows were invented. At Winchester, about three years ago, they had collected, three nights in succession, and broken two hundred windows as a political protest.

"Were they imprisoned?" I inquired.

"No, of course not. As a medical student I have taken part in political protests myself. On one occasion I broke in a door with a hatchet. We were expected to pay something for the damage done, but that was all."

"Then if our window-breaking has done nothing else," I suggested, "it has surely shown the public that what a man may do with impunity is a crime if done by a woman?"

"Women are different," was all he said.

Evidently they are.

I read in the *Votes* paper that it is true about the Suffragette prisoners being forcibly fed. However, as I had surmised, none of them have given in, so it is still going on.

I wonder how long it will take the government to realise that a Cause for which people are ready to die can never be stamped out by violence. The direct result of this treatment has been that letters have been pouring in to Mrs. Pankhurst from women who have not hitherto joined the fighting line giving in their names as willing to take part in the next deputation.

Two friends who met me on my arrival last night said that of course they also would go now, as it was the duty of all women in a crisis like this to stand by each other. Personally I have settled definitely that if we are not imprisoned next month I shall join the next deputation in February or March. Meanwhile I must go off and dress for this procession. I am glad to see that the sun is shining brightly, which ought to be a good omen.

October 10th.

I suppose everyone will admit that the procession has been a great success and triumph, but if I had had any idea of how trying an ordeal my share in it would be, I doubt whether I should have volunteered so light-heartedly to join.

I had naturally supposed that I would take my place, unconspicuously beside many others, and walk along the street; but when I arrived at the rendezvous, where the characters were being touched up preparatory to taking their place in the pageant, I was informed that I should have to stand by myself on a lorry, which would be slowly driven, from the starting-place to the Waverly Market, a distance of more than a mile, where Mrs. Pankhurst's meeting was to be held.

The procession was about a mile long—women on horseback, others playing the bagpipes or carrying the different banners, hundreds on foot. Only the characters in the pageant were on lorries, one in front of the other. The streets were absolutely packed as far as one could see all the way, and on the whole the crowd seemed interested and sympathetic; but it would be difficult to describe the mental and physical discomfort of balancing oneself, standing alone, on a lorry during a drive through the streets, with every sudden movement of the horse calculated to upset one, literally and otherwise, not to mention the ten minutes before the procession started while the lorry was stationary and one stood on it surrounded by crowds of interested spectators discussing one's appearance as if one were a wax figure at Madame Tussaud's.

As we passed one corner some people among the crowd hissed, so I looked round and smiled at them. Instantly men waved their hats and women their handkerchiefs—one almost dropped a baby in her haste to show that she was not an "anti"—and I heard no more hissing.

When at last my conveyance stopped with a final jerk in front of the Waverly Market, and I was about to descend, feeling inexpressibly thankful that it was over, a policeman walked up and said: "Look here, you must get down. You can't stop there any longer, blocking up the thoroughfare." He apparently thought that I had enjoyed the ride and was anxious to prolong it. However, I offered no explanation, but put my hand on his shoulder and jumped off.

Talking of policemen, I wonder whether the day will ever come when I shall see one without thinking of June 29th.

The Waverly Market was crowded for Mrs. Pankhurst's meeting, which went off very well in spite of the efforts of some medical students in the background to break it up by singing and making a noise.

November 26th.

I have neglected my diary for a very long time, but the reason is that I have been too busy working for the Cause to write. I have had a most interesting time. What I have been most struck by lately is the altered attitude towards militant methods of the more constitutional members of this union.

When one remembers the horror and disapproval expressed over the conduct of those first stone-throwers, it is interesting to hear the same women arguing in their defence now, and, moreover, ready, if necessary, to go and do likewise. One of the government's biggest blunders has certainly been this forcible feeding. By it they have played into our hands once more by rousing the indignation of the men in the country.

Meanwhile, it has to go on, for to the everlasting honour of our women not one has failed, though almost thirty have been through it now. Many have had to be released owing to the acute inflammation of the throat or gastritis, but not one has submitted to second division treatment.

The attitude of the public towards the question has noticeably altered of late, as one cannot fail to perceive while selling the papers.

Of course, one still meets a person occasionally who will make a remark such as, "There is a window, why don't you throw a stone at it?"

A man said that to me only yesterday. I replied that being a woman, I should look upon it as a foolish sort of political protest to throw a stone at a window of a shop, the occupant of which was probably a Suffragist, adding that we had only thrown them where there was a Cabinet Minister's meeting from which we were excluded, or for some other definite reason; and never without taking all possible precautions to prevent injury to people, no one having ever been hurt so far except ourselves. His reply was that it would never do for women to be exactly like men.

December 3rd.

I was much impressed by a letter in today's *Votes for Women*, the sentiments of which I endorse absolutely. So before discarding the paper I feel constrained to quote from it the following extracts:—

Gentlemen,—Here in Birmingham we have made a little mild history. It has been determined to make a special public protest against the torture of Miss Charlotte Marsh by forcible feeding in Winson Green Gaol. The seat of Brummagem Majesty, the Victoria Square, was accordingly selected as being the most forbidden spot. By good generalship the police had been de-

303

coyed in all directions except that from which the sortie was to be made, and Miss Capper, by an adroit flank movement, gained the Square and stormed the sacred eminence of the Victoria Statue. In the few moments' respite, while the police stood helpless in the paralysis of failure, the protest was well and truly made.

The Press has favoured us with a reasonable publicity regarding the ensuing scenes. I will not offer any addition to these accounts. The writer, the mildest of men, was accused of scragging seven policemen, including a deputy chief constable. It is probably a base rumour. Gluttony is a sin. Now, I wish to put a heavy finger on this Birmingham business. The disturbances and the arrests differ in no wise from those which have occurred in other places, except in one particular—a man had been found who was ready to hit, and hit hard, a policeman in the execution of his duty.

The subsequent attitude of the police and Press are significant. At first I was supposed to be drunk. This attitude was abandoned on discovering me seated in the Charge Office reading *Omar*. Then that I was mad. The cogency of my arguments on the Suffrage did something to remove this impression (and I think at least two policemen are recommending the W.S.P.U. to their wives). A third suggestion that I was a pugilist, paid by the women to bash the police, received some acceptance. On this account I was refused bail. The general belief was that I was 'broke,' anyhow, and was defending the women for hire. In the eyes of the police, then, I was drunk, or mad, or a pugilistic ruffian, or broke!

Friends have shown or sent to me cuttings, wherein I am variously described as 'The Women's Champion,' 'In Plucky Defence of the Women,' and 'A Squire of Dames.' In the eyes of the Press, then, I had done something extremely brave and chivalrous.

Gentlemen, the attitude of the police was mean and despicable. The attitude of the Press was Tosh. I am just an ordinary commonplace man, and to suggest anything else is but a further insult laid upon the brave band of women who have done without me and such as me in their splendid struggle against injustice and tyranny, scorning to ask the help which should have been given unasked.

The attitude of police and Press is that the natural action of defending a woman is abnormal. That if I had not been either a ruffian or a gallant I should not have dared. My reply to this is that I have just given myself away—I had the alternative of a month in default of the fine. The fine has been paid and I am free. I was not afraid of prison, but I dared not face its horrible accompaniment, the hunger strike, with its inevitable treatment—torture by forcible feeding. Could I go to prison and do less than the women? I chose the lesser shame of avoiding prison.

I sat in my cell after trial and debated the thing—fine or prison? In all the grand things, the women have done, there is no greater testimony to their courage than the cowardice of the 'burly ruffian' or 'gentle Bayard' (which you will), who shrank from a little hunger and a little pain.

It has come to this: We have held our hands so long that when we do strike, languidly and deliberately, the cry arises that we are mad, or drunk, or hired. That there is not one decent man ready to stand between women and ill-usage. The stronger and the nobler sex! My faith, it is a fine commentary!

Brette Morgan.

What will always be to me a more amazing thing than the attitude of the police and Press (the former, in London, are now entirely sympathetic) is the fact that there are a large number of people who really think it is an easy thing the Suffragettes are doing, and that they rather enjoy it than otherwise. There have been nights lately when I have wakened thinking of those women in prison, and I confess that sometimes I have felt my heart sink at the prospect of going through those horrible weeks next March; but oftener I rejoice that soon I shall be privileged to share with them in the price that has to be paid, and I pray that when the time comes I shall be strong.

December 6th.

At a friend's house today I met a woman whom I last saw selling *Votes for Women* in London. We recognised each other at once, and, of course, began to exchange confidences. Her experiences in the fighting line have been most thrilling, though she told them as if they were everyday occurrences. I asked her whether she intended to take part in the next deputation, and she said she did not, explaining that she was not at all strong now, and would certainly not be able to stand a hunger strike, much less forcible feeding.

"It is paralysis I am getting, gradually," she said, quite unemotion-ally. "I have had treatment from several doctors, but they do not think anything can be done."

I felt dreadfully sorry for her.

"What caused it?" I asked. "Nothing to do with being knocked about in this work, I hope."

"Yes," she said, "all the vertebrae of the spine were damaged in the first place, and since then I have been gradually getting worse."

"But how damaged?" I inquired.

"From blows," she said, quietly.

I felt my face getting hot.

"It was by mistake in the crowd," I suggested, "not blows given deliberately on purpose."

She smiled.

"Yes, blows given deliberately, on purpose. Have you never inter-rupted a Cabinet Minister's meeting? If so, you must have seen it. Stewards deliberately hit us with their fists, or knock us down. Several kicked us while we were lying on the ground. People who were at the Albert Hall meeting, when Lloyd George spoke, have told me that they went home feeling sick at the sight of things done that night, and were powerless to stop it. A great many men joined the League for Woman's Suffrage on the strength of it, because they realised for the first time what it means to be unenfranchised in this country."

"I am so sorry about you," I said, "are you sure that nothing can be done?"

"It does not matter," said the Suffragette, gently, and her eyes shone. "I am glad to have had the privilege of fighting for such a Cause and for such women as the leaders of this movement. It would have been dreadful not to have been able to do anything."

Just then our hostess came up and I did not see my new friend again till I was leaving.

"Goodbye," she said, "we may meet perhaps at Bow Street later on. I have been thinking that after all I shall go in that deputation. If I am unable to stand the forcible feeding it does not matter so very much. One can only die once, and I have often thought it would help the Cause very much if someone were to be killed in this fight."

I did not answer. What could I say to her?

As I walked slowly home, some lines of Whittier's came into my head:—

Wherever through the Ages rise,
The Altars of self sacrifice,
Where Love it's arms has opened wide,
And man for man has gladly died,
I see the same white wings outspread,
That hovered o'er the Master's head.

December 10th.

I said a few months ago that if the day should ever come when I thought it right to throw a stone I would admit as much. Well, that day has come, for not only did I think it right and necessary, but I contemplate doing it myself.

I have been wondering for some time what we should do if we lose our case and the government decides to give Mrs. Pankhurst and Mrs. Haverfield a month's imprisonment and drop the charges against all of us. It is the sort of thing this apology for a government would do, as ninety-five women, all prepared to hunger strike, would be a large order for four or five over-worked wardresses and one doctor.

Last night it suddenly occurred to me that the best plan would be to make a protest against the decision by breaking government windows. They would have to imprison us then, and it could easily be managed with no injury to people and very little to property. Anyhow, I have decided that if they go to prison I for one will go with them.

December 10th.

I went yesterday to Mrs. Pankhurst's welcome home meeting in London. She has returned from America, where she seems to have had a very successful tour.

The Albert Hall was full up, and as usual the audience was most enthusiastic. Mrs. Pankhurst informed us that her fine had been paid by someone anonymously, so she will not go to prison. I believe the government has got something to do with it, as in several cases lately Suffragettes' fines have been paid by someone unknown. Anyhow, I am glad on this occasion, for, as I surmised, they are going to withdraw the charges against all of us and proceed no further, though we lost the case in the higher Court. I have definitely decided to take part in the next deputation in February or March. I wonder what they will do then, as there will be many more women than even on June 29th last.

January 24th.

I made a dreadful mistake today while working at this horrible General Election. Our policy is to keep the Liberal out, and it is quite wonderful how we do succeed in turning votes. The open-air meetings are so well attended, and one can see the crowd, which has often collected largely out of idle curiosity, gradually change its attitude to one of deep interest and attention. As a means of propaganda work this election policy is certainly most effective.

I was distributing leaflets to the various people who passed, describing the treatment of women by the Liberal Government, and the various reasons for voting against them, and I handed some to a man whom I took to be one of the electors. He walked on a few steps, reading the contents. Then he came back to where I was standing.

"Do you know who I am?" he asked.

"No," I replied, feeling vaguely uncomfortable.

"I am the Liberal candidate," he explained. "These are very interesting papers, but it seems a pity to waste them on me, since I am not in a position to vote against myself." And he held out the pamphlets.

I took them in silence, feeling quite incapable of speech, and, as he walked away I gave them to a young man wearing the Unionist colours, who winked at me and said he'd vote for the women.

What worries me is that most likely this Liberal candidate will get in tomorrow, in which case I shall be under the painful necessity of calling on him to ask him whether he will support the Woman's Cause by balloting in the coming Session of Parliament for the Women's Enfranchisement Bill. I have received a letter from Clement's Inn explaining that they want a Private Member's Bill to be introduced, and requesting me, as soon as the result of the poll is known, to personally interview the new M.P. and ask him this question. It is most important that a large number of favourable replies should be received, so of course I must do my best. The bill, as given in the letter, reads as follows:—

That in all Acts relating to the qualification and registration of voters, or persons entitled or claiming to be registered, and to vote in the election of Members of Parliament, wherever words occur which import the masculine gender, the same shall be held to include women for all purposes connected with and having reference to the right to be registered as voters, and to vote in such election; any law or usage to the contrary notwithstanding.

It sounds a reasonable enough thing to ask, and if the Unionist candidate gets in I shall not mind doing so. I hope he will, but it seems doubtful in the extreme.

January 26th.

Really, this is too horrible. The Liberal candidate has got in. What comfort is it to me to be told that the majority has been enormously reduced when the fact remains that tomorrow I have got to personally interview and ask a favour from a man who is pretty sure to remember that only two days ago I was working hard to make him lose his seat? The position is an impossible one. Of course he will refuse to ballot for this bill. It seems only a waste of time asking him about it, and I can think of nothing I should dislike doing more, but I have been asked to, and in the W.S.P.U. personal inclination counts for nothing. I have found his address in the directory, and written a note saying that I am anxious to have a few moment's conversation with him on a matter of business, and would be much obliged if he would make an appointment to see me tomorrow or next day. One ray of hope remains. Perhaps he will refuse. In that case I shall have to write instead. It would be so much easier to write. Meanwhile I shall post this note and try not to think about it.

January 27th.

His answer has come at last. Merely two lines hastily scribbled on half a sheet of paper, to the effect that he can see me this afternoon at 3.30. Really, this is very trying. It's nearly 1 o'clock now, and a woman is coming to tea with me, whom I know very slightly. I shall have to leave a message in case I should be late.

I must write no more now, for the time is short. Dear me! 3.30 and I have no idea where the house is even. This is worse than chalking pavements. I shall certainly drink something very strong at lunch, then I shall put on my new Suffragette hat; it is very becoming and militant-looking, so it gives me courage. I suppose I had better wear the "Votes for Women" badge; there must be no mistaking what I have come about, and I shall take the letter from Clement's Inn with me; that will save a lot of explanation, but, oh, dear! what am I to say if he recognises me?

9 p.m.

The interview was not half so trying as I had expected, and now that it is over I need do nothing further in the way of militant work till the next deputation. I shall briefly describe the events of this afternoon.

I found the house after some difficulty, and rang the front door bell with my usual feeling of cold apprehension. The maid who answered it seemed extremely reluctant to admit me, though I explained that I had an appointment for that hour and was expected. Perhaps my Suffragette hat and badge made her suspicious.

Finally, asking me to wait in the hall, she went into an adjoining room, where she remained for what seemed to me quite a long time, in conversation with someone. A wild desire to leave the house overcame me, but I resisted it, and at last she returned with the information that her master would be able to see me in a few minutes, and would I wait in the study?

Accordingly I followed her to the study, and remained there at least ten minutes longer, during which time I feverishly concocted suitable short speeches and opening remarks, while unconsciously I twisted and crushed in my hands the typewritten letter I had brought with me.

At last the door opened to admit the Liberal candidate. Of course he recognised me at once. I could see that the moment he looked at me, and every idea I had on the question of Woman's Suffrage deserted me instantly. I just stood and looked at him, wondering vaguely whether I ought to shake hands with him or not.

He waited a few moments for me to speak, and then said: "Won't you sit down?" which I did, feeling less than ever able to say a word.

He then observed that he was extremely busy. It was not a good opening. I smoothed out and handed to him the crushed remains of the letter, explaining that I had come to ask him to ballot for our bill, and that I was very sorry to bother him and would not stay longer than I could help.

He glanced at the contents of the letter and smiled. "You are a member of the W.S.P.U.—in other words, the militant section of the women Suffragists?" he asked.

"Yes," I explained; "that is why I have come. Our work during the election has been—" I stopped suddenly, and the new M.P. smiled again.

"I know," he said, pleasantly. "You have been working to keep the Liberal out. On this occasion you have failed."

I did not refer to the fact that we had helped to reduce the majority considerably, but asked him whether he disapproved of militant methods. He replied that most certainly he did, and that women who employed them were obviously unfit to vote.

This remark, while it took my breath away, gave me back the power of speech. "The only difference between our methods and those of other Suffrage Societies," I said, "is that while they desire the vote and realise its importance, we are taking steps to secure it for them and for ourselves. In other words, we have undertaken to pay the price, and it is a very heavy one."

"Indeed," he said, drily. "I imagine that you rather enjoy paying it than otherwise. Some people love excitement and notoriety."

"You suppose," I said, angrily, "that we like standing on a lorry at a street corner arguing with a mixed crowd of the British electorate that we enjoy going to prison with common criminals and starving for days, that it is from choice that we interview newly-elected Members of Parliament in the forlorn hope of getting them to see that one and one make two."

The M.P. smiled again. "I have no doubt," he remarked, "that you get as much pleasure out of the proceedings as do the British electorate, the prison officials, or the newly-elected M.P.'s," and he glanced at a clock on the mantelpiece.

This was distinctly crushing, but in spite of myself I laughed. "You scored that time," I admitted, as I rose to my feet and held out my hand for the crumpled letter. "I must make a note of the fact. It is so seldom that an 'anti' scores; they generally lose their temper."

"But I am not an 'anti'."

"You are in favour of votes for women?"

"Certainly. I have always been in favour of it."

"They all say that, but will you promise to ballot for the bill?"

"Yes, I will promise."

This reply was so unexpected that once more words almost failed me. "Thank you," I said; "I really am very much obliged. I will say goodbye now. I am sorry to have detained you so long."

"It has been a pleasure," he said, solemnly, as he accompanied me to the door, which he opened for me to pass out. "I am glad that you decided to pay this price, and came to interview me."

"So am I now," I replied, as we shook hands; "and what is more, I am glad that we failed yesterday."

Once again the M.P. smiled. "Thank you," he said, simply.

When I got home I found that my visitor had arrived. I apologised humbly, explaining that the duties of a militant Suffragette were exacting.

"Don't discuss Woman's Suffrage with me, please," she implored, holding up her hands as if to ward off a blow. "You never will make me approve of militant methods, so there is no use talking. I quite agree with you that if women want votes they should have them, but I can't see that they are justified in kissing policemen."

I decided not to discuss Woman's Suffrage.

January 28th.

In the *Votes for Women* paper today there is a letter by Lady Constance, describing her experiences in prison. She had disguised herself as a working woman and taken the name of Jane Warton, in order to escape the "special treatment" accorded her on both previous occasions by Herbert Gladstone on account of her rank. The result was that they did not take the trouble to examine her heart before letting her undergo the ordeal of forcible feeding. It is interesting in this connection to read in the *Memoirs of Prince Kropotkin* the following extracts:—

> The horror of such (hunger) strikes seemed not to appeal to the *gendarmes*. At Karkoff the prostrated prisoners were tied up with ropes and artificially fed."

The result of this treatment was that the governor, General Kropotkin, was shot dead. The central prison, at which the first hunger strike, and consequent artificial feeding, took place, was under his orders. Further on in the book Prince Kropotkin says that "no Englishman would have tolerated this brutal treatment of prisoners."

As I read Lady Constance's letter and remembered the writer as I saw her the other day in Edinburgh, a new sense of the wonderful love that this movement has created in women came to me. She describes herself as physically a coward. I feel that I cannot better express my view of her conduct than by quoting as follows from what Mrs. Pethick Lawrence has written about her in today's paper.

> Lady Constance Lytton was not thinking of Mr. Gladstone when she planned the conditions of her arrest and imprisonment. She was thinking of Selina Martin, of Mrs. Leigh, of many other women who have endured direr and more long-drawn-out suffering than that even, which she was called upon eventually to endure. She was thinking of great wrongs that are done in our police courts in the name of justice. She endured imprisonment, insult, and torture, that she might hasten the day when the dark stain of our present prison system should be wiped out of a cleaner civilisation.

She wrote upon the wall of her prison cell the words of Thoreau:

Under a Government that imprisons any unjustly, the true place for a just man (or woman) is also in prison.

The action of Lady Constance Lytton has a political bearing. It is a startling and significant event in the movement for the emancipation of women. But it has very much more than a political significance. It has a profound human and moral significance. It is an action that will not be forgotten. Some day, not just now, but before very long, the world will understand it, and then it will be written in letters of gold upon the tablets of human history.

In years to come this story of compassion and chivalry will be told in the schools to children yet unborn. And they will listen to it as we listened, when we were children, to the tale of the chivalrous knight, Sir Philip Sydney, when, self-oblivious, he passed the cup of water that had been raised to his lips to the dying soldier in the field, with the words:

His need is greater than mine.

And many a woman child will say in her heart:

I, too, will be fearless and chivalrous and brave.

As for Herbert Gladstone and the part he has played from the commencement in connection with this Movement, the sense of burning anger I used to have has gone, and my feeling for him is one of deep pity. Degrading and horrible as prison experience must necessarily be for any woman who enters the fighting line now, I would rather experience it, not only once, but half a dozen times, than be in the position of the Home Secretary today.

February 2nd.

I would like to copy down, for the sake of future reference, a letter which came out in yesterday's paper, and which may help to console some of the people who see in the prospect of Woman's Suffrage a danger to the nation.

It is entitled "Woman's Suffrage in Australasia."

(To the editor of the *Daily Telegraph.*)

Sir,—In the face of Mr. Asquith's recent *dictum* at East Fife that Woman's Suffrage would be bad for the State and bad for the women, this week's mail has brought me from Mr. Mark Cohen, one of the leading editors visiting last year's Imperial Press Conference, the copy of a resolution which was submitted by Mr. Deakin, and duly carried in the Commonwealth Parliament, on December 4th, "amid approving cheers from both sides of the House," *viz*.:—

1. That this House testifies to the fact that after sixteen years' experience of Woman's Suffrage in various parts of Australasia, and nine years' experience in the Commonwealth, the Reform has justified the hope of its supporters and falsified all the fears and prophecies of disaster voiced by its opponents.

2. That, as foreseen by its advocates, its effects have been: (a) To gradually educate women to a sense of their responsibility in public affairs, (b) to give more prominence to social and domestic legislation.

3. That Australasian experience convinces this House that to adopt Woman's Suffrage is simply to apply to the political sphere that principle of government that secures the best results in the domestic sphere: the mutual co-operation of men and women for the individual and general welfare.

I submit that this testimony should weigh with serious and unprejudiced people, and should encourage those fighting in the great Cause of woman's enfranchisement.—Yours faithfully,

B. Borrmann Wells.

Similar resolutions have been passed in other places where Woman's Suffrage has been adopted, notably in Wyoming, as quoted by Lady Constance in her pamphlet "No Votes for Women."

February 3rd.

As I was out shopping this morning I noticed on a poster outside a newsagent's shop, "Suffragettes abandon Militant Tactics." I did not trouble to go in and buy a paper, because I prefer to wait and see the truth on Friday. I do not think it is at all likely to be true, anyhow as regards the next deputation, the date of which has been fixed for on or about March 1st. I sincerely hope not, for I have made all arrangements to enable me to spare a month for prison before going abroad.

It is interesting to notice how public opinion alters on this Suffrage question as time goes on. First of all people said we went to prison because we were paid for it. Then, when it was proved that that was not so, they said we liked prison, that it was only a luxurious detention, and the notoriety made it worthwhile. That was what was being said when I joined the Movement. When the hunger strike first started everyone said that though one woman might be found to do such a thing the others would not follow her example. However, they all did; not one failed. Then people began to say that Suffragettes behaved in a disorderly way, and instead of submitting to the consequent imprisonment, refused to eat in order to be released. One writer in the *Westminster Gazette* even described it as a simple device for escaping punishment!

The fact that every one of these women had submitted to this punishment before, some several times, was overlooked, as was also the "luxurious detention" argument, and the weakness of the Home Secretary was commented on. I would like to invite the writer of that article to try the experiment of this "simple device" for six days, and then to explain why, if the prisoners wished to escape punishment, they did not adopt the much simpler device of paying the fine.

When the forcible feeding started, everyone said:

Now this will soon stop these ridiculous women. Not many will be found ready to submit to all that it entails for more than a day or two, if that.

Nevertheless, every one of them did, though in at least one case it lasted for three months, and on their release, after they had been nursed back to some measure of health, they professed themselves ready to go again. The latest thing I have heard said is that it is a species of insanity. If this be so, the outlook for England is a serious one, for not only is insanity enormously and rapidly increasing, but it is spreading where it might least be expected to be found.

February 7th.

I have just received a letter from Clement's Inn to say that the deputation to the prime minister will not go in March. It has been decided to stop militant tactics for the present, while the government is given a chance of showing whether they are now prepared to carry a measure recognising women's claim to the vote.

Never has the union been in such a strong position as today, both as regards funds and membership. Never have so many women volunteered to join a deputation, ready and glad to suffer anything for the Cause. Yet now, because it seems advisable, under existing circumstances, at a word from the leaders of this wonderful movement, all are ready to carry out instructions and wait. Personally my strongest feeling is one of horrible disappointment. I recognise this policy as a carefully considered tactical movement, and a sign of strength, and later on perhaps I shall be glad, but today I find it impossible to overcome a deep sense of remorse that I, who am so strong and could have done it, should never have taken my place in prison beside these women. The chance will not come again, since I am going abroad. It sounds absurd to say that my eyes keep filling with tears as I write, because I cannot bear the thought that I will not suffer pain and starvation and imprisonment next month, yet so it is. I do not think I can write any more today.

February 11th.

The time has come when I must make a final entry in my diary, for I shall soon be leaving this country, and packing must be attended to. For the present I shall be debarred by force of circumstances from taking any active part in the Woman's Campaign, but the joy of victory will go with me, and I shall read with interest of the progress of the movement. Bitterly as I shall regret all my life that I did not go to prison with these friends of mine, I shall always feel grateful that I was privileged for one short year to work with them, in however insignificant a way.

I have learnt many things during the past year, among others the heroism which women are capable of. In reviewing the conduct of the pioneers of this Movement, and of those who have recently taken their part in the fighting line, even I, who admire them so passionately and love them for what I know them to be, am astonished.

Most people, even the "antis," admit now that this Reform will come, and probably before very long, so one is often tempted to say:

Then, why not give it now, and stop any more of this needless suffering?

But I have learnt also that there is no such thing as needless suffering. We would not lose what this battle has given us of courage, self-confidence, unity, loyalty, and love. I perceive further that if Woman's Suffrage were never to come, it would have been worthwhile to have done these things and to have learnt to lose sight of self for the sake of a great ideal. The love, which is the motive power at the back of this Movement, is a wonderful thing. To have felt its influence makes one reverent. It has been said:

Women can suffer and sacrifice themselves for the sake of a

man, but not for each other, or for a Cause.

Surely this can never be said again. Now that we are learning what the Sisterhood of Woman means we catch glimpses of the Unity and Brotherhood of Man, which will surely come, when the new man and the new woman shall stand together unfettered and free.

But I must cease theorising. It is a temptation to confide one's moods to a diary, particularly in the evening when thoughts form themselves more readily into words, but tonight my thoughts are sad, so I shall resist the temptation. As a poet says:—

Laugh, and the world laughs with you,
Weep, and you weep alone.

I shall therefore laugh, once again, as I record a conversation which I had today with an old gentleman.

I decided to do a final day's work for the Cause by selling *Votes for Women* in the town. I find it easy now. The papers I was selling contained my life sentence of "No imprisonment for the Woman's Cause." I disposed of all the copies I had with me, and met with politeness and friendliness most of the time. One old gentleman, however, who confessed that he had bought a paper simply out of curiosity paused to argue with me.

He said that if women were accorded equal rights with men they would become unwomanly as an inevitable result.

I am getting tired of quoting Australia, so I pointed out that the stage is the only place where women have equal rights with men in their profession. I asked:

Yet is there any place, where women retain their womanliness more than on the stage? Suppose a John Burns were to pass a law now that men must in future act women's parts as well as their own, as used to be the case not so very long ago on the plea that the actress's place is in her home, what would the verdict of the public be? I am convinced that ten years after women have secured the vote it will sound quite as absurd to suggest that they ought to be disfranchised on the ground of sex as to argue that the Married Woman's Property Act should be annulled, and the history of this agitation will be read with amazement and incredulity.

The old gentleman hesitated. "It would never do for all women to go on the stage," he observed.

317

Of course not, because then there would be no audience, just as if we were all Suffragettes there would be no critics. It takes all kinds to make a world.

"Young woman," said the old gentleman, severely, "the best thing that you can do is to get married. You will find it more satisfactory than going on the stage, or fighting with policemen in the street."

"I can't do that," I explained, "because I am married already. My husband is a Suffragist, and so are my two small sons."

This was too much for my companion. He left without making any reply.

I have decided to tear up the parts of my diary which do not bear upon Woman's Suffrage, and to keep the remainder, however disjointed and spasmodic, as a souvenir of the time I have spent in the ranks of the Purple, White, and Green since that memorable day when I first looked with pity and surprise at a bright-faced brave girl selling papers at the corner of a street in the drizzling rain.